DATE DUE

MAY 7 1982			
DEC 3 1 1983			
MAY 1 2 1985			
MAR 2 0 1987			
JUL 1 0 1993			
MAR 0 3 2000			

GAYLORD   PRINTED IN U.S.A

Greenlease Library

ROCKHURST COLLEGE

The Commemorative Book Fund

STEPHEN M. BOOS
(Master's degree)
from a gift by

Mrs. Nora E. Bishop

MONEY AND RETIREMENT

How to Plan for
LIFETIME
FINANCIAL
SECURITY

MONEY
AND
RETIREMENT
How to Plan for
LIFETIME
FINANCIAL
SECURITY

Robert T. LeClair
Stephan R. Leimberg
Herbert Chasman
The American College

ADDISON-WESLEY PUBLISHING COMPANY

Reading, Massachusetts
Menlo Park, California
London • Amsterdam
Don Mills, Ontario • Sydney

Library of Congress Cataloging in Publication Data

LeClair, Robert T.
   Money and retirement: How to plan for lifetime financial security.

   Includes index.
   1. Finance, Personal.   2. Retirement income.
I. Leimberg, Stephan R.   II. Chasman, Herbert.
III. Title.
HG179.L414   332.024'01   81-1792
ISBN 0-201-04089-1   AACR2
ISBN 0-201-10710-4 (Pbk.)

ISBN 0-201-04089-1 (H)
ISBN 0-201-10710-4 (P)
ABCDEFGHIJ–DO–8987654321

CONTENTS

1 INTRODUCTION   1
   FINANCING YOUR RETIREMENT   1
   THE NEED FOR EARLY PLANNING   2
      Where to Begin?   2

2 YOUR RETIREMENT INCOME AND EXPENSES   5
   PLANNING FOR FINANCIAL SECURITY   5
   INCOME FOR YOUR ENTIRE LIFETIME   8
   YOUR RETIREMENT INCOME   10
   TAXES   13
   OTHER FIXED EXPENSES   16
   PROJECTING YOUR FUTURE INCOME   18
   HOW MUCH MONEY WILL YOU NEED?   20
   HOW LONG WILL THE MONEY LAST?   23
   IS THE GRASS REALLY GREENER?   25
   A STRATEGY FOR FINANCIAL SECURITY   28

3 SOCIAL SECURITY   29

   THE HISTORY OF SOCIAL SECURITY   29

   SOCIAL SECURITY TODAY   31

   SOCIAL SECURITY AND YOU   35

   ESTIMATING YOUR SOCIAL SECURITY RETIREMENT CHECKS   36

      You Need Work Credits   37

      How to Estimate the Amount   37

      A Word About Maximum Benefits   41

   WHAT EVERY WOMAN WORKER SHOULD KNOW   41

      While You Work   41

      If You Interrupt Your Career   43

      When You Retire   44

   WHAT A WIFE SHOULD KNOW   45

      A Wife   45

      Young Widow With Children   46

      Aged Widow   46

      Remarried Widow   46

      Divorcee   46

      Medicare for Widows   47

      If You Change Your Home   47

   SUMMARY   47

4 THE IMPACT OF INFLATION   49

   EFFECT OF INFLATION   49

      Decline in Purchasing Power   51

      Income Growth Needed   52

      Budget Information for Retired Couples   53

   SOURCES OF RETIREMENT INCOME   55

   YOUR PERSONAL INFLATION FACTOR   57

   NEED FOR LIFETIME FINANCIAL PLANNING   60

   SUMMARY   65

5 INVESTING FOR RETIREMENT   67

   ESTABLISHING EFFECTIVE FINANCIAL OBJECTIVES   68

   HOW MUCH CAPITAL WILL YOU NEED?   69

   ACCUMULATING WEALTH OVER TIME   71

   INVESTING FOR RETIREMENT   72

      Saving for Retirement?   75

Certificates of Deposit   76

Money-market Mutual Funds   78

Mutual Funds   81

Government Securities   85

Treasury Bills   86

Municipal Bonds   89

Corporate Bonds   92

Preferred Stock   96

Common Stock   96

Real Estate   99

Tax-sheltered Investments   100

CONCLUSION   102

6 LIFE INSURANCE   105

HOW MUCH LIFE INSURANCE DO I NEED?   106

Life Insurance to Create an Estate   106

The Unknowns in the Equation   107

WILL MY FAMILY BE SHORT OF INCOME?   108

ALL ABOUT TERM INSURANCE   109

Level Term Insurance   110

Decreasing Term Insurance   111

"Fresh Start" Term Insurance   111

Convertible Term Insurance   111

Deposit Term Insurance   113

PERMANENT LIFE INSURANCE   115

Living Benefits   115

Nonforfeiture Options   117

Policy Loan Provision   118

Automatic Premium Loan Provision   119

Incontestable and Suicide Clauses   120

Participating Versus Nonparticipating Life Insurance   121

Policy Dividend Options   122

Mutual and Stock Life Insurance Companies   123

OPTIONAL ADDITIONAL BENEFITS   124

Accidental Death Benefit   124

Waiver-of-premium Benefit   125

Guaranteed Insurability Option   126

Payment of Premiums   127

ADJUSTABLE LIFE INSURANCE   128
  Designing the Adjustable Life Coverage   129
  Drawbacks to Adjustable Life Insurance   130
  When Adjustable Life Insurance is Most Attractive   131
INFLATION-FIGHTING POLICIES   131
  Adjustable-premium Feature   132
  Automatically Increasing Whole Life Insurance   133
  Combination of Term and Whole Life Insurance   133
  Universal Life Insurance   134

7 PERSONAL RETIREMENT PLANS   139
  INDIVIDUAL RETIREMENT ACCOUNTS (IRA)   140
    Who is Eligible?   141
    Contributions   141
    Establishing an IRA Account   142
    Withdrawal of IRA benefits   143
    Rollover IRAs   144
  KEOGH PLANS   144
    Eligibility   147
    Contributions   147
    Withdrawals   148
    Defined-benefit Keogh Plans   150

8 ESTATE PLANNING   153
  WHO CARES?   154
  PEOPLE-PLANNING INDICATORS   154
  ASSET-PLANNING INDICATORS   155
  WHAT'S GOING TO STOP ME?   155
  WHERE DO I START?   157
    Step 1: Gathering the Information   158
    Step 2: Analyzing Needs   158
    Step 3: Formulating a Plan   158
    Step 4: Testing and Implementing the Plan   158
    Review of the Plan   158
  WITHOUT A WILL, WHAT?   159
  WHAT DOES A WILL WILL?   160
  I'D RATHER DO IT MYSELF   161
  TURN AROUNDS   162

DO'S AND DON'TS 165

PROBATE: WHAT'S TO AVOID? 165

TWISTED JOINTS 168

TRUST ME 170

    What's in it for me? 171

    Who Should Watch the Store? 172

ARMS IN THE ARSENAL 173

    Revocable Living Trust 173

    Irrevocable Living Trust 174

    Testamentary Trust 174

    Life Insurance Trust with Pour-over Will 174

IS IT BETTER TO GIVE? 175

    What's the Cost? 177

    What to Give 177

WILL I DIE FOR ALL I'M WORTH? 179

    What the Feds Get 179

    The State of State Death Taxes 182

THE ALPHABET SYSTEM OF ESTATE PLANNING 183

    C—Creation of Tax-exempt Wealth 183

    D—Dividing the Estate 184

    D—Deduct 185

    D—Defer 186

    D—Discount 187

    E—Elimination or Reduction of Tax on Existing Wealth 188

    F—Freezing Techniques 188

WRAPPING IT UP 189

9 TIMETABLE FOR RETIREMENT PLANNING 193

IN YOUR 40s 193

IN YOUR 50s 195

IN YOUR EARLY 60s 195

BEFORE RETIREMENT 197

AFTER RETIREMENT 198

10 IMPORTANT QUESTIONS AND ANSWERS — ABOUT SOCIAL SECURITY, IRAs, AND KEOGH PLANS 201

SOCIAL SECURITY 201

x   Contents

    INDIVIDUAL RETIREMENT ACCOUNTS (IRAs)   211
    KEOGH PLANS   214

    APPENDIX   217
    GLOSSARY   231
    INDEX   243

1
INTRODUCTION

I used to think that money was the
most important thing in life. Now that
I am old, I know it is!

Oscar Wilde

FINANCING YOUR RETIREMENT

Have you made adequate plans for your retirement? It's not easy to do, but it certainly is important. Unfortunately, most people fail to do it or put it off until it is too late to make any real difference.

If you think about it, it is probably because someone you know has recently retired or is about to do so. You probably will say, "I've got plenty of time for that," and go about your daily business. The end result is that very few people really *plan* for their financial security during retirement. When *you* retire, will you be *financially* prepared?

The purpose of this book is to see to it that you are. It is estimated that you will spend some 85,000 hours during your lifetime earning a living and building an estate. And yet, you will spend about 10 hours in planning for a successful retirement and distributing to your family all that you have worked for.

While financial security is only one aspect of retirement planning, it is essential to a secure and happy future. Only after you have provided the resources for retirement should you begin to think about travel, recreation, and other leisure activities.

THE NEED FOR EARLY PLANNING

The reason you have to start now to meet your financial needs after retirement is the length of time necessary to accumulate financial resources. If you're like most people, you have only limited dollars to put aside for your retirement needs. If you begin the process while you are still in your prime earning years you will have a much easier task and you are more likely to reach your retirement goals. Time and the power of compound interest are valuable allies in securing your financial future.

When should you begin to plan for your retirement? The best answer is "yesterday!" It is a tragic mistake to think that you will be able to start planning your retirement six months before you receive your last salary check. By that time it will be far too late to do anything that can substantially improve your retirement lifestyle and standard of living. You must begin to take action when you are in your forties and fifties to ensure the safety and financial security of yourself, your spouse, and your family.

The "Timetable for Retirement Planning" outlined in Chapter 9 lists actions that should be taken by persons in their forties and continues until after actual retirement. If you are older than 40, it is still possible to catch up, but don't delay!

Where to Begin?

The best place to begin your planning is to estimate your retirement income based on your present salary, your pension plan (if you have one), Social Security (assuming you will receive it), and other financial resources such as savings, investments, and inheritances. You may or may not be shocked to learn how much money you will have to live on at retirement five, 10, or 20 years from now, but at least you'll have some time to take corrective action.

Most people underestimate the amount of money they will need to live comfortably after retirement. It is generally *wrong* to assume that you will need much less than your present income to enjoy a reasonable standard of living.

While it is true that certain expenses, like commuting costs, may be lower after retirement, others like medical bills, will almost certainly increase to offset them. In addition, the factor of inflation has become so threatening as to jeopardize even the most careful financial planning. Each of these areas will be reviewed in this book and practical suggestions will be offered as to how you can best meet the challenges that lie ahead.

Once you have determined your retirement needs and the resources that will be available to meet them, you can begin to close the gap. For one thing, your investment strategy should change as you move through the normal life cycle. What was appropriate in your twenties and thirties may be an invitation to disaster in your fifties and sixties. You have less time to recover from your "mistakes" and the loss of capital is much more costly at 50 than it is at 30.

TAX PLANNING

Tax planning is one of the most important factors in securing a comfortable retirement. Every dollar that can be shielded from taxation provides a continuing benefit for retirement. Such planning, however, must take place when those high-income dollars are being earned—in the middle years rather than later on. Certain investments are more advantageous than others in avoiding taxes and building up your net worth.

RETIREMENT PLANS

You may have an opportunity to provide extra retirement benefits through your own personal retirement plans. If you are self-employed you may create a Keogh plan to accumulate retirement dollars that reduce the burden of taxes on current income. If you're not covered by a retirement plan offered by an employer, you may benefit from an Individual Retirement Account (IRA).

While these programs can be extremely attractive, there are limits as to the amount that can be contributed each year. These restrictions emphasize the need to begin contributing early in life and to follow through with your commitment.

ESTATE PLANNING

Finally, the area of estate planning will be examined. Have you shied away from estate planning because you equate it with "death planning"? Nothing could be further from the truth. Effective estate planning can make your *lifetime* more secure and greatly enhance your enjoyment of retirement.

However, this is another area where a premium should be placed on careful planning and getting an early start. It may take some time to arrange your affairs most effectively and to take advantage of legally authorized means of reducing taxes and transferring property to others so as to reduce potential estate taxes.

Hopefully, these introductory paragraphs have awakened your interest and started you thinking about your own financial security and retirement planning. Whatever your age and present financial circumstances, *isn't it time you began to plan for the rest of your life?*

Don't put this book down and say, "I'll worry about that next month, or next year when I have more time." Each of us has the same 24 hours each day, and, frankly, your retirement planning is overdue!

Now is the time to plan and take action for your financial future. Tomorrow may be too little and too late!

2
YOUR RETIREMENT INCOME AND EXPENSES

I'd like to live like a poor man with lots of money.

Pablo Picasso

PLANNING FOR FINANCIAL SECURITY

The most crucial financial question facing each of us as we prepare for retirement is, "Will I have enough to live on?" Most of us will have no easy time of managing our money during our working years, and the thought of providing for your needs without a regular wage or salary can be frightening.

We have all seen and read horror stories of elderly persons who are barely able to survive on tiny pensions and Social Security payments. You may know members of your own family who are struggling to keep pace with the rapid rise of inflation.

Many articles and books on retirement planning indicate that you will be able to get along with quite a bit *less* in income after you retire. Don't believe it! Unless you are ready to accept a much lower standard of living and give up many of the things you have worked a lifetime to acquire and enjoy, you will need approximately the *same* level of income as you had before retirement.

5

One of these retirement guides makes the comment that, "you won't need to belong to the country club, wear fine clothes, entertain your friends, or travel a great deal after retirement." Just why have you been working so hard for the last 30 or 40 years?

Should you be forced to sacrifice the style of living you have built up during your career just because you have retired? If you had to do so, would it have an impact on your mental health and physical well-being? These are difficult questions to ask, and even more difficult ones to answer.

Consider, for example, the case of Ben Watson, a retired insurance salesman. During his career Ben and his wife had regularly spent three or four weeks on winter vacations to Florida. Ben relaxed from the year-end rush of selling and Mary enjoyed golf and swimming in the ocean.

They felt well prepared financially for their retirement, but over time they found it more and more expensive to keep up their Florida vacations. At first they simply cut back from four weeks to three and then two. With inflation currently running at more than 12% annually they are depressed at the necessity of giving up their plans altogether.

Each of us will react differently to our retirement lifestyle. Some will find it easier to accept than others. But none of us should be forced to live a life we do not choose, or one that will be harmful to us in any way.

The problem we all face, however, is that we may not have much choice in the matter—that is, unless during our working years we do the planning that is necessary to provide for a comfortable and secure retirement. You must take personal responsibility for this problem that faces everyone of us as we get older. No one else will be able to help you very much.

Don't rely on your family, your friends, your employer, or the Federal government to see that you are well taken care of later on. If the government cannot operate without billions of dollars in red ink each year, it isn't too likely that they will be able to balance your budget either.

Even your employer may not be well prepared to discuss the needs of retired persons and their individual problems and questions. There is only one person who will really be concerned about your retirement: YOU!!

You are going to have to live with the results of your planning. You will have to make do with the resources you have accumulated during your working years supplemented by Social Security and, perhaps, a pension plan.

You must take the responsibility for preparing for your retirement. The time and effort you spend now can be one of the best investments you will ever make in terms of financial return and personal satisfaction. Financial security simply will *not* happen to most of us. If we leave the whole thing to chance the results will be as random as a roll of the dice.

A few will be lucky and approach retirement well-off and without worries. Another small group will find themselves in desperate circumstances which will prevent them from even considering retirement. Most of these people will continue to work somewhere, and go on struggling financially for all of their lives.

Between these two extremes will lie the great majority of older persons who had hoped to be near the upper group, but are deathly afraid that their real position is nearer to the bottom. Each year, as their income remains about the same and inflation pushes their expenses higher and higher, they will feel lower and lower on the economic ladder. Recent surveys of consumer expectations show that many working people and *most* retired persons expect to be less well off financially in the years to come.

Personal financial planning can make the difference in whether you are secure and comfortable in your retirement years or worried, unhappy, and afraid. If you plan to have an adequate income during your retirement you are infinitely more likely to accomplish your goal than someone who has no goal and no plan to begin with!

For example, Dave and Roy Edwards are brothers, both in their late forties. When they get together they spend a great deal of time talking about their plans after retirement. Dave has no real plans for his financial security, but maintains that "everything will work itself out." Roy has set a definite goal of having a $100,000 nest egg to supplement his Social Security and company pension. Which brother is more likely to have a secure retirement?

Roy Edwards may not accomplish his goal of a $100,000 retirement fund, but he's likely to come a lot closer to providing retirement security for himself and his family than his brother is. We'll have more to say about setting financial objectives throughout this book, and Chapter 5, Investing for Retirement, will offer some helpful ideas on how to construct practical investment objectives.

One of the great allies of any financial plan is time: time for plans to be made and evaluated; time for income to be earned and assets accumulated; and time for changes to be made when necessary. The reverse, however, is also and unfortunately true. No amount of determined planning can really make up for the errors of omission that have already been made, or for procrastination, or for the loss of years. *Now* is the time to plan for your retirement income.

INCOME FOR YOUR ENTIRE LIFETIME

We all want to live comfortably and securely for *all* of our lives. None of us can know just how long that will be, but the longer the better! The insurance industry has a term for living beyond your expected life span—"excess longevity."

Most of us would probably be glad to have as much of that "excess longevity" as possible! However, the term does have important implications in that we can live *longer* than our assets. We can live beyond our ability to finance a comfortable standard of living and a secure retirement. This is one of the first problems we must deal with in planning our retirement income.

One aspect of the problem is a personal one, and that is just when you plan to retire. Do you want to take an early retirement or do you want to continue your job as long as possible? Despite recent legislation permitting individuals to work beyond age 65, more and more persons are electing to retire before 65. Obviously, this will lengthen the total retirement period and put more emphasis on your personal plans for financing that retirement. It will likely mean taking reduced Social Security benefits and a smaller pension as well. Your personal resources will have to make up the difference.

How long will you live? No one can say for certain, but we can look at average statistics for the population as a whole. A recently issued table of life expectancies for persons 65 to 85 years of age is shown in Table 2.1. These numbers are based on a large sample of persons who lived until age 65 and beyond. Since persons who died prior to age 65 are not included in the table, the life expectancies shown there are considerably *longer* than frequently published statistics for the population as a whole. In simpler terms, if you make it until age 65, you are likely to have many more good years ahead of you.

For example, an average male who survives until he is 65 years old can expect to live another 13.4 years, or until about age 79. The man who is presently 70 years of age can look forward to an average of 10.7 additional years of life. Even the man who has reached 75 years of age can expect to live well into his eighties.

For a variety of reasons women can expect to live even longer, and *outlive* their husbands of similar age by four to five years. This makes it even more critical for both husbands and wives to plan, not only for their future together, but also for her future *alone*. Wives who are younger than their

TABLE 2.1 LIFE EXPECTANCY, AGES 65 TO 85

AGES	MALE	FEMALE
65	13.4	17.5
66	12.8	16.7
67	12.2	16.0
68	11.7	15.3
69	11.2	14.6
70	10.7	13.9
71	10.2	13.2
72	9.7	12.6
73	9.2	12.0
74	8.8	11.4
75	8.4	10.8
76	8.0	10.0
77	7.6	9.5
78	7.2	8.9
79	6.8	8.4
80	6.4	7.9
81	6.0	7.4
82	5.7	6.9
83	5.4	6.5
84	5.0	6.0
85	4.7	5.7

SOURCE: U.S. Dept. of Health, Education and Welfare

husbands should anticipate an even longer period of widowhood and plan accordingly.

As an example, the woman who reaches age 65 can expect to live another 17.5 years on average until she is in her early eighties. A 75–year-old woman can expect better than 10 more years of life, and since many wives are several years younger than their husbands, she must be prepared for upwards of 10 years of personal financial reponsibility.

Of course, many women are now better able to anticipate a more secure financial future in their own right. This is due to better employment, their own Social Security benefits, higher survivor's benefits in pension plans, and greater financial sophistication and understanding.

On the basis of your present age and the information in Table 2.1, you can estimate both your remaining accumulation period and how long your resources must last. Of course, the estimate of your personal payout period may have to extend beyond the average figures shown in the life expectancy table. What shape will you be in financially if you live "too long"? The answer to this question will have an impact on the manner in which you hold your resources and the investments you may choose during the accumulation period. The longer you live, the more your retirement income will be subject to the cumulative impact of inflation over the years. We will have more to say on this topic in Chapter 5, "Investing for Retirement."

YOUR RETIREMENT INCOME

The first step in preparing for your future financial security is to analyze your present income and to estimate what you will have available when you retire.

Most of us probably have a pretty good idea of what our gross income amounts to, but not what is left after certain fixed expenses are paid. In preparing for retirement we must pay close attention to the expected change in our *disposable* income, not the gross amount.

For a variety of reasons which we will consider, the change in our disposable income is not likely to be as great as the change in our total income. Table 2.2 presents three examples of before-and-after retirement income changes. These income statements are highly simplified but will give you an idea of what is likely to happen to you economically after retirement.

Salaries and wages represent the great majority of your income before you retire. Most people earn some additional income through dividends, interest, and other sources, but as a percentage of your total income these extras are relatively small.

Even the figures shown in Table 2.2 are probably optimistic as to the amount of income from other sources. Not many persons have savings or investments equal to one year's salary. You may be among the majority of Americans who have virtually no "savings" beyond what they may be forced to contribute to a pension plan, the equity in their homes, or the cash value of their life insurance.

Don't let this discourage you, however, as with a little planning and a lot of determination you can make a big difference in your retirement income.

The situations outlined in Table 2.2 cover a wide range of personal income. The $20,000 income level is approximately the median income level in the United States during 1981. This means that half of us have a family income of less than $20,000 and half earn more than this amount. The top

TABLE 2.2 INCOME COMPARISONS: BEFORE AND AFTER RETIREMENT

	A		B		C	
INCOME:						
SALARY	$20,000	——	$40,000	——	$60,000	——
PENSION (1)	——	$ 5,000	——	$16,250	——	$29,250
SOCIAL SEC. (2)	——	8,000	——	9,750	——	9,750
OTHER INCOME (3)	1,600	1,600	3,200	3,200	4,800	4,800
TOTAL	$21,600	$14,600	$43,200	$29,200	$64,800	$43,800
TAXES:						
REAL ESTATE	$ 1,000	$ 1,000	$ 2,000	$ 2,000	$ 3,000	$ 3,000
FED. INC. (4)	2,643	——	7,400	498	15,400	1,672
2% STATE INC. (5)	432	32	864	64	1,296	96
SOC. SEC. (6.65%)	1,330	——	1,975	——	1,975	——
TOTAL	$ 5,405	$ 1,032	$12,239	$ 2,562	$21,671	$ 4,768
OTHER EXPENSES:						
MEDICAL EXP. (6)	$ 1,087	$ 1,196	$ 1,342	$ 1,476	$ 2,323	$ 2,555
INTEREST CHGS. (7)	1,836	184	2,200	220	2,500	250
CONTRIBUTIONS (8)	542	407	646	485	939	704
MISCELLANEOUS (9)	400	200	600	300	800	400
TOTAL	$ 3,865	$ 1,986	$ 4,788	$ 2,481	$ 6,562	$ 3,910
DISPOSABLE INC.	$12,330	$11,582	$26,173	$24,157	$36,567	$35,122
% OF PRE-RETIRE-MENT INCOME	93.94%		92.30%		96.05%	

(1) 65% OF SALARY LESS SOC. SEC.; 50% TAXABLE
(2) HUSBAND AND WIFE, EACH AGE 65 in 1981
(3) 8% INTEREST ON ASSETS EQUAL TO ONE YEAR'S SALARY
(4) 1980 TAX RATES, MARRIED FILING JOINTLY
(5) EXCLUDES SOCIAL SECURITY AND PENSION INCOME
(6) INCREASES BY 10% AFTER RETIREMENT
(7) REDUCED BY 90% AFTER RETIREMENT
(8) REDUCED BY 25% AFTER RETIREMENT
(9) REDUCED BY 50% AFTER RETIREMENT

figure of $60,000 is at or near the top of the income distribution in our country. Less than 5 percent of the population earns more than this amount annually. Of growing importance to retirement planning is the number of two income families. More than half of the women in the U.S. are now employed and this percentage is almost certain to increase substantially in the future. The figure is much higher for younger age groups where the median income level for two-income families is closer to $30,000. You should analyze your own disposable income situation based on your income, your spouse's income, if any, and other income such as dividends and interest.

After retirement the majority of your income is likely to come from Social Security, pension benefits, and unearned income from savings and investments. It is impossible to generalize as to how much the average person receives from his or her pension plan. Some are quite generous and provide benefits equal to 50–75% of a person's normal income. Other plans are very marginal and provide a low level of retirement income.

Many pension plans are "integrated" with Social Security benefits. This means that your private pension benefits will be adjusted for the level of Social Security you qualify for at retirement. For example, one plan provides that a person will receive 50% of their final year's salary as a retirement benefit. Not all of this amount is paid by the employer, however. The employer will make up the *difference* between the given level of Social Security benefits and 50% of the employee's final salary.

For example: Joe Livingston is about to retire from a firm with a pension plan that will pay half his final year's salary, integrated with his Social Security benefits. Joe's salary is currently $3000 per month and he estimates that his Social Security income will be $500 per month.

Under his pension plan, Joe will receive a total monthly income of $1500. $500 will come from the U.S. Government and his employer will make payments of $1000.

With the sharp increase in inflation and the accompanying increase in Social Security payments, "integrated" plans are becoming less popular with employees. Some plans call for an automatic reduction in benefits at age 62, or whenever an individual is eligible to begin receiving Social Security payments.

If you are a participant in a pension plan, it is *your* responsibility to become familiar with its provisions and procedures. This is essential whether or not you actually contribute to the plan.

Your employer or personnel office is the place to start getting information on the details of your pension. But don't be afraid to get in touch with friends or former employees who have already retired. They will be able to give you firsthand experiences and advice on any problems they encountered in arranging for their pensions.

The examples in Table 2.2 assume that when combined with your Social Security benefits, your pension will amount to 60–65% of your working income. We again assume that you will have some additional income from other sources, but that it will continue to be only a small part of your total retirement income.

At this point you may be shocked and disappointed at the comparison between your current income and what you will have available to live on after you retire. You may be asking yourself, "How will I ever live on two-thirds of my current income?" Even with the kids gone and the mortgage likely paid off it seems like a frightening proposition. Hold on! What we have examined so far is your gross income before and after retirement, not what you will actually have to spend.

TAXES

The first big category of "fixed" expenses that faces every one of us is, of course, taxes. During our working years we spend almost three hours out of every day earning what we have to pay the Federal government, the states, and local governments in various taxes. This includes income taxes, both Federal and state, property taxes, and other miscellaneous taxes. The taxes shown in Table 2.2 represent a major expense both before and after retirement. Fortunately, the impact of tax payments will be considerably less once you retire. This is due to the changed nature of your income and the special tax treatment accorded to older persons by the Federal government in particular.

Taxes on any real estate that you may own, however, will not provide any relief from the tax burden. These are based on the value of your property rather than your income and will continue at the same level, if not higher, during your retirement years. The figures shown in Table 2.2 remain the same after retirement, but you may need to increase real estate taxes after retirement based on the experience in your own community or the area where you may wish to retire. Real estate taxes may be reduced if you elect to move to an area with generally lower taxes, or if you plan on selling your home and moving into an apartment.

Federal income taxes are likely to be considerably less as a percentage of your retirement income than they were when you were working. There are several important reasons for this reduction. First, Social Security payments are exempt from Federal and state income taxes. This is due to the fact that you were taxed on your contributions to the system when the monies were earned during your working years. The government does *not* tax you again when you receive your benefits. (It is worth noting that some Congressmen have proposed taxing individuals on the portion of Social Security represented by the employer's payments into the system. Such action is not likely at the present time, but it may become necessary if the Social Security system continues to experience reduced contributions and higher payouts to retired persons.)

Secondly, some or all of your pension benefits may not be taxed. This will depend on whether or not you contributed to the pension plan while you were working. If you did make payments into the plan, your contributions have already been taxed and will be paid out to you tax-free. Only that portion of your pension benefit that represents your employer's contributions plus earnings will be taxed.

Your employer will provide you with information that separates your contribution from your employer's. Many plans consider all of the initial payments a return of your contribution. This means that you will not be taxed at all until all of your contributions have been paid out to you in the form of benefits. However, from that point on, your full pension benefit will be subject to federal income taxes.

A third important factor that reduces the burden of income taxes on retired persons is the additional exemption available to persons who are 65 years of age or older. You may take an extra exemption on your Federal income tax return if you were 65 years of age or older on the last day of the tax year. You are considered 65 on the day before your 65th birthday.

At the present time each personal exemption is worth $1000, and a husband and wife both aged 65 or older would be able to claim their regular exemptions plus old age exemptions for a total exemption of $4000. This means that a married couple filing a joint return could have income up to $7400 (the $4000 exemption plus the "zero bracket amount" of $3400) before they would have to even file a return or pay any tax. Social Security payments would not be included in calculating their taxable income.

State income taxes are levied by all states except Florida, Nevada, New Hampshire, South Dakota, Washington, and Wyoming. Table 2.3 summarizes the tax rates charged by the various states on personal income. These vary considerably from state to state as does the definition of taxable income used by each state. You should become familiar with the details for your own state or any state you may be considering for a retirement residence. In any case, the states do not tax Social Security payments, and many do not

TABLE 2.3 STATE INCOME TAX RATES

STATE	RATE (%)	STATE	RATE (%)
Alabama	1.5–5	Minnesota	1.6–17
Alaska	3–14.5	Mississippi	3–4
Arizona	2–8	Missouri	1.5–6
Arkansas	1–7	Montana	2–11
California	1–11	Nebraska	18*
Colorado	3–8	New Jersey	2–2.5
Connecticut	7	New Mexico	1–9
Delaware	1.5–16.5	New York	2–14
Dist. of Col.	2–11	North Carolina	3–7
Georgia	1–6	North Dakota	1–7.5
Hawaii	2.25–11	Ohio	0.5–3.5
Idaho	2–7.5	Oklahoma	0.5–6
Illinois	2.5	Oregon	4–10
Indiana	2	Pennsylvania	2
Iowa	0.5–13	Rhode Island	19*
Kansas	2–9	South Carolina	2–7
Kentucky	2–6	Tennessee	6
Louisiana	2–6	Utah	2.25–7.25
Maine	1–10	Vermont	23*
Maryland	2–5	Virginia	2–5.25
Massachusetts	5–10	West Virginia	2–9.6
Michigan	4.6	Wisconsin	3.5–10

SOURCE: P-H Inc. All States Tax Guide, *1980*
Percentage applies to Federal Income Taxes paid

tax pension benefits as well. Therefore, the portion of your income that will be taxed at the state level after you retire is likely to be small.

The final item in Table 2.2 under Taxes is that represented by OASDI, or Social Security taxes. These amounts have risen sharply in the past few years and are scheduled to increase even more in the future. (We will come to a schedule of future tax rates for employees and the corresponding wage base in Table 3.1. Similar information for self-employed persons is shown in Table 3.2.)

Unless you continue to work on a part-time basis after you retire, you will no longer pay Social Security taxes. If you work in covered employment you will be required to contribute to Social Security even though you are receiving benefits at the same time. Depending upon how much you earn from employment after you retire you may find your Social Security benefits reduced or eliminated. This will be discussed in greater detail in Chapter 2, "Social Security."

OTHER FIXED EXPENSES

In addition to taxes certain other expense items should be reviewed before you determine your disposable income before and after retirement. The four categories shown in Table 2.2 under "Other Expenses" are the major items of deductible expenses for Federal tax purposes. The figures for medical expenses, interest charges, contributions, and miscellaneous expenses are the latest averages reported by the Internal Revenue Service.

As we might expect, persons in higher income categories generally have more in the way of itemized deductions. They tend to have higher-priced medical care, and give away more in the form of charitable contributions. Also, despite their upper level income, the affluent tend to borrow more resulting in larger interest deductions at income tax time.

In developing Table 2.2 we have assumed that certain expenses will increase while others will go down. Medical costs, for instance, are likely to increase after you retire. Not only are medical expenses one of the fastest rising parts of the family budget, but you are also likely to require more frequent care as you get older. This is a particularly important reason why you will need to maintain your level of income after you quit working. Medicare and medicaid programs may provide some help, but you should not count on these government programs to pay all of your medical bills. Private medical insurance will still be necessary for most of us, and even then we can probably count on having to pay some medical costs from our regular income.

At the other extreme, interest costs are typically much lower during the retirement years. The main reason is that most families will have paid off the mortgage on their homes by that time. Secondly, any borrowing necessary to finance your children's education will likely be behind you by that time. You may still be paying some carrying charges on credit cards and charge accounts, but they will normally be much lower as compared with interest paid in earlier years.

You will likely reduce your charitable giving once you retire. In the first place, you won't be there to "give at the office" any longer. There will be fewer occasions to make donations and less social pressure to do so. The figures shown in Table 2.2 are average charitable deductions claimed by persons at the three income levels. We have assumed that these will be reduced by 25% after retirement. You will have to decide for yourself what charitable giving you want to continue and what might best be eliminated for your own welfare.

Miscellaneous expense deductions are often related to a person's occupation. Some examples include union dues and expenses, uniforms, tools and supplies, home office expenses, and certain educational costs. After retirement these expenses should fall quite a bit. We have cut them in half for the purposes of the examples shown in the table, but you can best judge your own expenses and decide what these are apt to be after you retire.

Now that we've looked at all of the individual income and expense items, let's see what the general results turn out to be. In the first place, it is pretty obvious that our *gross* incomes are likely to fall rather sharply. Our pensions and Social Security benefits are likely to provide only 60–70% of the income that we had while we were working. Even with other assets equal to a year's salary or wages we are not going to have all of the income that we might want.

Before real panic sets in, however, you should also notice that your taxes and other expenses will be much lower as well. Federal income taxes will fall most sharply due to the exclusion of Social Security and some part of your pension from taxable income. The progressive nature of our tax system will also work in favor of those persons who had relatively high incomes during their working years. While their incomes will fall significantly, their taxes will go down even more as they move lower on the tax rate schedule.

State income taxes and Social Security (FICA) contributions will virtually disappear. Most states do not tax the principal sources of retirement income, and, unless you continue to work, you will not be contributing to Social Security. Most persons will pay only 20–30% of the taxes they paid while they were working, and many will pay even less. This fact will go a long way toward balancing your reduced income with your ongoing needs for a stable level of disposable income. In addition, despite higher medical costs, other expenses should decline after retirement. The sharp reduction in interest expenses will free a lot of money for other purposes.

With all of these things considered you may be pleasantly surprised to find that your "disposable income" is not too far below the pre-retirement level. For example, let's assume that Column B of Table 2.2 represents the situation faced by Ed Carter as he begins to analyze his retirement income. Ed's retirement income is projected at $29,200 which is only 68% of his $43,200 income while he was working.

PROJECTING YOUR FUTURE INCOME

If he were to stop there, Ed Carter would be a miserable man indeed. With only two-thirds of his regular income he might expect to give up much of his desired lifestyle and to worry constantly about paying for necessities such as food or medical care. But, Ed has to analyze his expenses as well as his income to see the complete picture of his retirement situation.

His overall tax bill will be reduced by almost 80%, due to lower income taxes and elimination of his Social Security contributions. In addition, the category of "other expenses" will be cut in half by reduced interest charges, smaller contributions, and lower miscellaneous expenses.

The result of his analysis will show Ed that his retirement income will be only slightly less (92%) than his *disposable income* prior to retirement. Similarly, Columns A and C of Table 2.2 show only modest changes in disposable income after retirement. Such declines in spendable income are manageable in that they can be offset by increased income from savings and investments.

The first step in providing for this reduction in disposable income is to recognize that it will occur for almost everyone and to begin to make plans to compensate for it. The best way to do this is to analyze your current spending and to estimate how much of a reduction *you* will experience when you retire.

Figure 2.1 provides you with a detailed form for examining your income and for projecting what it is likely to be in the future. This is *not* a budget, nor an attempt to put you into some kind of financial straight-jacket; it is a tool that you can use to see just where your money comes from, both now and in the future.

The form provides for a variety of fixed and variable expenses common to most of us. See if you can come up with reasonable estimates of where you are currently spending your income. If you are like most of us your first attempt will fall far short of your figures for annual income. You may be tempted to ask yourself, "What happened to all the rest of it?" If you go back over the list of expenses more realistically, you will probably increase most expense categories to the point where you are spending most of, or all of—or even more than—your total income.

A particular danger signal is the increased use of credit cards, charge accounts, installment loans, and "bill consolidation" loans. All of these may indicate that you are spending far above your level of income. This may be

INCOME/EXPENDITURE—CURRENT/PROJECTED

ANNUAL INCOME	CURRENT	PROJECTED ONE YEAR	ACTUAL ONE YEAR	PROJECTED THREE YEARS	ACTUAL THREE YEARS
Salary, Bonus, etc.					
Self-Employment (Business)					
Real Estate (net after taxes, etc.)					
Dividends—(a) Close Corporation Stock					
(b) Investments					
Interest—(a) Bonds					
(b) Savings Accounts					
Trust Income					
Life Insurance Settlement Options					
Other Sources					
TOTAL ANNUAL INCOME					

ANNUAL EXPENDITURES

FIXED:

Housing (Mortgage/Rent)					
Utilities and Telephone					
Food, Groceries, etc.					
Clothing and Cleaning					
Income Taxes, Social Security, etc.					
Property Taxes					
Transportation (Auto, Commuting)					
Medical/Dental/Drugs (include insurance)					
Debt Repayment					
Housing Supplies/Repairs/Maintenance					
Life Insurance					
Property and Liability Insurance					
Current School Expenses					
TOTAL FIXED EXPENSES					

DISCRETIONARY:

Vacations, Travel, Camps, etc.					
Recreation/Entertainment/Club Dues					
Contributions/Gifts					
Household Furnishings					
Fund for Education					
Savings					
Investments					
Other					
TOTAL DISCRETIONARY EXPENSES					
TOTAL ANNUAL EXPENDITURES					
NEW BORROWING OR ASSET LIQUIDATION (total expenditures minus total income)					

FIGURE 2.1

possible while you are still working, but it will make it all the more difficult to cut back once you retire. And it will be virtually impossible for you to put away any money to build up your retirement fund. This fund is critical if you are to overcome the reduction in your disposable income that will take place when you actually do retire.

Keeping disposable income at the same level before and after retirement is an important financial goal. Happily, it is within reach of most of us if we plan carefully and begin early on to prepare for our future financial security.

HOW MUCH MONEY WILL YOU NEED?

Most of us will be disappointed in comparing our disposable incomes before and after retirement. Even if the difference is less than we might have thought, the amount is probably less than we will want to live on.

Keep in mind our earlier comment that unless you are willing to give up many of the things that make your present lifestyle a comfortable one, you will need about the same amount of income. Certain expenses may decline or even be eliminated on retirement, but others will definitely increase and inflation will be operating all the time. You should plan to have approximately the same level of income before and after retirement. This is *not* an easy task, but can be accomplished with careful preretirement planning and stick-to-it determination.

You should expect that your pension income and Social Security payments will provide about 60–65% of your preretirement income. At least, that is the objective of many corporate benefit plans and retirement counselors. However, their goals are to provide you with a "minimum acceptable level" of income. They will be satisfied if you can keep a roof over your head, have warm clothes, and eat three decent meals a day. Will you be satisfied with that? Probably not! Most of us have more in mind for our retirement years. We want to enjoy the additional leisure time by traveling, pursuing our hobbies, learning new skills, taking longer vacations, and generally enjoying ourselves. All of this will take money far beyond the level necessary to maintain a minimum standard of living. Even that low level of existence will be a challenge when inflation is factored into the equation. More will be said about inflation and its impact on retirement planning in Chapter 4, but you should accept the fact now that it won't make your plans any easier to accomplish.

Your challenge then is to make up the difference between what your employer and the government may provide and the money you will need to live the way you want. The most obvious source of any shortfall in your desired level of income will be the assets you have accumulated during your working years. Whether you are "wealthy" or not, these assets should be invested in a safe and secure way that will provide the maximum return on your investments. After all, it will have taken you a lifetime to acquire them, and they will have to provide for you for the rest of that lifetime.

How much will you need to fill the gap between your pension plus Social Security and your current income? You should be able to get an estimate of your future pension benefits from your employer. Chapter 3, "Social Security," will help you to estimate the benefits you will receive from the Federal government. Subtracting the total of these two amounts from your present income will leave the amount that must be provided from your invested capital. As an example, let's look at the figures for Individual B back in Table 2.2. The difference in disposable income before and after retirement is about $2700, but this already included $2800 in other income from assets. Therefore, the total investment income required would be closer to $5500 per year.

How much capital would be required to provide a secure return of $5500 per year? Obviously, this will depend a great deal on the rate of return available from various investment sources and whether or not we want to dip into the capital itself to make up any shortages in income. Assuming we want to preserve our capital, the entire $5500 will have to come from earnings on our investments.

At one extreme let's put all of our capital into a passbook savings account at the local savings and loan or savings bank. The rate of interest paid on these accounts is currently 5.5%. Dividing this rate into the desired $5500 shows us the amount of capital necessary to reach our goal:

$$\frac{\text{Desired income}}{\text{Rate of return}} = \text{Principal amount}$$

$$\$5500/5.5\% = \$100,000$$

To put it another way, if you had $100,000 in a savings account earning 5.5% interest, you would receive $5500 per year in interest. However, the rate paid on insured savings accounts is generally the lowest available return in the financial marketplace. Many other investments are available and will be discussed in Chapter 5, "Investing for Retirement."

For the moment let's assume that you can invest your funds and earn 10% per year. In this case you will need only $55,000 to provide the desired amount of income:

$$\$5500/10\% \ = \ \$55,000$$

In December 1980, six-month U.S. Treasury bills were yielding 15%; an investment in them would reduce the necessary capital even further:

$$\$5500/15\% \ = \ \$36,666$$

The point here is that as the rate of return goes up, the amount of capital required to provide a given level of annual income is reduced. We have also assumed that the rate of return is fixed, while, in reality, these rates vary considerably over time. You cannot assume that you will always earn the highest rates available and you should not build a lifestyle on that assumption.

During the past several years, rates of interest have been at their highest points in the 20th century. These rates can fall quite rapidly, however, as witnessed in early 1980 when short-term rates fell from more than 16% to a little over 8% in just three months (see Fig. 2.2).

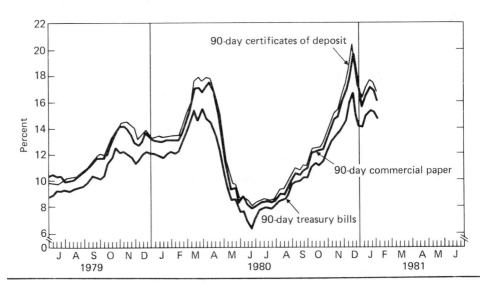

FIG. 2.2 INTEREST RATE FLUCTUATIONS

It is probably better to plan on some reasonable average return than to forecast either very high or very low rates of return on invested assets.

Another assumption in the previous examples was that the figure of $5500 also remained fixed. This "zero-inflation" assumption is obviously unrealistic, and we should expect to need additional income throughout our retirement period in order to maintain the same standard of living.

As we will see in the next chapter, Social Security payments are likely to increase with inflation as measured by the Consumer Price Index (CPI). Many pension plans have a cost-of-living adjustment (COLA) clause which increases retirement benefits to offset inflation. However, these are likely to be limited to 2–3% annually, which is far below the present level of inflation in the United States.

All things considered, we will probably have to rely on our assets for an increasing proportion of our income during retirement. The alternative is to reduce our income itself in the face of rapid increases in prices.

HOW LONG WILL THE MONEY LAST?

Another painful possibility that we may have to consider is using up some of our assets in order to provide an adequate income. This brings us back to the problem of "excess longevity," and whether we will outlive our assets. Obviously, as we eat away at our capital we will have less and less available to generate income. Our income from investments will decline unless we have a higher rate of return. If not, we enter the vicious circle of less capital providing less income—which requires us to use up more capital which results in even less income.

We can evaluate this critical situation by using Table 2.4, which combines the rate of return we expect to earn on our assets with the rate of withdrawal we need to provide an adequate income. The expected rates of return are shown diagonally along the top of the table. The various rates of withdrawal are indicated on the vertical axis at the left. The figures in the body of the table indicate the *number of years* that a given amount of capital will last under different sets of conditions.

For example, Rose Selby plans on taking 10% of her capital each year to supplement her Social Security and pension income. How long will her money last? Look at the row across from the figure for a 10% rate of withdrawal. If she were earning only 5% on her money it would run out at the

TABLE 2.4 HOW LONG WILL YOUR MONEY LAST?

Expected rate of return

Rate of withdrawal:

	5%	6%	7%	8%	9%	10%	11%	12%	13%	14%	15%
6%	37	6%									
7%	25	33	7%								
8%	20	23	30	8%							
9%	16	18	22	29	9%						
10%	14	15	17	20	27	10%					
11%	12	14	15	17	20	25	11%				
12%	11	12	13	14	16	19	24	12%			
13%	10	11	11	12	14	15	18	23	13%		
14%	9	10	10	11	12	13	15	17	22	14%	
15%	8	9	9	10	11	12	13	14	16	21	15%
16%	8	8	9	9	10	10	11	12	14	16	20
17%	7	7	8	8	9	9	10	11	12	13	15
18%	7	7	7	8	8	9	9	10	10	11	13
19%	6	7	7	7	7	8	8	9	9	10	11
20%	6	6	6	7	7	7	8	8	9	9	10

Example: Assume that you are able to earn a 10% rate of return on your invested capital, and that you are withdrawing 15% of it each year. Read down the column for a 10% rate of return until you reach the row which represents the 15% rate of withdrawal. The figure shown is "12" which means that your capital would be used up at the end of 12 years.

If your expected rate of return is equal to or greater than the rate of withdrawal, your funds will last indefinitely, or even increase over time.

end of 14 years. If she could increase the return to 9% it would take some 27 years before her capital would be exhausted.

What happens at rates higher than 9%? If the rate of return is equal to or greater than the rate of withdrawal, the funds will last indefinitely, and may even increase. Ideally, most of us would like to be in a situation where we could live adequately on our income without invading the principal value of our assets. This may not be possible, and so you should give some thought to how much capital you will need, what rate you are presently earning on your assets, and whether you can increase the overall return by making changes in your investments.

After reading Chapter 5, "Investing for Retirement," you may find that you can adjust your investments to earn a substantially higher return without excessive risk. Hopefully, such actions will increase the life expectancy of your capital and possibly your own life since you won't have to worry as much about outliving your assets.

IS THE GRASS REALLY GREENER?

Can you really live better for less in some other part of the country? Living costs do vary considerably from one region to another and from city to country living. You may be giving some thought to whether or not you should move after you retire in order to get more mileage out of your relatively fixed income.

Many persons do move for a variety of reasons or spend part of the year in a seasonal residence. This is a major decision that involves far more than just economic considerations. In fact, the financial factors may be the least important ones to consider. Your social, emotional, and personal lives are definitely tied very closely to where you live and the relationships that you have built up over the years. It is a very difficult process to loosen or cut those ties and try to reestablish them elsewhere.

If you do decide to move, however, you will want to look carefully at the cost of living in a particular area before you make up your mind. Table 2.5 will give you a general idea of how various parts of the nation compare to your present home in regard to living costs. The average urban area has an index cost equal to 100. More expensive locations will have a cost index greater than 100 while cheaper areas will be less than 100. For example, most of the major cities in the northern U. S. are above average in cost. Living costs in Boston are 19% higher than the average community. Cities everywhere, however, tend to have a higher cost of living than nonmetropolitan areas.

Fortunately, most areas in the southern U. S. and some western locations have lower than average living costs. These are typically the parts of the country considered by retired persons when they think about moving their home. Orlando, Florida, for example, has a cost of living index of only 92, and nonmetropolitan areas in the south average only 81 on the scale.

TABLE 2.5 COST OF LIVING FOR A RETIRED COUPLE IN SELECTED CITIES AND AREAS[1] (Average cost in all U.S. cities = 100)

AREA	INDEX
Urban United States	100
Metropolitan areas	105
Nonmetropolitan areas[2]	86
Northeast:	
Boston, Mass.	119
Buffalo, N.Y.	110
Hartford, Conn.	115
New York-N.E. New Jersey	118
Philadelphia, Pa.-New Jersey	107
Portland, Me.	104
Nonmetropolitan areas[2]	98
North Central:	
Cedar Rapids, Ia.	100
Chicago, Ill.-N.W. Indiana	101
Dayton, Ohio	96
Green Bay, Wis.	99
Minneapolis-St. Paul, Minn.	101
St. Louis, Mo.-Ill.	100
Nonmetropolitan areas[2]	89
South:	
Atlanta, Ga.	91
Austin, Tex.	90
Baltimore, Md.	98
Baton Rouge, La.	88
Dallas, Tex.	94
Durham, N.C.	94
Houston, Tex.	93
Nashville, Tenn.	96
Orlando, Fla.	92
Washington, D.C.-Va.-Md.	103
Nonmetropolitan areas[2]	81
West:	
Bakersfield, Calif.	95
Denver, Colo.	97
Los Angeles-Long Beach, Calif.	103
San Diego, Calif.	99
San Francisco-Oakland, Calif.	110
Seattle-Everett, Wash.	104
Honolulu, Hawaii	113
Nonmetropolitan areas[2]	89

[1] *Based on an intermediate budget for a retired couple (husband 65 or over), Autumn 1972. Preliminary estimates developed by U.S. Department of Labor, Bureau of Labor Statistics.*
[2] *Places with population of 2,500 to 50,000.*

Living costs are also increasing at different rates in various parts of the country. While certain areas may be cheaper now, they may not continue to be so in the future. Table 2.6 shows the 1979 increase in the Consumer Price Index (CPI) for various metropolitan areas. Surprisingly, the figures for northeastern cities such as Buffalo, New York, and Philadelphia are among the lowest reported. Prices increased most rapidly in Kansas City, Dallas-Fort Worth, and Los Angeles.

While it is possible to stretch your retirement budget by moving to an area with lower living costs, you should not count on doing so to solve all of your financial problems. In the first place, it may be expensive to move your possessions and you may add substantially to your travel costs if you constantly are returning "home" for visits to family and friends.

A better approach is to plan to have enough income to live comfortably wherever you want to live. Then if you decide to move to a cheaper area it will come as a "bonus" rather than something that you are forced to do. Moving after you retire should be a voluntary decision based on personal desires, not a forced one based on economic hardship.

TABLE 2.6 1979 ANNUAL INCREASE IN THE CPI FOR VARIOUS METROPOLITAN AREAS

Atlanta	12.3%
Buffalo	10,8%
Chicago Metropolitan Area	15.0%
Cleveland	13.0%
Dallas-Fort Worth	16.1%
Detroit	15.3%
Honolulu	12.3%
Houston	13.2%
Kansas City	17.6%
Los Angeles Metropolitan Area	15.7%
Minneapolis-St. Paul	12.2%
New York Metropolitan Area	10.6%
Philadelphia	11.2%
Pittsburgh	11.7%
San Francisco-Oakland	14.6%

SOURCE: U.S. Bureau of Labor Statistics

A STRATEGY FOR FINANCIAL SECURITY

At this point you should be convinced of the importance of careful planning for your future financial security. We all want to be at least secure, if not well off, for the rest of our lives. This concern certainly grows as we reach our retirement years, particularly if we have not done any advance planning. Hopefully, you have done so, or have enough working years left to make plans now and put them into action. Even a small increase in your retirement income may make a great deal of difference to your overall standard of living. Through careful planning now you can ensure that your disposable retirement income will be at least as much as your preretirement income.

Analyze your present income and expenditure patterns. Not with the idea that you are going to have to cut back and be miserable, but with the determination to use your income efficiently and to accumulate retirement resources. Estimate the income and assets that you will need once you retire. Set some financial goals! Even if you don't succeed completely, you'll probably come a lot closer to your objectives than if you had none in the first place. Obviously your plans will change over time and you may have to rethink your goals as conditions change. But *you* will be in control, rather than at the mercy of our changing economy.

The remaining chapters in this book will provide additional information for you to consider. More importantly they will provide the tools and techniques by which you can design your own personal strategy for financial security.

3
SOCIAL
SECURITY

If a free society cannot help the many
who are poor, it cannot save the few
who are rich.

John F. Kennedy

HISTORY OF SOCIAL SECURITY

The Social Security system of the United States was created on August 14, 1935, when President Franklin D. Roosevelt signed legislation passed by Congress. The legislation was based on recommendations of a Committee on Economic Security which was created to study the effects of the Great Depression of the 1930s. Prior to that time only 15% of all workers in the U.S. were covered by any type of retirement plan.

The Social Security Act of 1935 provided old-age insurance only for retired workers. The survivors and dependents of those workers were not included in the program until amendments to the original legislation were passed in 1939. Coverage in the early days of Social Security was aimed primarily at industrial workers and those in similar occupations. During the 1950s, farm workers, self-employed persons, household employees, and certain disabled persons came under Social Security coverage.

Coverage has continued to spread throughout the labor force until the great majority of workers in the United States are now included in the system. Perhaps the single largest group *not* included in the plan are public employees of state, local, and federal governments. Congress, which passed the original Social Security bill, has voted not to be included under its coverage! The Congress has its own retirement plan which many have criticized as being much more generous in its benefits than the Social Security system.

One of the most widespread changes in the Social Security system occurred during the 1960s when new legislation added Medicare benefits to the retirement insurance program. Medicare consists of two separate plans: hospital insurance and supplementary medical insurance. Medicaid provisions were also introduced whereby retired persons were eligible to have physicians' charges included for an additional monthly fee deducted from their Social Security checks.

Most recently, Congress has passed new laws which have revised the contribution formulas and benefits schedules which will apply to all participants in the program. Both the Social Security tax percentage and the amount of income to which it applies have been raised and will continue to increase in the future.

Table 3.1 shows the Social Security tax rate, the maximum wage base, and the maximum tax to be paid by employees and their employers. Table 3.2 provides similar information for those persons who are self-employed. Without such increases it was feared that the entire Social Security system would have gone bankrupt within the next few years.

TABLE 3.1 SOCIAL SECURITY TAX ON EMPLOYEES

YEAR	% RATE (OASDI + HI)	MAX. WAGE BASE	MAX. TAX (EACH)	MAX. TAX (BOTH)
1981	6.65 (5.35 + 1.30)	29,700	1,975.05	3,950.10
1982–84	6.70 (5.40 + 1.30)	29,700*	1,989.90	3.979.80
1985	7.05 (5.70 + 1.35)	29,700*	2,093.85	4,187.70
1986–89	7.15 (5.70 + 1.45)	29,700*	2,123.55	4.247.10
1990–2010	7.65 (6.20 + 1.45)	29,700*	2.272.05	4,544.10
2011–	7.65 (6.20 + 1.45)	29,700*	2,272.05	4,544.10

Maximum Wage Base subject to automatic adjustment in 1982 and after based on changes in wage levels.

TABLE 3.2 TAX ON SELF-EMPLOYED PERSONS

YEAR	% RATE (OASDI + HI)	MAX. EARNINGS BASE	MAX. TAX
1981	9.30 (8.00 + 1.30)	29,700	2,762.10
1982–84	9.35 (8.05 + 1.30)	29,700*	2,776.95
1985	9.90 (8.55 + 1.35)	29,700*	2,940.30
1986–89	10.00 (8.55 + 1.45)	29,700*	2,970.00
1990–2010	10.75 (9.30 + 1.45)	29,700*	3,192.75
2011–	10.75 (9.30 + 1.45)	29,700*	3,192.75

Maximum Earnings Base subject to automatic adjustment in 1982 and after based on changes in wage levels.

SOCIAL SECURITY TODAY

The original intent of Social Security was to provide a "floor" of benefits which would be guaranteed to covered individuals based on their contributions during their working years. Thus, persons who earned higher incomes and made greater contributions to the system could expect to receive more in benefits when they retired. It was presumed that individuals would provide additional retirement income through their own savings and investment programs. Finally, group plans offered by employers would provide the third leg of the "tripod of financial security."

This concept of Social Security as a base upon which the individual could build his or her own retirement security has been changed substantially over the years. In recent years the system has been criticized for providing benefits that would not support an individual with a minimum degree of comfort and economic security. Retired persons have made increasing demands that Social Security payments alone should enable them to have an adequate standard of living. Such demands have come at a time when Social Security has been hard pressed to pay even the present level of benefits, let alone a substantially higher level that would provide for all of a person's economic needs during a period of rapid inflation.

Many persons still believe that their Social Security contributions go into their own "account" which is held for them until they retire. This has *never* been the case, and would certainly be impossible under the financing conditions that exist today.

Retirement benefits have always been paid to retired persons from the contributions of those individuals who were still working. During the early years of operation, the payroll taxes from working persons far exceeded the amounts paid to those receiving benefits. The surplus was "invested" in securities of the Federal government and shown as assets of the Social Security system. At times this trust fund approached $50 billion in assets.

Over the years, however, the number of persons receiving benefits has increased dramatically, as have the various benefit levels. Finally, in 1975, benefits paid exceeded payroll tax contributions by some $2.7 billion. These deficits have continued to mount putting pressure on the Congress to revise the funding of Social Security. Recent changes in the Social Security tax and wage base have been introduced to put the system back on a pay-as-you-go basis. Even with these changes it is very uncertain that contributions can keep up with benefits which have been indexed to the levels of inflation. Benefits are increased yearly on the basis of changes in the Consumer Price Index (CPI) during the previous year. Recently, as inflation has moved up rapidly, benefit levels have grown dramatically. It has been suggested that the government turn to general revenues to make Social Security payments and to guarantee older persons that the system will never go broke.

Continuous changes in the financing of Social Security will probably be required as the population of the United States "ages" during the coming years. There are more and more persons reaching retirement age with fewer new workers to provide payroll tax revenue. Figure 3.1 shows how our population has changed by age and sex from 1950 to 1979, with a forecast of what it will look like in the year 2030.

In 1935, when Social Security began, there were 11 people in the adult labor force for everyone who was 65 years of age or older. Today, the ratio is about three to one—95 million Americans working and some 32 million receiving Social Security benefits.

Figure 3.2 shows how the relationship between covered workers and beneficiaries has changed over the years since 1950 and what we can expect to happen in the future. Also, the number of older persons in our population will increase faster than the population as a whole. This is shown dramatically in Table 3.3, which indicates that the number of persons 60 years old and over will grow five times as fast as the under-60 population. Each of these factors will put an additional strain on the Social Security system.

Is it any wonder that taxes on workers must increase rapidly to keep up the payments to the ever larger group of retired persons? Other suggestions

AGE

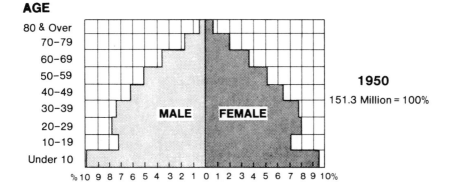

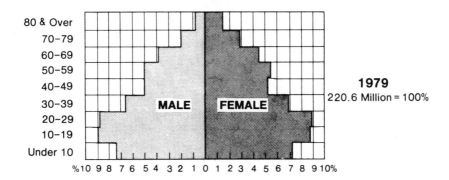

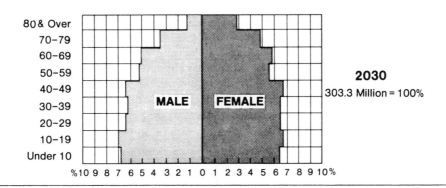

FIG. 3.1 DISTRIBUTION OF THE U.S. POPULATION *SOURCE:* U.S. Bureau of the Census, *Current Population Reports*, Series P-25, Nos. 311 (July 2, 1965), 704 (July, 1977), and 870 (January, 1980).

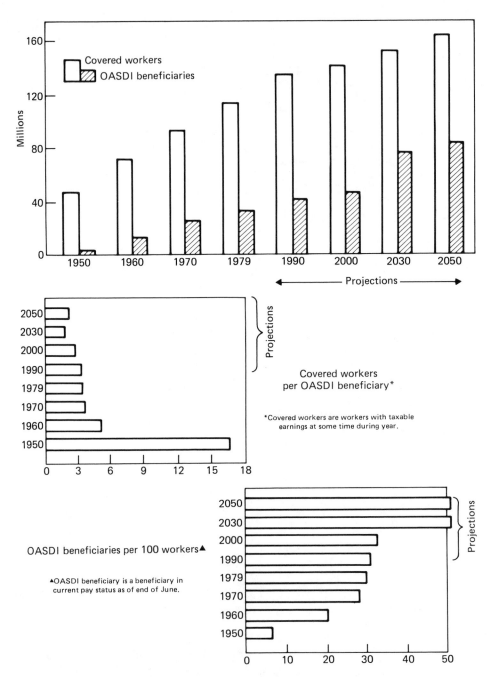

Note: Projections are based on an intermediate set of assumptions. The Trustees' Report also presents projections based on two other sets of assumptions — "more optimistic" and "more pessimistic" than the intermediate set.

FIG. 3.2 COVERED WORKERS AND OASDI BENEFICIARIES

TABLE 3.3 PROJECTED POPULATION GROWTH

	PROJECTED NUMBER IN 2030 (MILLIONS)	PERCENT INCREASE, 1979 to 2030
Total U.S. Population	300.3	+ 36%
Under 60 years old	229.6	+ 23
60 years old and over	70.7	+107
80 years old and over	12.7	+149

for balancing the Social Security budget have included proposals to reduce retirement benefits, to increase the age at which a person would begin to receive benefits from 65 to 68, and to include more persons in the system who are not now covered by Social Security payroll taxes. Needless to say, all of these suggestions have met with howls of protest and outrage from those who would be affected by the plans. Within the next 20 years, however, some or all of these suggestions may have to be carried out to keep the system in balance.

SOCIAL SECURITY AND YOU

For most of us the Social Security system represents our single largest financial asset. Now you may well ask how that can possibly be when the system seems to be barely chugging along. Well, it is necessary to *assume* that the Federal government will not let the system go bankrupt and will take action to maintain the flow of benefits to retired persons and their dependents. If so, the flow of potential benefits to a person or their family is the equivalent of a very large amount of capital. How much? In order to provide the current maximum family benefits of $1028.40 per month that family would have to have $205,680 earning an after-tax return of six percent. Of course, this assumes that they would use only the income and the capital base could be preserved forever. Even so, it should be clear that the "asset" represented by full Social Security benefits is a substantial one indeed.

Perhaps a more relevant case would be that of, for example, Steve Forbes, who is about to retire at age 65. Steve has been giving some thought to the real value of his Social Security benefits. As we saw in Table 1.1, Steve's life expectancy is a bit more than 13 years. A retirement benefit of $400 per month would be equal to $4800 annually. If he wished to match his Social

Security benefits with his own funds, how much capital would Steve need to provide 13 years of comparable benefits?

Assuming Steve were able to earn 7% after taxes on his capital he would need $40,117 to provide $4800 per year for 13 years. Even then, he would have used up all of his funds and would face the problem of "excess longevity," or outliving his resources. This is a distinct advantage of Social Security in that it provides a *lifetime* income based on millions of participants rather than any one individual account.

Overall, then, Social Security represents a very important part of your strategy for financial security. Another of its advantages is the nonvoluntary nature of your participation in the program. If you are working in covered employment you *must* participate, and so will earn credits toward full coverage. As your income increases your average indexed monthly earnings (AIME) will also increase, leading to higher benefits when you eventually retire. All of these things occur automatically with the exception that you must file an application to begin receiving benefits.

Still another advantage to the system is the fact that you cannot invade the principal value of your "account" whenever you wish to make a major purchase, or even to send your children to college. You are assured that the funds will be there when you retire, given the assumptions we made about the government's desire to maintain the solvency of the program. Let's take a look now at how you can estimate the amount you will receive in retirement benefits and try to answer some of the important questions you may have concerning Social Security.

ESTIMATING YOUR SOCIAL SECURITY RETIREMENT CHECK

Retirement just around the corner? You're probably wondering how much your Social Security checks will be. You'll find an approximate answer in this section.

A retired worker and spouse can get full monthly checks if they wait until 65 to start getting benefits. This is true even though the method used to figure payments is based on when a worker reaches 62. The information given here is limited to retirement checks for people who reach 62 in 1980 through 1983. Social Security also pays disability and survivors' benefits, but for information about these benefits, call any Social Security office.

This section can give you a rough estimate, not an exact figure, of what your retirement check will be. Retirement benefits for people who reach 62 in 1980 through 1983 will be figured two ways: first, by the method described here; second, by a new method. The benefit payable will be the higher of the two calculations. For the next few years, the method described will result in a higher benefit rate for most people.

Under the new method, actual earnings for past years will be adjusted to take account of changes in average wages since 1951. These adjusted earnings will be averaged together and the benefit rate figured from this average. You will receive at least as much as the rate you get by using the method described here. You will get more if the new method results in a higher benefit rate. Once your retirement checks start, your benefit rate will be increased automatically as the cost of living increases.

You Need Work Credits

Before you can get a Social Security retirement check, you need to have credit for a certain amount of work under Social Security. The table shows how much credit you need. No one ever needs more than 10 years of work.

IF YOU REACH 62 IN	YOU NEED CREDIT FOR THIS MUCH WORK
1981	7-1/2 years
1982	7-3/4 years
1983	8 years
1987	9 years
1991 or later	10 years

If you stop working under Social Security before you have this much credit, you can't get retirement benefits. But the credit you've earned will stay on your record, and you can add to it if you return to work in a job covered by Social Security.

How To Estimate the Amount

Follow the directions below and you'll find out the approximate amount of the monthly checks you'll get from social security after you retire.

STEP 1

Your retirement check is based on your average earnings over a period of years. For the year you were born, pick the number of years you need to count from the following table:

YEAR YOU WERE BORN	YEARS NEEDED
1917	23
1918	24
1919	25
1920	26
1921	27

Write the number of years here _____.

STEP 2

Fill in the worksheet in Fig. 3.3. Column A shows maximum earnings covered by Social Security. In Column B, list your earnings beginning with 1951. Write "0" for a year of no earnings. If you earned more than the maximum in any year, list only the maximum. Estimate your earnings for future years, but *do not* include earnings for the year you reach 62 or later.

STEP 3

Cross off your list the years of your *lowest* earnings until the number of years left is the same as your answer to Step 1. (You may have to leave some years of "0" earnings on your list.)

STEP 4

Add up the earnings for the years left on your list. Write this figure in the space marked "Total" at the bottom of the worksheet and here. $_____.

STEP 5

Divide this total by the number you wrote for Step 1. The result is your average yearly earnings covered by Social Security. Write the figure here. $_____.

STEP 6

Look at the benefit chart, Table 3.4. Under the heading "For Workers," find the average yearly earnings figure *closest* to your own. Look over to the column listing your age at retirement to see about how much you can expect to get. Write the figure here. $_____.

YEAR	A	B
1951	3,600	
1952	3,600	
1953	3,600	
1954	3,600	
1955	4,200	
1956	4,200	
1957	4,200	
1958	4,200	
1959	4,800	
1960	4,800	
1961	4,800	
1962	4,800	
1963	4,800	
1964	4,800	
1965	4,800	
1966	6,600	
1967	6,600	
1968	7,800	
1969	7,800	
1970	7,800	
1971	7,800	
1972	9,000	
1973	10,800	
1974	13,200	
1975	14,100	
1976	15,300	
1977	16,500	
1978	17,700	
1979	22,900	
1980	25,900	
1981	29,700*	
TOTAL		$

*Maximum amount of annual earnings that count for Social Security will rise automatically after 1981 as earnings levels increase. Because of this, the base in 1982 and later may be higher than $29,700.

FIG. 3.3 SOCIAL SECURITY WORKSHEET

TABLE 3.4   SOCIAL SECURITY BENEFIT CHART

MONTHLY RETIREMENT BENEFITS FOR WORKERS WHO REACH 62 in 1979-83

Average yearly earnings	For Workers				Spouse at 65 or child	For Dependents[1]			Family[2] benefits
	Retirement at 65	at 64	at 63	at 62		at 64	at 63	at 62	
$923 or less	121.80	113.70	105.60	97.50	60.90	55.90	50.80	45.70	182.70
1,200	156.70	146.30	135.90	125.40	78.40	71.90	65.40	58.80	235.10
2,600	230.10	214.80	199.50	184.10	115.10	105.50	95.90	86.40	345.20
3,000	251.80	235.10	218.30	201.50	125.90	115.40	104.90	94.50	384.90
3,400	270.00	252.00	234.00	216.00	135.00	123.80	112.50	101.30	434.90
4,000	296.20	276.50	256.80	237.00	148.10	135.70	123.40	111.10	506.20
4,400	317.30	296.20	275.00	253.90	158.70	145.40	132.20	119.10	562.50
4,800	336.00	313.60	291.20	268.80	168.00	153.90	140.00	126.00	612.70
5,200	353.20	329.70	306.20	282.60	176.60	161.80	147.20	132.50	662.70
5,600	370.60	345.90	321.20	296.50	185.30	169.80	154.40	139.00	687.10
6,000	388.20	362.40	336.50	310.60	194.10	177.80	161.70	145.60	712.10
6,400	405.60	378.60	351.60	324.50	202.80	185.80	169.00	152.10	737.10
6,800	424.10	395.90	367.60	339.30	212.10	194.30	176.70	159.10	762.30
7,200	446.00	416.30	386.60	356.80	223.00	204.30	185.80	167.30	788.90
7,600	464.60	434.60	403.60	372.50	232.80	123.30	194.00	174.60	814.70
8,000	482.60	450.50	418.30	386.10	241.30	221.10	201.10	181.00	844.50
8,400	492.90	460.10	427.20	394.40	246.50	225.80	205.40	184.90	862.60
8,800	505.10	471.50	437.80	404.10	252.60	231.40	210.50	189.50	883.80
9,200	516.00	481.60	447.20	412.80	258.00	236.40	215.00	193.50	903.00
9,400	520.40	485.80	451.10	416.40	260.20	238.40	216.80	195.20	910.40
9,600	524.60	489.70	454.70	419.70	262.30	240.30	218.50	196.80	918.00
9,800	530.40	495.10	459.70	424.40	265.20	243.00	221.00	198.90	928.00
10,000	534.70	499.10	463.50	427.80	267.40	245.00	222.80	200.60	935.70

[1] If a person is eligible for both a worker's benefit and a spouse's benefit, the check actually payable is limited to the larger of the two.

[2] The maximum amount payable to a family is generally reached when a worker and two family members are eligible.

STEP 7

If you have an eligible spouse or child, or both, look under the heading "For Dependents" to find about how much they can get, based on the same average yearly earnings you used to figure your check. Write the amount of any dependents' benefits here. $_____.

STEP 8

Finally, add the figures you wrote for Steps 6 and 7 to see about how much your total family retirement benefit will be under Social Security. (The total cannot exceed the amount in the "Family benefits" column.) Write the figure here. $_____ .

Figure 3.4 gives an example for a person who was born in 1919 and plans to retire in 1981, and who has regularly made the maximum Social Security contribution.

A Word About Maximum Benefits

Some people think that if they've always earned the maximum amount covered by Social Security they will get the highest benefits shown on the chart. This isn't so. The reason is that the maximum amount of earnings covered by Social Security was lower in past years than it is now. Those years of lower limits must be counted in with the higher ones of recent years to figure your average earnings and thus the amount of your monthly retirement check.

WHAT EVERY FEMALE WORKER SHOULD KNOW

A woman who works earns Social Security protection not only for herself but also for her dependents. Even if she is single and has no dependents, the Social Security credits she earns while she works count toward monthly benefits for the family she may have in the future. This section explains the Social Security benefits payable when a woman worker becomes disabled, dies, or retires.

While You Work

You have Social Security disability and survivors' insurance protection while you are working. This means that monthly benefits would be payable if you

Step 1	25 years needed (birth year = 1919)
Step 2	See completed worksheet below
Step 3	Eliminate years 1951–1955
Step 4	$236,000
Step 5	$236,000/25 = $9440
Step 6	$416.40 (figure for $9400)
Step 7	$195.20 (figure for $9400; spouse age 62)
Step 8	$611.60 total retirement benefit

Year	A	B
1951	3,600	~~3,600~~
1952	3,600	~~3,600~~
1953	3,600	~~3,600~~
1954	3,600	~~3,600~~
1955	4,200	~~4,200~~
1956	4,200	4,200
1957	4,200	4,200
1958	4,200	4,200
1959	4,800	4,800
1960	4,800	4,800
1961	4,800	4,800
1962	4,800	4,800
1963	4,800	4,800
1964	4,800	4,800
1965	4,800	4,800
1966	6,600	6,600
1967	6,600	6,600
1968	7,800	7,800
1969	7,800	7,800
1970	7,800	7,800
1971	7,800	7,800
1972	9,000	9,000
1973	10,800	10,800
1974	13,200	13,200
1975	14,100	14,100
1976	15,300	15,300
1977	16,500	16,500
1978	17,700	17,700
1979	22,900	22,900
1980	25,900	25,900
1981	29,700*	
TOTAL		$ 236,000

FIG. 3.4 SAMPLE SOCIAL SECURITY CALCULATION

become disabled or die after having worked long enough under Social Security. If you become disabled and can't work for a year or more, you can get disability checks. Your disability payments would start with the sixth full month of your disability—there's a five-month waiting period for disability benefits—and would continue as long as you are disabled. When you've been eligible for disability payment for two consecutive years, you also will have Medicare protection. (*Note:* While you work, you also earn credits toward Medicare protection for yourself and your dependents in the event that you or they ever need dialysis treatment or a kidney transplant for permanent kidney failure.)

Your children can get benefits, too, when you're disabled. Under the Social Security law, the term "children" includes stepchildren and legally adopted children. Monthly checks are payable to unmarried children who are under 18 (or under 22 if they are full-time students) and to children who became disabled before age 22 and remain disabled.

If he is 62 or older, your husband may qualify for payments when you're disabled. Both your widower and your children can get monthly survivors' checks if you should die. Survivors' checks may be payable even if you only have one-and-a-half years of work in the three years before you die. If there are no children, your widower must be either 60 or older or between 50 and 60 and disabled to get survivors' benefits on your work record. There's also a lump-sum death payment of $225 that can help pay for funeral expenses. And if you have dependent parents 62 or older, they may be eligible for payments if you die.

If You Interrupt Your Career

To get any Social Security benefits, you need credit for a certain amount of work. The amount of credit you need generally depends on your age when you become disabled, die, or retire. If you stop working before you earn enough Social Security credits, no benefits will be payable. But credits you have already earned remain on your work record, and you can always go back to work and earn any additional credits you need to get benefits. This rule applies to both women and men, but it's particularly significant to a woman simply because she may prefer to stay home while she's raising children.

One thing to keep in mind, though, is that the amount of any monthly benefit payable on your record could be affected by years of no earnings.

The amount of your benefit—and your family's benefits—is based on your average earnings over a period of years. If several years of no earnings (or low earnings) have to be included in figuring your average earnings, then your benefit may be lower than what it would be if you worked throughout your life.

When You Retire

You can retire as early as age 62, if you want to take reduced benefits. Payments to people who retire before age 65 are *permanently* reduced to take account of the longer period of time they get checks. If you wait until age 65 to retire, you get full retirement benefits.

If you're married, you can get retirement payments either on your own record or on your husband's. By the same token, your husband can get retirement benefits at 62 or older either on his record or on yours. But whenever a person is eligible for benefits on more than one work record, the benefit payable is equal to the larger amount. (This same rule applies to children who are eligible for benefits when their parents retire.)

Of course, if you've worked all your adult life and had high earnings, it's likely that your own benefit will be higher than a wife's benefit. At 65, a wife gets 50 percent of what her husband is entitled to at age 65. On the other hand, if you stopped working for several years or had low earnings, the wife's payment may be higher. When you apply for retirement benefits, the people in the Social Security office can tell you whether you will get a higher payment on your own record or on your husband's record.

A wife who has earned her own Social Security credits also has certain options at retirement. For example, suppose your husband continues to work past 65 and earns too much to get benefits. Or suppose he's younger than you. You can go ahead and retire on your own record. Then, when he retires, you take wife's payments if they would be higher.

Or regardless of your husband's age, you can take reduced benefits on your wage record before age 65. But remember, your payment will always be reduced—even if you take reduced benefits on your own record and then take wife's benefits when your husband retires. (*Note:* These same benefit rules and options apply to a husband who is eligible for retirement payments on both his own and his wife's work record.)

Finally, there's Medicare. If you are entitled to monthly Social Security benefits—either on your own record or on your husband's—you will have Medicare hospital insurance protection automatically at age 65. If you're not entitled to benefits, you'll need some credit for work under Social Security to get hospital insurance without paying a monthly premium. To get Medicare medical insurance, you enroll for it and pay monthly premiums.

WHAT A WIFE SHOULD KNOW

What about the woman who chooses to make her home and family her career? She and her family have Social Security protection through her husband's work, and they can get benefits when he retires, becomes disabled, or dies. This section explains the benefits payable to a wife. A working wife is entitled to these same benefits, but if she's working, she may be earning too much for benefits to be payable to her.

A Wife

Regardless of your age, you can get payments when your husband becomes disabled or retires if you are caring for a child under 18 or a disabled child who is entitled to benefits. If you don't have a child in your care, you must be 62 or older to get benefits when your husband becomes disabled or retires. If you get retirement benefits before 65, the payment is reduced. If you wait until age 65 to retire, you get the full wife's benefit, which is 50 percent of the amount your husband is entitled to at 65.

Both you and your husband will have Medicare hospital insurance at 65 if he is entitled to monthly benefits. You can enroll for medical insurance. You will have Medicare at 65 even if your husband is younger than you and still working, provided he files an application to establish that he will be entitled to benefits when he retires. If your husband is deceased, you'll have Medicare if he would have been entitled to benefits or had worked long enough under Social Security. (*Note:* While your husband is working, he earns credits toward Medicare protection for your family in the event any of you ever need dialysis treatment or kidney transplant for permanent kidney failure. Also, if he becomes disabled and is entitled to benefits for two years, he would have Medicare protection.)

Young Widow with Children

You can get a widow's benefit at any age if you are caring for a child who is under 18 or disabled and entitled to benefits. Survivors' benefits on your husband's record are also payable to unmarried children under 22 who are full-time students. Your benefits will stop when you no longer have a child in your care who is either under 18 or disabled. Usually your benefits also will stop if you remarry. But even if you do remarry, benefits to your children will continue so long as they remain eligible for payments.

Aged Widow

Even if you do not have dependent children when your husband dies, you can get widows' benefits if you are 60 or older. The amount of your monthly payment will depend on your age when you start getting benefits and the amount your deceased husband would have been entitled to or was receiving when he died.

Widows benefits range from 71.5 percent of the deceased husband's benefit amount at age 60 to 100 percent at 65. So if you start getting benefits at age 65, you'll get 100 percent of the amount your husband would be receiving if he were still alive. If you're disabled, you can get widows' benefits as early as age 50, but your payment will be reduced.

A point to remember: If you are entitled to retirement benefits on your own work record and you receive reduced widows benefits between age 50 and 65, your own retirement benefit at 65 also would be reduced.

Remarried Widow

Ordinarily, a widow loses her Social Security rights when she remarries. But if you remarry at 60 or older, your widow's benefits could continue. The amount you would get would be 50 percent of the retirement benefit your deceased former husband was entitled to. If your new husband gets Social Security checks, however, you can take a wife's benefit on his record if it would be larger than your widow's payment.

Divorcee

You can get benefits when your ex-husband starts collecting retirement or disability payments if you are 62 or older and were married to him at least

10 years. You may also get payments if your ex-husband dies, provided you are 60 or older (50, if you're disabled) and were married 10 years or more or have young children entitled to benefits on his record.

Medicare for Widows

If you are 50 or older, and you become disabled while getting checks because you have young children in your care, contact Social Security about eligibility for Medicare. Even though you haven't filed a claim for payments based on disability (since you are already getting payments as a mother), you could be eligible for Medicare protection if you have been disabled for two years or longer.

If You Change Your Name

One important thing to remember about Social Security is to make sure that your Social Security record shows your correct name. This is particularly important if you are employed, because your employer reports your earnings under the name you give him or her. Whenever you change the name you use in employment—whether because of marriage, divorce, or other reasons—you should report the change to Social Security. Otherwise, your earnings won't be properly recorded and you may not receive all the Social Security due you for your work.

Of course, if you choose to continue using your maiden name after marriage, as many women do today, you don't have to report your marriage. Just be sure you use your maiden name consistently throughout your employment.

Even if you don't work, you should report any name change so that your record will show the correct name when you apply for benefits. To report a name change, all you have to do is fill out a *Request For Change in Social Security Records*. You can get this form at any Social Security office.

SUMMARY

In summary, Social Security represents the single most important element of retirement security for most people. In addition to providing a lifetime income that increases when the cost of living goes up, the System offers some protection against the rapidly rising cost of medical care. The mandatory nature of participation and the protection from invasion of principal are also valuable characteristics.

And yet, you should not count on Social Security to "do it all" when you retire. Remember, Social Security started out as a base to build on, and you should not consider it anything more than that. You still have a job to do in preparing for your retirement. The remainder of this book will alert you to some of the problems you are going to face and advise you on how to plan for your financial security. The primary responsibility is still yours, not the United States government's. You must determine the strengths and weaknesses of your own situation and then set out to improve that situation until the day you retire.

Answers to some of your most important questions concerning Social Security can be found in Chapter 10, the last chapter of this book.

4
THE IMPACT OF
INFLATION

I've been rich and I've been poor.
Rich is better.

Mae West

Chapters 2 and 3 have been concerned with determining the amount of income you can expect to have when you retire. The result is an estimate of the actual *dollars* you will have available to spend. Unfortunately, simply knowing how *many* dollars you will have available is not enough to determine whether or not you will have a comfortable retirement. The purchasing power of those dollars, year after year, is much more significant in measuring the quality of your retirement. Measuring the ability of those dollars to purchase goods and services brings us to the important topic of inflation and the effect that it will have on your financial security and retirement income.

EFFECT OF INFLATION

A simple, economic definition of inflation is "a period of rising prices." Most of us would be hard put to remember a time when prices *weren't* rising! Inflation has been a common part of our everyday economic lives since at least the end of World War II. Looking back over that period we can see that since 1945 the purchasing power of the dollar has declined in every year but two (1949 and 1955)! Is there any good reason to believe that this situation will change substantially in the years to come? Probably not, and it is something that every person planning for financial security and retirement must take into account. While we have seen that your disposable income may be more than you expected, the value of those dollars is almost certain to shrink a great deal as each year passes.

Figure 4.1 shows how steady and serious the impact of inflation has been in the United States since 1949. The value of a dollar has declined to only 28.1 cents when compared with its purchasing power in 1949. Even worse is our experience with inflation in more recent years. The current Consumer Price Index (CPI) is based on the purchasing power of the dollar in 1967. As of November 1980 it would take $256 to purchase the same amount of goods and services as could have been purchased for $100 in 1967.

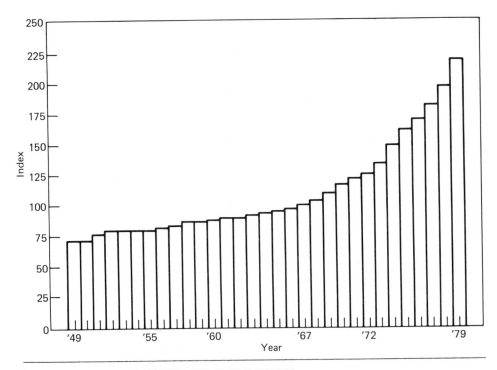

FIG. 4.1 CHART OF CONSUMER PRICE INDEX

Throughout 1979, 1980, and 1981 the inflation rate has ranged from 12% to 18% annually. Officials of the federal government have admitted that they do not see national economic conditions changing enough in the near future so as to reduce this level to less than a 10% annual rate. Such an inflationary climate is a disaster for those persons who are living on a relatively fixed income. This includes most retired persons who have less ability to increase their incomes to offset the effects of high inflation. For those of us who are still working, inflation makes planning all the more difficult and jeopardizes our hopes for the future. While Social Security benefits are currently indexed to changes in the CPI, they may not always keep pace with inflation. And because of the rapidly escalating costs of the Social Security system, even this benefit may be reduced in the years to come.

Relatively few pension plans have any cost-of-living adjustments built into them, and even when they do, it is often a token amount such as 1% or 2% per year. The average retired person, therefore, can expect to be made a little bit *poorer* each year because of inflation! Realizing this fact, however, should make you even more anxious to plan carefully for your future. Inflation will not go away. Let's see just what it will take for you to keep up with the decline of the dollar.

Decline in Purchasing Power

Table 4.1 projects the decline in purchasing power of the dollar for the next 15 years at various rates of inflation. Keep in mind that these rates are lower than the present rate of inflation which may be considered abnormally high by historic standards.

Remember also that the average man who survives until age 65 and then retires can expect to live for an additional 14 years. Women can expect an even longer life span, 18 years. It is the cumulative effect of inflation over this time period with which we must be so concerned. Your later years should be just as secure and enjoyable as the earlier ones, but it will take careful planning to offset inflation.

As an example, let's look at Brian Winters, who is about to retire at age 65. He will receive a monthly pension of $1000 beginning in 1981, but has no cost-of-living clause built into his plan. If inflation were to average 8% annually for five years, what would Brian's purchasing power be in 1986?

Looking at Table 4.1 for the year 1986 and an inflation rate of 8% we

TABLE 4.1 DECLINE IN PURCHASING POWER OF THE DOLLAR

YEAR	RATE OF INFLATION				
	6%	7%	8%	9%	10%
1981	$ 1.00	$ 1.00	$ 1.00	$ 1.00	$ 1.00
1982	0.94	0.93	0.92	0.91	0.90
1983	0.88	0.86	0.85	0.83	0.81
1984	0.83	0.80	0.78	0.75	0.73
1985	0.78	0.75	0.72	0.69	0.66
1986	0.73	0.70	0.66	0.62	0.59
1987	0.69	0.65	0.61	0.57	0.53
1988	0.65	0.60	0.56	0.52	0.48
1989	0.61	0.56	0.51	0.47	0.43
1990	0.57	0.52	0.47	0.43	0.39
1991	0.54	0.48	0.43	0.39	0.35
1992	0.51	0.45	0.40	0.35	0.31
1993	0.48	0.42	0.37	0.32	0.28
1994	0.42	0.39	0.34	0.29	0.25
1995	0.40	0.36	0.31	0.27	0.23
1996	0.37	0.34	0.29	0.24	0.21

see a factor of 0.66. Multiplying Brian's original benefit of $1000 by this factor gives us an inflation-adjusted total of $660.

Brian's hard-earned pension benefits would have *lost* one-third of his purchasing power in just five short years! At the end of 15 years, or his approximate life span, his 1996 pension of $1000 per month would buy the equivalent of only $290 worth of 1981 goods and services.

Income Growth Needed

It may be easier for most of us to look at this problem in terms of dollars rather than rates of inflation. Table 4.2 shows the amount of income growth necessary to keep pace with given levels of inflation. These figures are consistent with those in Table 4.1, but show the required growth in income to maintain a particular level of consumption rather than the decline in the purchasing power of the dollar.

If Brian Winters wanted to maintain his 1981 standard of living, how much income would he need in 1986 to keep pace with an 8% rate of inflation? Looking at Table 4.2 for 1986 and an inflation rate of 8% we see a figure of $147. This means that every $100 of income in 1981 must increase

TABLE 4.2 REQUIRED INCOME GROWTH TO KEEP PACE WITH INFLATION

YEAR	RATE OF INFLATION				
	6%	7%	8%	9%	10%
1981	$ 100	$ 100	$ 100	$ 100	$ 100
1982	106	107	108	109	110
1983	112	114	117	119	121
1984	119	123	126	130	133
1985	126	131	136	141	146
1986	134	140	147	154	161
1987	142	150	159	168	177
1988	150	161	171	183	195
1989	159	172	185	199	214
1990	169	184	200	217	236
1991	179	197	216	237	259
1992	190	210	233	258	285
1993	201	225	252	281	314
1994	213	241	272	307	345
1995	226	258	294	334	380
1996	240	276	317	364	418

to $147 by 1986 in order to keep up with inflation. Multiplying Brian's pension amount of $1000 by 1.47 produces an inflation-adjusted figure of $1470. Unless his income has increased in other ways to reach the figure of $1470, his purchasing power will have declined. And all due to a rate of inflation that is *significantly lower* than current rates of inflation!

BUDGET INFORMATION FOR RETIRED COUPLES

Another perspective on the impact of inflation may be gained by examining budget information for retired couples (husband and wife over age 65) published by the U.S. Bureau of Labor Statistics (BLS). For 1978, the BLS estimated that the income amounts needed for various levels of consumption would be as shown in Table 4.3.

These figures apply to a retired couple living in a major metropolitan area such as Philadelphia, Boston, or New York. The individual budget items which showed the largest percentage increases were medical care and food. Each of these necessities, essential for *every* retired person, increased by approximately 13%!

TABLE 4.3 THREE BUDGETS FOR A RETIRED COUPLE, AUTUMN, 1978

BUDGET CATEGORY	LOW BUDGET		MEDIUM BUDGET		HIGH BUDGET	
Food	$1,891	35%	$2,566	31%	$ 3,184	26%
Housing	1,466	27	1,878	23	2,802	23
Furnishings and operating costs	440	8	975	12	1,694	14
Transportation	79	1	615	8	1,197	10
Clothing	184	3	308	4	455	4
Personal care	147	3	209	3	308	3
Medical care	750	14	758	9	765	6
Other consumption	232	4	386	5	776	6
Total consumption	$5,189	96%	$7,695	94%	$11,181	92%
Other items	234	4	492	6	910	8
Total budget	$5,423	100%	$8,187	100%	$12,091	100%

SOURCE: *Bureau of Labor Statistics, U.S. Department of Labor, August 20, 1979.*

As an example of the demands put on your retirement budget by inflation, let's assume you expect to retire and maintain a "high" level of consumption. Using the BLS statistics for 1978, this means a required annual income of $12,091. Indeed, many current retirees have indicated that they had hoped to have a retirement income of $1000 per month. They felt that this level of income would make them "secure" and able to enjoy their retirement years. Just how secure will they be in the years ahead with this level of income?

Let's use the figures from Tables 4.1 and 4.2 to calculate the impact of inflation on Paul and Mary Taylor's retirement budget of $12,091. The inflation factor for five years of 8% inflation is 66%. Assuming no increases, the Taylor's income of $12,091 would buy only $7980 ($12,091 × 0.66) of current goods and services. Using Table 4.2 we can see that they would have to increase their income to $17,774 ($12,091 × 1.47) if they wished to to maintain their present standard of living.

The figures are even more startling if we look out to the full retirement period of 15 years. With no increase in income the Taylors will be living on the equivalent of $3506 ($12,091 × 0.29) or would need $38,328 ($12,091 × 3.17) to maintain their present lifestyle! Whether you expect to have a higher or lower retirement income, it is obvious that inflation will have a major effect on how much you can buy with your retirement dollars.

SOURCES OF RETIREMENT INCOME

As we noted earlier, it is extremely difficult for the average retiree to increase his or her income. We can expect that Social Security will continue to be indexed to increases in the CPI. However, Social Security does *not* represent all of a person's retirement income. A report published by the Social Security Administration gives the breakdown of income for retired persons shown in Table 4.4.

Even if Social Security keeps pace with inflation it represents less than half of many retirees' incomes. Private pensions and other income from savings and investments generally will *not* increase, and may even decline after retirement. This is especially true if capital must be used to supplement income in order to maintain an adequate standard of living. Many women have been shocked to find that when their husbands died, *his* pension benefits ceased altogether or provided only a drastically reduced widow's benefit.

The category of income from Table 4.4 that offers the best chance of keeping up with inflation is obviously that of Earnings. As long as you are still employed to some degree you have the likelihood of wage or salary increases. They may be modest increases, but they will help to offset the certain reduction in purchasing power that accompanies inflation. For those retired persons who do not have any income from earnings, however, even ths slim hope is removed.

Some type of work, even on a part-time basis, may be necessary for you to maintain an adequate standard of living over the years to come after retirement. Such activity can have many important psychological bene-

TABLE 4.4 SOURCES OF RETIRE—MENT INCOME

Social Security	34%
Earnings	29%
Assets	15%
Public Pensions	7%
Private Pensions	5%
Public Assistance	4%
Veterans Benefits	3%
Charity & Other	3%

SOURCE: Social Security Administration

fits in addition to providing needed income. It will almost certainly provide you with desirable social contacts with others and prevent a feeling of isolation that often accompanies retirement. As shown in Table 4.4, the largest proportion of income received after "retirement" is from earnings. This indicates that a large number of persons continue to work past retirement age and that many others still work on a part-time basis.

The Federal government has recognized the social and economic needs of older persons through recent changes in the laws governing mandatory retirement age. Amendments to the Age Discrimination in Employment Act passed by Congress on March 23, 1978, effectively raised the age limit for mandatory retirement of employees from age 65 to 70 years. Private industry is likely to follow the federal government in this action and enable individuals to add several additional years to their working career. Still, recent statistics on the labor force indicate that an increasing number of persons choose to retire before age 65. Hopefully, these "early" retirees will have their plans made for a secure financial future.

Whether you choose to retire at age 62, 65, 70, or at any earlier or later age is one of the most important and personal decisions you will ever have to make. Before you consider such a decision you should be confident of the economic circumstances into which you will retire and your ability to maintain a desirable standard of living. If you aren't confident in making this decision, you have a pretty good reason for continuing to work and for continuing to build up your retirement assets.

If you expect to retire and *not* continue to work, even part-time, your current planning *must* take into account the effects of inflation on your retirement income. Unfortunately, this probably means that you must put away more of the income earned during your active, working years. This is difficult to do as most of us probably feel that we need almost every dollar we take in to keep up our present standard of living. Still, Americans, on average, save far less as a percentage of their income than the citizens of most other developed countries. Table 4.5 compares the current savings rate in the United States with other representative countries.

You may have to plan on a different distribution of the income received throughout your lifetime. Consuming less during the early and middle years may be necessary in order to save more so that you can have an adequate income during retirement years. Again, the federal government has recognized this fact of economic life in the recent changes that have been made in the Social Security system. Contributions on the part of employed persons and

TABLE 4.5 SAVINGS RATES IN SE-LECTED COUNTRIES, 1979	
COUNTRY	SAVINGS AS A % OF DISPOSABLE INCOME
France	17%
Great Britain	13%
Japan	25%
West Germany	15%
United States	4%

SOURCE: *U.S. Savings & Loan Association*

employers have risen sharply and will continue to increase rapidly in the future (see Table 3.1). These increased contributions represent a shifting of income from one's early, high-earning years to the later retirement years when additional income will be needed. Obviously, it means less income can be spent early in life, but that more should be available later on. Even with these changes in Social Security funding, it is not clear that the sytem will be in balance over the long run.

The legislated changes in Social Security are imposed by law on most wage earners. Even so, it may not be sufficient to provide the level of desired income you calculated in Chapter 2. A similar action will have to be taken voluntarily by many persons if they wish to have an adequate retirement income. This means that you may have to forego even more consumption spending today so that an adequate retirement fund can be accumulated during your working lifetime. Failure to do so almost guarantees that inflation will take a heavy toll on your retirement income and erode the value of goods and services that you can purchase with a fixed monthly income.

YOUR PERSONAL INFLATION FACTOR

A recent article on financial planning pointed out that the impact of inflation does not affect every individual or family in the same way. The types of expenses that one family or person has may be quite different from those of others. In such cases, it is likely that inflation will have more of an impact on one set of expenditures than the other.

The most common example of this distinction is the inflationary effect on rent versus mortgage payments. A family which rents its home is subject to continual increases in rent that are justified by inflation. In contrast, the family which owns its home and has a conventional mortgage pays a fixed amount that will not increase over time. Both families may be subject to inflation in utilities and other operating costs, but the homeowner is "protected" from inflation to a much greater degree than the person or family that rents a home.

In a similar fashion other budget items may be more or less subject to the problems of continuing inflation. Food prices certainly will be, while life insurance premiums generally remain fixed over the years. You can calculate your own Personal Inflation Factor (PIF) by analyzing your various monthly expenses and classifying them into "inflationary" or "noninflationary" categories. If most of your expenses are in the inflationary category you will be more susceptible to inflation than someone with a lower percentage in that category.

Figure 4.2 is based on the same set of monthly or annual expenditures that we discussed earlier in Chapter 2. Using this table, review your monthly spending pattern and identify which expenses fall into each category. Then add up the total for each column and determine the percentage each column represents of your total budget.

The percentage for the "inflationary" column is your Personal Inflation Factor (PIF) and can be used to measure just how vulnerable you actually are to the impact of inflation. This can be done by multiplying your own PIF times the widely publicized inflation rates released by the Federal government.

For example, if 80% of your expenditures are in the inflationary category, and government figures show that inflation is running at a 10% annual rate, your personal inflation rate would be 8% (10% × 0.80; or, if you prefer: 0.1 × 0.8). If only 60% of your expenses were subject to the impact of inflation, however, and the national rate were 10%, your personal inflation rate would be just 6% (10% × 0.60).

The personal inflation factor is a more accurate barometer of the impact of inflation on your own economic situation than the general government statistics. You should use this figure in planning for your future financial security and in determining income needs for retirement. At this point you may want to go back to Chapter 2 and recalculate your desired retirement income on the basis of the Personal Inflation Factor you have determined in Fig. 4.2.

ANNUAL EXPENDITURES

Fixed:	Inflationary	Noninflationary
Housing (mortgage, rent)	$	$
Utilities and telephone		
Food, Groceries, etc.		
Clothing and cleaning		
Income taxes, Social Security, etc.		
Property taxes		
Transportation (auto, commuting)		
Medical, dental, drugs (include insurance)		
Debt repayment		
Housing supplies, repairs, maintenance		
Life Insurance		
Property and liability insurance		
Current school expenses		
Total Fixed Expenses		

Discretionary:		
Vacations, travel, camps, etc.		
Recreation, entertainment, club dues		
Contributions, gifts		
Household furnishings		
Fund for education		
Savings		
Investments		
Other		
Total	$	$

Inflationary total   = $
+ Noninflationary total = $
_____
Total budget   = $

$$\frac{\text{Inflationary total} = \$}{\text{Total budget} = \$} = \quad \% \ \text{(PIF)}$$

FIG. 4.2 CALCULATION OF PERSONAL INFLATION FACTOR (PIF)

NEED FOR LIFETIME FINANCIAL PLANNING

It should be clear by now that planning for your future financial security is no easy task. Not only must you take account of your potential needs and future sources of income, but these estimates must be continually updated to reflect changes in your personal plans, government programs, and the impact of inflation. Therefore, no matter what your age, whether it be 40, 50, or 70, you should get yourself into the habit of regularly reviewing your personal financial situation.

An annual review is certainly a necessity, and more frequent examinations may be called for by any change in your personal economic situation. A wage or salary increase, unexpected expenses, a job change, or a new investment opportunity are events that should trigger a comprehensive review of your financial plans. You may want to schedule this "financial checkup" at the end of the year or whenever you prepare your income tax returns. Another good time for a review is when you receive a salary increase. You may be able to put aside some of the additional money before it gets "built into" your regular budget. Remember that *when* you plan a financial review is not as important as the fact that you actually *carry it out.*

You should regularly review your income and compare it with estimates you have made in the past. The same is true with your pattern of expenditures including savings and investments. The worksheets contained in the last chapter of this book provide space for a comparison of projected and actual results. If you are not meeting the financial goals that you have set for yourself, you can take immediate action to correct the situation. You may have to revise your saving and spending plans to keep on track with your financial objectives.

The worksheet labeled "Accumulation for Specific Objectives" is designed to be used on a regular basis to measure progress toward long-term financial goals such as a college fund for a child's education or the creation of a retirement fund. It enables you to keep a record of your fund's growth during the year and to compare the present amount with the amount desired in the future. If there is a deficit from the planned amount, it can be analyzed and plans can be put in place to offset it.

For example, your retirement fund may not have grown as rapidly as you estimated because of lower contributions during the past year. You may have had unexpected expenses that prevented you from putting away as much as you intended at the beginning of the year. Using the worksheet you can determine how far behind you are and what amount will be necessary to get caught up. You may find in doing your analysis that you are actually ahead of the game. Higher interest rates earned on your savings may have resulted in a larger retirement fund at the end of the year than you had expected. Thus, a regular review can provide emotional and financial security as well as identify problems.

An example of the use of this worksheet is shown in Fig. 4.3. The objective set here is to establish a $50,000 retirement fund over the next 15 years. Let's assume that Paul Brown already has $5,000 set aside to fund his retirement in 15 years. If he can earn an after-tax rate of return of 8% on these funds they will grow to $15,861 when he retires. (This is an after-tax rate of return which assumes that taxes on interest earnings will be paid from income and not taken from capital.)

How much will Paul have to put away in order to reach his goal of $50,000? The "deficit" will be $34,139, but he has 15 years to make it up. Therefore, he can put away $1257 annually, a little over $100 per month, and reach the objective of $50,000. Again, we assume that he will be able to earn 8% interest on his annual contributions to the retirement fund. If the rate earned is lower than 8%, additional contributions will be needed. But if he can get a higher return, he will not need to save as much.

The worksheet also enables you to plan the management of your funds. Simply knowing *how much* you will have available and what your regular contributions should be is important to reaching your future financial goals. But you must also be concerned with *how* these funds are to be invested and the different opportunities that are available in the marketplace. The worksheet has three separate sections that will help you plan the most effective utilization of your money.

The first of these sections is labeled, "Types of Investments and Expected Return(s)." Here you should list the various types of investment alternatives that are available and the current return that each provides. The choices may include savings accounts, government securities, mutual funds, common stocks, bonds, commodities, or a wide range of other possibilities. Many of these investments will be discussed in greater detail in Chapter 5, Investing for Retirement. Once you are aware of the different opportunities that are available, and the returns that each one will provide, you can begin to select those that are suitable to your own specific needs and your own particular investment personality.

In recent years the variety of available investments has increased dra-

ACCUMULATION FOR SPECIFIC OBJECTIVE(S)

Specific Objective: ___Retirement Fund___

Target Date for Accumulation (p. 5)	1996	
Years from Present to Target Date (p. 5)	15	years
Amount of Capital Desired (p. 5)...	$ 50,000	
Capital Currently Available for this Purpose... $ ___5,000___		
Amount Present Capital Will Grow to During Accumulation Period at ___8___% Interest	– $ 15,861	
Estimated Balance to be Provided..	$ 34,139	

To Provide for Deficit (if any):

    Amount of Annual Invested Capital @ ___8___%
    to Achieve Objective .... $ ___1,257___

Details of Plans:

Type(s) of Investments and Expected Return(s): _____

_____

_____

_____

_____

_____

Funding Vehicles, Trusts, Etc.: _____

_____

_____

_____

_____

_____

Special Considerations: _____

_____

_____

_____

_____

_____

_____

FIGURE 4.3

matically as has the range of returns that each provides. Savings accounts now provides 5.5% interest, certificates of deposit yield 8–10% depending on maturity, bonds are selling to yield 12–15%, as are some U.S. Treasury obligations. Each investment has its own risk characteristics, however, and many may not be appropriate for your particular needs. We will have more to say about this later, but for now you should simply be aware that higher returns are generally accompanied by higher risk. The reverse is also true.

This concept of risk versus return is illustrated in Fig. 4.4. Each type of investment has certain risks associated with it and compensates for those risks by promising a certain level of investment return. While we have not attached specific numbers to the investments on the chart, the order in which they are shown is significant.

Beginning with savings accounts, they increase in risk and potential return up to speculative common stocks. A savings account ensures safety of principal but offers only a relatively low rate of return on the investment. Common stocks can provide a considerably higher level of return, but you must be willing to suffer a substantial loss in principal if the market declines. In between these extremes are a wide variety of other investments with different risk and return characteristics.

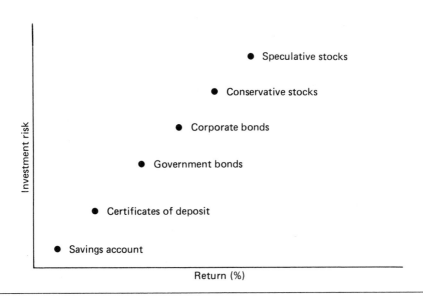

FIG. 4.4 RISK/RETURN CHARACTERISTICS

The second planning section of the Accumulation worksheet is labeled, "Funding Vehicles, Trusts, Etc." Here you can give consideration to various arrangements that may improve your overall returns by a careful *structuring* of how you manage your money. Most of these procedures have as their objective the elimination or reduction of taxes which will improve the overall return on the investment. Some techniques may be quite complex and require the services of an accountant or an attorney in setting them up. There are others, however, that are quite simple to arrange and can be done very easily by anyone. Among the simpler arrangements are the effective use of gifts to minors and the creation of short-term trusts, often referred to as "Clifford trusts." Both can be used effectively even where the dollar amounts involved are not large. Don't forget! *It's your money, and every dollar is important to you and your future financial security.*

Making a gift to a minor of cash, securities, or other assets will normally increase the return on the investment due to the minor's generally lower income tax bracket. If additional control over the funds is desired, a short-term trust can be arranged whereby the income will be taxed to the minor child and the capital will be returned to the person creating the trust when it expires at the end of a specified period of time.

Of particular importance to certain persons will be the opportunity to create a personal retirement fund through a Keogh plan or an Individual Retirement Account (IRA). These plans permit individuals who qualify to set aside some of their current income for retirement purposes and to postpone payment of income taxes until the money is actually withdrawn and used. Much more will be said about these arrangements in Chapter 7, Personal Retirement Plans.

The final section of the Accumulation worksheet permits you to note special factors that may affect your financial plans, particular investments, or the funding arrangements you select. Obviously, you will want to tailor your financial affairs to take account of special needs and your own particular desires. Many factors that bear on your personal and family situation will have to be considered. You may wish to involve an independent financial counselor in the process to provide additional information and objectivity. Even if you seek professional help, however, you should be completely comfortable with any recommendations made to you before you proceed to implement them.

SUMMARY

In summary, then, this chapter has attempted to alert you to the impact of inflation on your future financial security. Inflation is not going to go away, and you had better make your plans accordingly! An important part of your strategy for financial security must be to consider what the effects of that inflation will be for the rest of your lifetime. It must be considered when you decide how much to spend and how much to save. It will have an impact on the investments you select and how well they perform. And most certainly it will have an important role in the security and comfort you enjoy during your retirement years.

5

INVESTING FOR RETIREMENT

*The safest way to double your
money is to fold it over once
and put it in your pocket.*

Kin Hubbard

The preceding chapters of this book have been aimed at determining your financial needs in retirement. After estimating your retirement income and expenses (Chapter 2), allowing for what you will receive from Social Security (Chapter 3), and factoring in the impact of inflation (Chapter 4), you should have a pretty good idea of what additional income, if any, will be needed.

As we noted in Chapter 2, pension plans and Social Security will often provide 60-70% of our preretirement income. We also indicated, however, that you should aim to have the *same* level of income after retirement if you want to maintain the same standard of living. This is particularly true since inflation will continue to take its toll on your disposable income while pension and Social Security benefits may not keep pace with the rising cost of living.

Almost all of us will have to plan on additional income over and above our pensions and Social Security. Where will these important "extra" dollars come from? They must be provided from savings and investments accumulated during your prime earning years. The sooner you start putting away a portion of your current income for retirement purposes the easier it will be to accumulate the necessary capital.

The sooner you set a goal for yourself, the easier it will be to reach it! Remember, time and compound interest are on your side if you start now to plan for your future financial security. If you fail to make effective use of these advantages now, you give them up forever!

ESTABLISHING EFFECTIVE FINANCIAL OBJECTIVES

Setting a retirement objective may not be an easy task, but by following certain established guidelines we can get the job done. First, our objective must be *well defined* and clearly understood. Unless we really know and understand what we are trying to accomplish it isn't likely that we will be very successful.

One way of working toward a clear and useful objective is to try writing it down. Does it make sense when you read it? Also, have your wife or husband and other family members look it over. Does it make sense to them? Is it something that they all feel is a worthwhile goal and something they will be willing to make some sacrifices to accomplish?

Be sure that your financial objective for retirement is not just wishful thinking. The statement, "I want a safe and secure retirement income," is *not* a very useful objective. It does not provide much guidance in planning what you should do now in order to accomplish it. Also, what do words like "safe" and "secure" really mean? Such statements may try to capture the spirit of what we want, but they are not very useful in setting up a program for financial security.

A better financial objective is one stated in *quantitative terms.* Only by attaching numbers to our plans can we measure whether or not we are making any real progress toward reaching our goals. As we saw in Chapter 2, we can calculate the income we need from our investments and then determine the capital needed to produce that income. By adding these numbers to our objectives we can not only measure our progress but we will find that it is much easier to understand.

For example, Beth Adams, age 50, has determined that she will need an additional $10,000 per year in retirement income before taxes in order to maintain her desired lifestyle. She assumes that she will be able to earn 10% on her investments. Putting these two factors together results in a retirement objective for Beth of accumulating $100,000 ($10,000/10% = $100,000).

Beth has already accumulated $25,000 and hopes to reach her goal of $100,000 within the next 10 years. Her present capital will have grown to about $65,000 by that time so she will need to accumulate another $35,000 over the next ten years. This is a much more useful objective; well defined and easy to understand. Such a statement will help her to reach her goal!

Beth's objective also follows another important rule in setting up financial objectives. Each goal or plan should have a *time dimension* attached to it! Beth needs to know when she plans to reach her goals, how much time she has to work with, and where she needs to be along the way. Once you have set an objective with a time dimension, you can break it down into subobjectives with shorter time spans.

For example, if Beth Adams wants to accumulate $35,000 at the end of 10 years, how much does she need to have at the end of five years? Or at the end of one year? A little analysis using the tables in Chapter 10 of this book will show that she needs to invest about $170 per month, or about $2050 per year. Obviously, this is a much more workable objective than one spread over 10 years or an even longer time span.

In summary, our financial objective or objectives for retirement should have three characteristics if they are to be helpful in meeting our needs. First, they should be *well defined* and clearly understood by everyone involved. Second, they should be stated in *quantitative terms* whenever possible to aid in measuring our progress. And, third, they should have a reasonable *time dimension* attached to them so that we can monitor them over time and make any necessary adjustments to our plans.

Evaluate your own retirement objectives using these three rules. By now you should be thinking of some goals even if you haven't written them down or analyzed them carefully. Do they meet these three criteria for effective planning? If not, try revising them so that they do qualify. Keep reworking them until they become clearer and more useful in managing your retirement plan. Aim for a monthly program you can follow *now* no matter how long it is until you plan to retire.

HOW MUCH CAPITAL WILL YOU NEED?

Before you can begin to examine the various investment media that can be used to accumulate capital you should have some idea of the target you are shooting for. You need to know how much capital will be required to produce your desired income. How much wealth you want to have when you retire will be an important factor in selecting from among the many different types of investments that are available in the marketplace.

The Income/Expenditure form we introduced in Chapter 2 (Fig. 2.1) is the starting point for estimating your retirement income needs. Use the blank forms contained at the end of the book to estimate your expected income and planned expenditures. Try to be realistic about what you will *have* to spend and also what you will *want* to spend when you retire. If you have budgeted a much lower level of spending after retirement, take a second look. You may be doing some wishful thinking about your expenses and what you will have left over as disposable income.

Most people will find that their pensions and Social Security do not cover their estimated expenses. It is this deficit that you must make up from your own resources. If you cannot do so then you will have to make some sacrifices and cut back on various categories of your expenses. You may be able to do so, but you are not likely to be very happy about it. Why not plan *now* to have the income you need when you retire?

An even simpler approach to determining your future income needs is to compare your present income with what you expect to receive from a pension and Social Security. This technique assumes that you want to have exactly the same amount of income before and after retirement. This method does not require you to estimate your future living expenses.

If you are a typical wage earner your pension plan and Social Security benefits will provide 60-70% of your pretirement income. Therefore, your own investments must make up the difference of 30-40%. How much capital would you need to earn 30% of your current income? Answering this question will take you a long way toward setting your future financial objectives.

Dave Brown is a corporate executive whose current salary is $30,000 per year. After checking with his personnel department and the Social Security Administration he has projected that his retirement income from those sources will be about $20,000. He wants to keep his income at the same level as when he was working and wants to determine how much he must put away to fund his retirement plans.

How much will Dave need in the way of assets to provide an extra $10,000 per year? This will depend a great deal on what Dave does with his money once he retires and the risks he is willing to take with his investments. As we noted in Chapter 4, return and risk are very closely related. The more risk you are willing to take, the greater return you are likely to earn. The problem here is that most of us do not want to take excessive risk with our retirement funds. We may be willing to speculate a bit while we are accumulating the money during our working years, but not after retirement.

Most retirees are also greatly concerned with using up their assets and would prefer to live only on the income from their investments. Even if they are forced to slowly eat into their capital, most persons would like to avoid doing so if possible. Table 2.4 will give you an estimate of how long your money will last if you plan to make withdrawals from your capital.

If Dave Brown wants $10,000 only from investment income, the required capital will depend on his assumed rate of return from his investments. If he were to place all of his funds in an insured savings account earning 5.5% interest, he would need about $182,000. This is determined by dividing the required income by the assumed rate of return as follows: $10,000/5.5% = 10,000/0.55 = $181,818.

He could reduce the required capital considerably by investing in certificates of deposit with a higher rate of return. Purchasing an 8% savings certificate would reduce the necessary capital to $125,000. And if he were willing to purchase corporate bonds yielding 12% interest he could get by with only $83,333.

As we will soon see, there are many other investment opportunities that are available to people like Dave Brown. Each has its own particular characteristics which may or may not be attractive to you as a retirement investment. Your choice will depend not only on your personal financial needs but also on your emotional and psychological feelings about investment and risk.

ACCUMULATING WEALTH OVER TIME

Don't be too surprised if you are somewhat discouraged at this stage of our analysis. You may be saying to yourself, "I'll never be able to save $85,000!" Perhaps not, but could you save $1000 a year, or about $80 each month? If so, and you start early enough to fund your retirement, you'll be surprised what you can accomplish.

With enough time and compound interest on your side, even $80 per month can assure you a more safe and secure retirement. If you put $1000 per year into an investment yielding 8.5%, and maintain that program for

25 years, the result will be more than $85,000 in total capital! Table 5.1 provides other examples of wealth accumulation based on different time periods and various rates of return.

Think about the number of years remaining until you plan to retire. What could you accomplish if you had a regular program of savings and investment over that period of time? If you are now 50 years of age and plan to retire at age 65, you should be able to add $30,000–40,000 to your retirement fund by saving $1000 per year.

Use the strategy we suggested earlier when we discussed setting financial objectives. Instead of working with large amounts and long periods of time, break your objectives down into smaller and smaller units. Develop a yearly plan rather than one that focuses on the next 20 years. Set a monthly retirement funding goal instead of thinking about the thousands of dollars that you will need to provide your desired retirement income.

You will be surprised to see how near you are to your goal. And compound interest will be doing most of the work! In the example above, where we built up a retirement fund of $85,000 over 25 years, our actual contributions were only $25,000. Compound interest provided the remaining $60,000! The lesson to be learned here is to start early and to stick to it. What you do now and in the years to come can make a tremendous difference in your retirement security and happiness.

INVESTING FOR RETIREMENT

Once you have determined the amount of capital you will need, and when you will need it, you will have accomplished a great deal. But important considerations lie ahead, and critical decisions still need to be made. What will you do with the money you are accumulating? Where is the best place to keep it? How should it be invested for the next 10, 15, or even 20 years? What rate of return should you expect to earn on your investments? The remainder of this chapter will answer these questions and provide important information for you to use in making investment decisions.

The first thing to realize is that there is *not* just one place to invest your money. There are many. Each savings or investment vehicle has its own particular characteristics. Each has its own unique advantages and disadvantages for different types of investors. Various investments may be more attractive than others at a particular time.

TABLE 5.1

BUILDUP RATE

WEALTH ACCUMULATED

	5 Yrs.	10 Yrs.	15 Yrs.	20 Yrs.	25 Yrs.	30 Yrs.	35 Yrs.	40 Yrs.
3%	$ 5,468	$11,807	$ 19,156	$ 27,676	$ 37,553	$ 49,002	$ 62,275	$ 77,663
3.5	5,550	12,141	19,971	29,269	40,313	53,429	69,007	87,509
4	5,632	12,486	20,824	30,969	43,311	58,328	75,598	98,826
4.5	5,716	12,841	21,719	32,783	46,570	63,752	85,163	111,846
5	5,801	13,206	22,657	34,719	50,113	69,760	94,836	126,839
5.5	5,888	13,583	23,641	36,786	53,965	76,419	105,765	144,118
6	5,975	13,971	24,672	38,992	58,156	83,801	118,120	164,047
6.5	6,063	14,371	25,754	41,348	62,715	91,989	132,096	187,047
7	6,153	14,783	26,888	43,865	67,676	101,073	147,913	213,609
7.5	6,244	15,208	28,077	46,552	73,076	111,154	165,820	244,300
8	6,335	15,645	29,324	49,422	78,954	122,345	186,102	279,781
8.5	6,429	16,096	30,632	52,489	85,354	134,772	209,081	320,815
9	6,523	16,560	32,003	55,764	92,323	148,575	235,124	368,291
9.5	6,618	17,038	33,441	59,263	99,914	163,907	264,648	423,239
10	6,715	17,531	34,949	63,002	108,181	180,943	298,126	486,851
11	6,912	18,561	38,189	71,265	126,998	220,913	379,164	645,826
12	7,115	19,654	41,753	80,698	149,333	270,292	483,463	859,142
13	7,322	20,814	45,671	91,469	175,850	331,315	617,749	1,145,485
14	7,535	22,044	49,980	103,768	207,332	406,737	790,672	1,529,908
15	7,753	23,349	54,717	117,810	244,711	499,956	1,013,345	2,045,953
20	8,929	31,150	86,442	224,025	566,377	1,418,257	3,538,009	8,812,629
25	10,258	41,566	137,108	428,680	1,318,488	4,033,967	12,320,951	37,610,819

Example: If you put $1,000 per year into investments yielding 8%, and continue to do so for 20 years, the amount of capital available at the end of that period would be $49,422.

The investments that suit your needs and fit your personality are almost certain to change as your personal situation changes. Just as you personally go through a "life cycle" which involves many changes, your investments should as well. The level of risk you were willing to take at age 20 or 30 may have changed a great deal as you got older.

There are also many more investment vehicles available today than there were even 10 years ago. At one time a person planning for retirement might have invested in stocks or bonds, or planned to use the cash value of his or her life insurance policies. Today there are literally dozens of different types of savings and investment plans that can be used to fund the retirement objective. Over the last few years the financial community has become very creative in introducing new products and providing new services.

Options, money-market mutual funds, single-premium deferred annuities, and mortgage-backed bonds are only some of the new products that are now available to use in retirement planning. Which ones you select will depend on your particular needs, the resources you have available, and your feelings about risk and return. We can be certain, however, that as these conditions change throughout your lifetime, your investment program should change as well.

You should also plan to have a diversified portfolio of investments to fund your retirement goals. No one investment product is likely to provide for all of your needs. Also, a variety of investments will reduce the overall risk of your portfolio. Now you may be saying to yourself, "I don't have enough money for a whole portfolio of investments!" Whatever amount you have is *all* that you'll have and you should try to manage it in the most efficient manner possible. By selecting a variety of savings and investment plans you will provide for your changing needs and have a better chance of accomplishing your overall retirement objectives.

Whatever investment vehicles you include in your retirement plan, you should reinvest your earnings back into the plan. As we noted, compound interest is on your side, but only if you leave the money in your plan to be compounded. Too many persons invade their retirement funds for too many reasons. You cannot expect to use these funds "temporarily" for every good reason that comes along and then still find them ready to provide the needed income on retirement.

Make a commitment to reinvest earnings within your retirement portfolio. As we demonstrate in the remaining sections of this chapter, there are many ways to accomplish this objective. Interest on savings accounts will automatically be credited to your account. Leave it there! If you own common stocks as a part of your retirement plan, inquire as to whether the company has a dividend reinvestment program which will take your dividends and purchase additional shares of stock. All mutual funds will reinvest both income and capital gains dividends in the purchase of additional shares. You should plan to use all of these devices which keep you from getting your hands on the earnings from your retirement fund. Every dollar that you *don't* spend today will be two, three, or four dollars that you will have available when you retire.

Saving for Retirement?

Most often when we think about putting money away for our retirement we think of some sophisticated investment product, real estate, or some other long-range program. However, we should also give some thought to the value of a simple savings account as well. In addition to being virtually risk free (almost all savings accounts in the U.S. are guaranteed by some government agency), they can provide a great deal of flexibility in managing your money.

A savings account can be used to accumulate and temporarily store small retirement contributions until they can be reinvested in other media. This can be particularly effective if you can arrange automatic withdrawals from your salary and have them deposited directly into your savings account.

We determined earlier that Beth Adams needed to put away $170 per month in order to fund her retirement plan. If she can arrange to have this amount put away through a payroll deduction she will have taken a big step toward accomplishing her goal.

Many persons are not emotionally comfortable with investments that involve even a small degree of risk for their capital. The story is told of the man who purchased common stocks but worried about his investments constantly and could not get any sleep at night. In discussing his investments one day with a friend he told of his problems and asked for advice. His friend suggested that he "sell down to the sleeping point." An investment may seem to have many advantages, but if it does not fit your psychological profile you should avoid it.

Persons with a very small retirement fund also need to protect every dollar that they do have from the risk of loss. For these persons as well a simple savings account can be the best place for their retirement funds. Almost all of us should have some of our retirement money in a savings account so that we can quickly take advantage of investment opportunities as they arise.

However, the low risk nature of a savings account means that the return we earn will also be relatively low. The typical account offered by commercial banks, savings and loan associations, mutual savings banks, and other thrift institutions currently pays about 5.5% interest. This is far below the rate available on other investments, even those of similar risk levels. Short-term certificates of deposit, money market funds, and other liquid and safe investments may provide almost twice the return as the ordinary savings account.

For this reason you generally should keep the funds in a savings account to a minimum. If you have been using such an account to accumulate retirement money, regularly review your balances and determine what other investments should be made and the rates of return that are available in the marketplace. Also, keep your account with an institution that pays interest from the day of deposit to the day of withdrawal. This will avoid the loss of interest which would occur if you use an institution that pays only quarterly or semiannually.

Certificates of Deposit (CDs)

Most savings institutions also offer one or more types of certificate accounts in addition to the traditional savings account. A certificate of deposit is simply a note from the institution that promises to pay a specified rate of interest for a stated period of time, and to return the original principal at the end of the period.

During the past several years institutions have offered certificates with maturities ranging from six months up to eight years in length. In general, the longer the period of time until maturity, the higher is the rate of interest paid. Such certificates are also free of default risk, but do require that you tie up your funds for an extended period of time. This should not be a problem with funds earmarked for retirement, and may even be an advantage if you are too often tempted to dip into those funds for other purposes.

One of the most popular forms of such certificates has been the six-month maturity with an interest rate based on that provided by U.S. Treasury bills. These certificates have a required minimum purchase of $10,000 and have attracted billions of dollars in deposits during the past four years. Savers and investors have both been attracted by the high rates paid on these certificates in recent years, particularly in comparison with the fixed rates available on savings accounts.

Six-month rates have fluctuated a great deal, however, and longer term certificates are also proving to be popular with investors. The so-called "30-month certificate," which guarantees a rate of interest for two and one-half years has attracted large amounts of money to financial institutions in the relatively short time it has been offered. The rates on these certificates are also based on Treasury securities and do vary from time to time.

Certificates of deposit can be an important part of your retirement planning program. This is particularly true for those persons who have accumulated considerable amounts of money and who desire a low-risk investment that still provides a rate of return based on current market rates rather than a specified savings account rate. Short-term rates generally reflect the current inflation rate. Short-term certificates will yield more in the way of return when inflation increases, driving up short-term interest rates.

Again, you should plan to reinvest any interest earned on your short-term certificate investments. This will enable you to compound interest on interest during your personal accumulation period prior to retirement. Most financial institutions will simply roll over a certificate of deposit when it matures into another certificate of the same maturity. Usually the interest earned on the first certificate will be added to the original principal and reinvested in the new certificate.

Once you reach retirement you may find short-term certificates even more useful in financing your retirement plans. Even if you have not used them up to that time you may want to shift some funds from other investments into CDs. Other investments such as common stocks and mutual funds may not provide the current income you will need once you retire. Shifting funds from such investments to certificates of deposit can provide the spendable income you will require and protect your principal from any unnecessary risks.

However, you should be aware of the often rapid changes in short-term interest rates and the resulting impact on your disposable income. If you invest in CDs when rates are high and assume that your income will always remain at those levels, you may be disappointed when rates fall and your income shrinks.

Don't assume that you will always be earning the highest rates of return that are publicized. Set your spending level around an average rate of return so that the "extra" income you receive when rates are high will help to make up for less income when rates decline.

Money-Market Mutual Funds

Mutual funds which invest in so-called "money-market" instruments have proven to be the most successful innovation in fund history. Investing their money in short-term Treasury bills, large bank certificates of deposit, banker's acceptances, and other liquid assets, these funds have amassed over 100 billion dollars during the past few years. This is twice the amount invested in all other types of mutual funds.

Money-market funds owe much of their popularity to the very high interest rates which have prevailed during the past few years. The rate offered by these funds have reached as high as 15–17% while savings accounts have been pegged at 5.5%. And while six-month certificates require a minimum investment of $10,000, money-market funds have minimum investments of as low as $1000.

While not guaranteed by any federal or state agency, the short-term, highly liquid nature of these funds' assets makes them quite secure as an investment. In addition to being low-risk investments, money-market funds offer a number of features attractive to retirement planning. They will reinvest all earnings on the fund automatically, so that you can compound your investment and not be tempted by getting your hands on the money. Also, the shares you own in the fund do not "mature" in the same way that a six-month certificate has a definite maturity date. The management of the fund takes care of reinvesting its assets while you simply own your shares until you choose to sell them.

Most funds make it quite easy to redeem part or all of your shares whenever it is necessary to do so. You can redeem shares by mail, by telephone, or even by writing a special check provided by the fund. Such convenience is very attractive, particularly for the retired person who wants to receive a regular monthly income by selling some of his or her shares in the money-market fund.

The rate of return earned by a money-market fund will be very close to the current short-term interest rate. This is due to the highly liquid, short-term nature of the instruments in which the fund invests. As we stated earlier, such instruments will closely reflect the current inflation rate. As inflation increases the returns from money-market funds will go up, but as inflation declines so will the return on these funds. Overall, these funds provide an excellent means of matching your returns with the level of inflation.

While money-market funds emphasize the short-term nature of their assets, they can be used very effectively in an overall retirement planning strategy no matter what your age. Because they do such an effective job of matching the inflation rate you may want to make long-term investments in these funds. They provide safety, liquidity, and convenience in a package that is hard to match. Almost all of these funds are "no-loads" in that they do not have a sales charge associated with their purchase. They do charge a management fee, however, which is paid by the fund and is reflected in the rate of return earned by investors such as yourself.

However, you may also want to take advantage of the fact that many of these funds are part of a mutual fund "family" that contains a number of funds with differenct investment objectives. These fund groups permit you to switch from one fund to another within the group at very little or no cost. You can even make these transfers with a simple phone call to a toll-free number.

Here is an example of how you might work with such a family of funds to plan an effective investment program aimed at retirement. John Crawford is a business executive who wants to start funding a retirement plan. He does not have any particular investment experience, but he feels that the stock market is a good bet over the long run. He has selected a mutual fund group that offers a stock fund, a bond fund, and a money-market fund among others.

John has determined that he needs to put away $100 per month to meet his retirement objectives. After making the initial required purchase of $1000, John can make subsequent investments in the money-market fund of as little as $100. He plans to accumulate money in the money-market fund until he feels that it would be appropriate to shift into the common stock fund. He does not plan to shift all of his investment at one time, and he figures to continue the $100 monthly contribution to the money-market fund.

Of course, he will reinvest all of the earnings in both funds to take advantage of compounding the earnings of his investment. John also anticipates that there will be times when he feels that the stock fund has appreciated and that the market may be due for a fall. He expects to sell some or all of his shares in the stock fund at that time and to reinvest them in the money-market fund.

John's plan is really a modern version of the old adage of "buy low—sell high" tied in with the family-of-funds concept. While continuing his regular retirement savings program he can take advantage of swings in the stock market and hopefully improve his overall rate of return. While his plan cannot guarantee against losses in the stock market, he should be able to take advantage of the long-term, upward trend in stocks. At the same time, he has a convenient method of accumulating his regular retirement contributions.

Once he does retire, John can continue to use the same family of funds to provide the dollars he will need to supplement his pension and Social Security benefits. At that point he is likely to reduce the amount he has invested in the stock fund. Such funds generally provide a fairly low dividend yield, and John may want to emphasize income as opposed to future capital gains.

He can reinvest the proceeds of his sale of the stock fund into the money-market fund or into the bond fund. Either one is likely to provide a much higher level of current income than the stock fund. He may wish to split his investment between the bond fund and the money-market fund. The bond fund would offer a high current income while the money-market fund, with its short-term, interest-sensitive orientation, would provide some protection against inflation.

This example shows how a money-market fund, as part of a mutual fund group, can be used over the retirement planner's life cycle. You should give serious consideration to making such funds a part of your retirement planning program. They offer safety, convenience, and a much higher return than savings accounts.

You should never have more than a few thousand dollars in a regular savings account. Any savings over and above this level should be transferred to a money-market mutual fund. The extra return available on these funds, even if it is only a few percentage points, will make a real difference in the amount you will have available when you retire.

Before leaving the topic of money-market funds we should note that the switching strategy described above can have tax implications for John Crawford and other investors. Every time a switch is made, shares of one fund are sold and another purchased. These sales are "tax events" and result in a taxable gain or loss to the investor. Such gains and losses, whether short-term (less than one year) or long-term (more than one year), must be reported to the Internal Revenue Service on the indvidual's tax return. You should consider your own tax situation before purchasing shares in these funds, and before you decide to switch from one fund to another.

However, if you own mutual fund shares in the context of an IRA or a Keogh plan, you may switch without any immediate effect on your income taxes. In these situations, taxes are postponed until funds are withdrawn from the plan—which normally occurs after age 59½. We will have considerably more to say about individual retirement accounts and Keogh (HR-10) plans in Chapter 7, Personal Retirement Plans.

Mutual Funds

Money-market mutual funds have certainly attracted the spotlight during the last year, but there are many other types of funds also available. Fund performance has been generally good during the past few years as compared with most of the 1970s. For most of the decade mutual funds mirrored the weak-to-mediocre performance of the stock market in general. Growth stocks in particular were poor performers, and many of the high flying funds of the 1960s suffered substantial losses.

The mutual fund industry has countered this cyclical stock market behavior with the introduction of new funds that offer investors a variety of investment opportunities. In addition to the traditional bond and stock funds there are now option funds, tax-free bond funds, funds of mortgage-backed securities, and, of course, money-market funds.

Mutual fund organizations have advanced the concept of the "family of funds" whereby a single organization will sponsor a variety of funds. In doing so they hope not only to attract more investors to their funds, but also to keep those same investors even when their needs change. When this occurs you are encouraged to merely switch from one fund to another rather than sell out of the organization altogether.

There are literally hundreds of mutual funds in existence today and their investment objectives vary considerably. Some funds invest for growth while others stress income and the preservation of capital. One fund invests only in energy-related stocks, and another in the shares of companies that are trying to develop undersea resources. Funds also range in size from a small fund with less than one million dollars in assets to giant organizations which manage billions of dollars of investors' money.

Mutual funds have traditionally offered small investors: (1) diversification of their portfolio; (2) professional management services; and (3) convenience. By pooling the small investments of a large number of investors the funds have been able to purchase more shares in more companies than would have been possible for any single individual. Presumably, such diversification reduces the risks of investing and stabilizes the overall returns.

In addition, the fund portfolios are managed by professional organizations staffed with portfolio managers and security analysts. Such talent, however, does not guarantee exceptional performance. Hopefully, professionally managed funds will perform better than a portfolio managed by the individual investor. This may take time, though, and you should consider any investments in mutual funds as long-range commitments. The one exception would be shares of money-market funds that can be used in a short-term cash-management program as well as for longer-term investments.

Mutual funds vary considerably in the charges they levy on investors. The main distinction which exists is between funds that charge a sales "load" and those that do not, or "no-load" funds. These sales charges can be as high as 8.5% of your original investment. In comparing the performance of load versus no-load funds there does not appear to be a substantial difference. That being the case there is little justification for paying the load fee and starting out with a negative return. Due to investor resistance to paying the load charges, many such funds have recently switched to a no-load form of organization.

Most fund organizations offer a variety of convenient services to their investors. Among these are automatic reinvestment of dividends (both capital gains and income), monthly payout plans which may be a great advantage in planning your retirement, and the opportunity to switch from one fund to another at little or no cost. This last feature is the key one in using mutual funds as an important part of financing your retirement fund.

Your investment program is likely to undergo many changes during the accumulation period prior to retirement. Younger people tend to place most of the emphasis on capital growth, and possibly on tax shelter. Later on the emphasis may shift to preservation of capital. Finally, it turns to the generation of income to supplement a pension and Social Security. At one time if you wanted to make these shifts with mutual funds you would have had to use more than one fund and several fund organizations. This is no longer the case.

Today you can move money from one fund to another within the same fund group by a simple, toll-free phone call. The bookkeeping is taken care of by the fund's computers and you are provided with an accurate record of any transactions. Over the years you may find yourself investing in most, if not all, of the funds offered by a mutual fund group. Which funds you invest in and when you decide to switch will depend on your own personal feelings and financial situation.

As an example, let's look at the investment "life cycle" of Carol Morgan, a sales representative of an office equipment manufacturer. At age 28 Carol started to plan for her future financial security. She felt that she could put away $100 per month, but had little or no idea what to invest in. As a start she opened an account with the Omnibus Fund Group (a fictitious name) and began purchasing shares in their money-market fund.

Realizing that she had a very long time horizon to consider until her retirement, Carol concluded that at least part of her funds should be invested in common stocks. She hoped to benefit from an upward trend in the market, and realized that capital gains would be taxed more favorably than the income dividends on the money-market fund. By simply calling Omnibus she was able to shift most of her money-market fund balance into the Group's common stock fund. She planned to continue her regular contributions to the money-market fund.

During the next few years Carol continued her monthly purchases of money-market fund shares. But she also "switched" her investment between the two funds from time to time when she thought the market was over- or undervalued. She did not attempt to guess exactly when the high or low point of the market would take place, but was content to follow the major swings in price movements.

Later on Carol married a successful physician and continued to progress in her own career. These actions resulted in Carol and her husband being in a combined tax bracket of 50%. At that point Carol decided to shift some of the funds she had invested into the Omnibus Group's tax-free income fund. She continued to reinvest all of the earnings on her investments and also maintained her regular monthly contributions as well.

As funds built up in the money-market fund she would channel them into either the stock fund or the tax-free fund, depending on her outlook for the stock market. Occasionally she would sell most of her shares in the common stock fund in anticipation of a decline in the market. Normally she would reinvest the funds in the money market, but once in a while she would add to her holdings in the tax-free fund.

As she and her husband approached retirement Carol began to systematically cut back on her investments in the common-stock fund. She placed additional funds into the tax-free bond fund where she was more confident of preservation of capital, and because their combined incomes were still quite high and still subject to high tax rates.

Carol and her husband both retired at the same time. At that point she sold almost all of her shares in the common stock fund and transferred the money into the Omnibus money-market fund. She liquidated her holdings in the tax-free income fund and switched the proceeds to the Omnibus bond fund, which produced a much higher yield given her now lower tax rate. She elected to receive the income from both funds rather than to reinvest it. A diagrammatic view of Carol Morgan's investment "life cycle" is shown in Fig. 5.1.

This example demonstrates how mutual funds can be used to fund a retirement plan over your full life cycle. However, you should not assume that this is the *only* plan to use, or that it will necessarily result in the greatest amount of money for your retirement. Our purpose here is to demonstrate the mechanics of the plan and to highlight the flexibility it provides as your investment needs change.

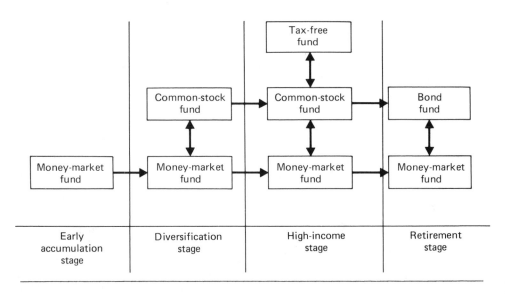

FIG. 5.1 INVESTMENT LIFE CYCLE

Mutual funds can be an effective tool in designing your personal retirement program. If used properly they can offer many advantages, particularly to the small investor who is looking to build up his or her resources over the long run. If you follow the suggestions of working within a "no-load" fund group, reinvesting all of the earnings from the funds, and switching funds at appropriate times, you will have organized an effective plan for your future financial security.

Government Securities

The United States Government is the largest single issuer of securities in the world. In financing its many activities the Federal Treasury uses a wide variety of financial products in enormous volume. The Treasury uses these instruments to raise money, but the other side of the coin is the fact that these securities offer a means of investment for countless institutions and individuals.

One reason for the popularity of government securities as investments is their risk-free character. Because the Treasury can simply print money or raise taxes to pay its obligations, Treasury securities are almost entirely free of default risk. Also, the U.S. Government has never defaulted on one of its obligations in its more than 200-year history.

Because of the secure nature of U.S. Government securities, many institutions such as banks and savings and loans are required to keep at least a part of their assets in these issues. Other institutional investors and many individuals are also attracted by the low risk of owning a government obligation. The same thinking is applied in only a slightly lesser degree to the securities of U.S. Government agencies such as the World Bank, the Postal Service, and the Federal Home Loan Bank. These and other agencies issue many billions of dollars of securities each year, providing additional investment opportunities.

As we have noted several times, however, whenever we see low risk, we can also expect to find relatively low returns associated with it. This is certainly true for government securities, which generally provide the lowest yields in comparing investment securities. Because other issuers such as major corporations are considered riskier than government, their securities must provide a higher return. The difference may not be substantial for the larger firms, such as American Telephone and Telegraph or General Motors, but it can be quite large for smaller, less well-known organizations.

Can you name the most widely held U.S. Government security? If you said the dollar bill, give yourself a high mark in financial expertise. Yes, cash in circulation is an obligation of the U.S. Treasury even if we do not generally think of it as an investment security. The nation's money supply is essential to the smooth functioning of our economy, even though about 98% of our payments are made by check!

Another important category of U.S. Government security is that made up of savings bonds. Many billions of dollars worth of Series E and the new Series EE bonds have been purchased over the years. Even now, when they offer a relatively low 9% interest after eight years, they are still sold in large quantities. During 1979 some $7 billion worth of these bonds were issued, mostly through payroll savings plans, or so-called "bond-a-month" plans.

Savings bonds have generally lost their appeal as an investment vehicle due to their low yield and the requirement that the purchaser hold them eight years or more in order to receive even that low level of return. However, they do have one unusual feature that should be mentioned for those who may have accumulated these bonds over the years. Series EE bond owners may exchange their bonds—alone or in combination with Series E bonds or Savings Notes (Freedom Shares)—at current redemption values, for current-income HH bonds. EE bonds are eligible for exchange six months after issue; E bonds remain eligible for exchange until one year after final maturity.

Bond owners who have deferred reporting the interest on the EE and E bonds for tax purposes may continue to defer such reporting to the taxable year in which HH bonds issued in exchange are redeemed, disposed of, or reach final maturity, whichever happens first. Thus, you can continue to defer reporting of the interest you have earned on Series EE or E bonds while at the same time you receive income from the conversion into HH bonds. Of course, the interest received from the HH bonds is taxable immediately and should be reported to the Internal Revenue Service on your annual tax return.

Treasury Bills

The most widely held Treasury security, and the one that has received so much publicity during recent years, is the Treasury "bill." These are short-term instruments auctioned off by the Treasury each week in enormous volume. Literally billions of dollars worth of bills are traded each day in the "money market." Most of this activity involves large financial institutions and corporations as well as the Treasury itself, which makes large purchases and sales for its own account. In addition to financing government activities the Treasury is also concerned with managing the nation's money supply. In carrying out this responsibility the Treasury will buy or sell securities in order to influence bank reserves and interest rates.

Treasury bills are generally issued with a maturity of 13 or 26 weeks. That is, you are literally making the government a loan for that period of time. At the end of that period the Treasury promises to repay your loan along with an appropriate amount of interest. Interestingly, T-bills as they are often called, are sold "at a discount." This means that they are sold for less than their redemption value. The difference between what you pay for the bill when you purchase it and what the government pays you when it matures is the interest earned.

Like six-month CDs, the minimum denomination for a Treasury bill is $10,000. As a matter of fact, the six-month certificates issued by banks, savings and loans, and savings banks have their interest rates set by the action of the Treasury each week at its bill auction. Whatever rate is set for the 26-week Treasury bill is the maximum rate that can be paid on six-month certificates of deposit issued that week. Obviously, the rate can change each week, and has changed dramatically during the past year or so. (When the Treasury bill rate is less than 9%, thrift institutions can offer ¼% more interest on their certificates than those offered by commercial banks.)

Treasury bills offer the advantage of extreme safety of principal, and a return that is at least competitive with other money market instruments. Another bonus is the fact that interest on Treasury securities is not taxed by the states or local governments. This can be significant if you live in an area with a substantial state income tax or local income tax. This tax advantage may make it more attractive for you to purchase Treasury bills instead of six-month certificates even if they pay the same rate of interest.

The principal disadvantage of Treasury bills is the minimum purchase obligation of $10,000. They do not lend themselves to gradual accumulation programs which are important to retirement planning. Once you have built up a retirement fund, or have actually retired and are looking for safety and a reasonable return, they can be an attractive investment alternative.

In addition to short-term Treasury bills the government also issues longer-term securities in large volume. Treasury "notes" generally mature in from one to five years while government "bonds" have maturities of more than five years and frequently of 20 years or longer. In addition, government agencies issue long-term bonds to finance their various activities. These securities offer the same high level of safety as do Treasury bills and are available in smaller denominations, frequently $1000. However, we should note that only fully guaranteed issues of the Treasury are exempt from state and local income taxes.

The main drawback to investing in long-term government bonds is that such obligations pay a fixed rate of interest—a fixed amount of dollars—that will be eroded over time by the effects of inflation. This can be particularly severe if the bonds are purchased at a time when the general level of interest rates is low. As we saw in Chapter 4, inflation can do considerable damage to your purchasing power over the years. Whenever possible you want to invest in securities that will keep pace with inflation, either through increased income, capital gains, or both.

A few government bond issues have a unique feature that may be of special importance to your retirement and estate planning. These issues may be used at their full par value in payment of federal estate taxes. Even if they were purchased at a substantial discount they may be applied to the payment of such taxes as if they were fully valued at their maturity. Such issues have been given the term "flower bonds" for fairly obvious reasons.

Therefore, if you anticipate having a substantial estate tax to be paid, you may want to consider the purchase of one of these special issues for later use in discharging that obligation. For example, Paul Jones expects to have a considerable estate tax due upon his death. He wants to leave as much of his estate as possible for his children, and to reduce the amount paid in taxes. He could consider the purchase of "flower bonds" at a discount. If he could purchase a $1000 bond for $900 and have the full $1000 applied to the payment of his taxes, his estate would benefit considerably.

The number of government securities that qualify for this special estate tax treatment is limited and no new issues with this feature are currently offered. So if you feel your estate tax obligations might be large, you may want to place some of these particular issues in your retirement portfolio.

In the final analysis, government securities are *not* attractive for most retirement plans. You can earn considerably higher returns without much extra risk, and you should be focusing on investments that will protect your purchasing power against inflation. They also lack the convenience of money-market funds or mutual funds as a means of building up your retirement fund through a regular program of small contributions.

Municipal Bonds

Municipal bonds are issued by the states and by thousands of local governments throughout the country. Funds are used to finance a wide variety of projects such as roads and bridges and also to provide municipal services such as sewage treatment, water, and public utilities.

The principal attraction of these bonds is the tax-exempt nature of the interest they pay. Interest received on municipal bonds is exempt from federal income taxes, and, indeed, is not even reported on your tax form. The various states generally do include municipal bond interest for state income-tax purposes, with one major exception. Most states do not tax interest paid by municipalities within the state.

As an example, Pennsylvania would not tax the interest paid by the City of Philadelphia on its municipal bonds, but would tax interest paid by New York City.

This tax-exempt feature of municipal bonds is obviously more valuable the higher your income-tax bracket. A dollar of taxable interest is worth only 60 cents to someone in the 40% tax bracket, and only 50 cents to a person in the 50% bracket. (The maximum tax rate on earned income is 50%, but can rise to 70% on so-called *unearned income* such as dividends and interest.)

Table 5.2 shows how much you would have to earn from a taxable security to compare with various tax-exempt returns. The figures in the body of the table show taxable returns, assuming various individual tax brackets from 43% up to the maximum 70%.

For example, Earl Bishop is considering two alternative investments that have been recommended to him by his broker. The first investment is a corporate bond that would pay Earl *taxable* interest at the rate of 12% annually. A second possibility is to purchase a municipal bond that yields 7% tax free. If Earl is in the 49% tax bracket, which investment should he choose?

Go to Table 5.2 and select the column headed "7.00." Move down this column until you reach the row for the 49% tax bracket. The figure shown is "13.73%," which means that in Earl's tax bracket a tax-free return of 7% would be equivalent to earning 13.73% in taxable interest. Since the taxable bond pays only 12%, Earl would be better off with the tax-free municipal bond.

Another way of evaluating the attractiveness of tax-free income is to

TABLE 5.2

TAX BRACKET	TAX-EXEMPT YIELDS (%)									
	4.00	4.50	5.00	5.50	6.00	6.50	7.00	7.50	8.00	8.50
43%	7.02	7.89	8.77	9.65	10.50	11.40	12.28	13.16	14.04	14.91
44	7.14	8.04	8.92	9.82	10.71	11.61	12.50	13.39	14.29	15.18
46	7.41	8.33	9.26	10.19	11.11	12.04	12.96	13.89	14.81	15.74
49	7.84	8.82	9.80	10.78	11.76	12.75	13.73	14.71	15.69	16.67
54	8.70	9.78	10.87	11.96	13.04	14.13	15.22	16.30	17.39	18.48
55	8.89	10.00	11.11	12.22	13.33	14.44	15.56	16.67	17.78	18.89
59	9.76	10.98	12.20	13.41	14.63	15.85	17.07	18.29	19.51	20.73
63	10.81	12.16	13.51	14.86	16.22	17.57	18.92	20.27	21.62	22.97
64	11.11	12.50	13.89	15.28	16.67	18.06	19.44	20.83	22.22	23.61
68	12.50	14.06	15.63	17.19	18.75	20.31	21.88	23.44	25.00	26.56
70	13.33	15.00	16.67	18.33	20.00	21.67	23.33	25.00	26.67	28.33

compare it with other categories of income as reported to the Internal Revenue Service. Table 5.3 shows the *after-tax* return in various tax brackets for four different types of income. As you can see, "Tax-Free Income" is the only category in which a dollar is worth a dollar, after taxes, no matter what tax bracket you are in.

Ordinary income, which includes taxable dividends and interest, is the least favorable type of income in that it is subject to the highest tax rates. As noted above, the maximum tax rate on earned income such as salaries and wages is 50%. Capital gains are also taxed favorably since even in the highest brackets you will be able to keep 72¢ of every dollar after taxes.

Only the first 40% of long-term capital gains are taxable. Even if you should be in the highest tax bracket (70%) the result would be a 28% tax on your capital gains (40% × 70% = 28%).

As with all other types of investments, municipal bonds can vary considerably in quality. The national rating agencies evaluate state and local governments and assign them a rating based on the analysis. While most municipalities have a good record of paying their debts, some do not. You should always inquire as to the rating of any municipal bond you may consider buying, and ask about its payment history as well.

During the past several years the interest rates paid on good quality municipal bonds have been at all-time highs. Tax-free returns of more than 10% have not been unusual. For individuals and families, including two-

TABLE 5.3 COMPARISON OF TAX-FREE VERSUS TAXABLE INCOME

TAXABLE INCOME JOINT RETURN	TAX-FREE INCOME	ORDINARY INCOME	EARNED INCOME	CAPITAL GAIN
$ 5,500– 7,600	$1.00	$0.84	$0.84	$0.936
7,600– 11,900	1.00	0.82	0.82	0.928
11,900– 16,000	1.00	0.79	0.79	0.916
16,000– 20,200	1.00	0.76	0.76	0.904
20,200– 24,600	1.00	0.72	0.72	0.888
24,600– 29,900	1.00	0.68	0.68	0.872
29,900– 35,200	1.00	0.63	0.63	0.852
35,200– 45,800	1.00	0.57	0.57	0.828
45,800– 60,000	1.00	0.51	0.51	0.804
60,000– 85,600	1.00	0.46	0.50	0.784
85,600–109,400	1.00	0.41	0.50	0.764
109,400–162,400	1.00	0.36	0.50	0.744
162,400–215,400	1.00	0.32	0.50	0.728
over $215,500	1.00	0.30	0.50	0.720

income families, who are at or near the 40–50% tax bracket, this is equivalent to almost 20% return on taxable securities.

However, municipal bonds share some important disadvantages with other types of fixed income securities. The return, even though it may be relatively high at the present time, is fixed, and its purchasing power will decline as the years go by. Also, buying bonds directly does not lend itself to an accumulation program as easily as some other investments. This disadvantage can be overcome to some degree by investing in tax-exempt mutual funds on a regular basis.

Corporate Bonds

Most of the major corporations in the United States borrow money from investors through the issuance of bonds. These securities can be an important part of your program to finance a secure retirement. You will need to know some of the basics, however, before you can consider them for your portfolio.

First, the quality of corporate bonds can range from excellent to poor to very poor. The highest quality corporates are those rated "AAA" or its equivalent by Standard and Poor's, Moody's, or Fitch's. These are three of the nation's largest and best-known rating agencies.

Generally these top-rated issues come from telephone companies, other public utilities, and the very strongest industrial corporations. These obligations are second only to securities of the Federal government in their freedom from risk of default. As this risk increases, the bond's rating declines to AA, A, BBB, and so on down to bonds with a C rating, which are in default.

How far down the ratings scale should you go, and why? Well, as you can probably guess by now, the lower the rating the higher the yield available from the bond. Risk and return are related and investors will not put their money into lower quality issues unless they are compensated by higher returns. The yield difference between a AAA bond and one rated BBB can sometimes be two percentage points or more. This may not sound like much, but a bond paying 12% will give you 20% more income than one paying only 10%. Banks and savings banks are generally restricted to investing in securities with at least a BBB rating.

Most corporate bonds pay interest semiannually, but different bonds make these payments at different months of the year. For example, some bonds pay interest in January and June while others make payments in

March and September. This feature enables you to diversify your portfolio and receive interest payments throughout the year. By purchasing a portfolio of six bonds with different payment schedules you could arrange to receive a regular monthly income from your investments.

While corporate bonds can provide a high level of current income, that income is again fixed in amount. For example. AT&T has a bond issue paying 8.75% which matures in the year 2000. This means that the company will be paying $87.50 in interest to the owner of each $1000 of bonds until the year 2000. Specifically, the company will make payments of $43.75 in May and November of each year. The bonds will mature in the year 2000, at which time AT&T will redeem each bond at its par value.

Since AT&T is a AAA rated issuer you can be quite sure that you will receive your money every six months. But what will that series of $43.75 payments buy for you over the years? Twenty years ago it might have purchased a good quality dress or suit; it will not do so today! It will purchase even less in the years to come and so should not be relied upon to maintain your standard of living or to accumulate your retirement fund.

We cannot emphasize too strongly the need to maintain your retirement fund in assets that will keep up with the rate of inflation. In general, bonds are not the best investment to accomplish this objective. You may be able to invest or reinvest the interest payments and keep up with inflation, but what about the value of your capital when the bond matures? We may use $1000 1981 dollars to purchase the bond in 1981, but by the year 2000 a 10% inflation rate would have reduced the purchasing power of that money to $163.51.

Even after you retire you should *not* invest all of your funds in corporate bonds, no matter how attractive the yield may seem. The reason for this is the life expectancy chart we discussed in Chapter 2. If you reach age 65 you can expect to live another 15 to 20 years, and you will still have to be concerned with protecting your purchasing power over that period of time. You should keep at least some of your retirement fund in assets which will reflect inflation and maintain their purchasing power. This may mean a "permanent" investment in stocks, equity mutual funds, real estate, or money-market funds.

DISCOUNT BONDS

One strategy that can be used in buying bonds is to purchase only so-called "discount bonds." These are bonds that were originally issued at a par value of $1000 per bond, but which are now selling for less than that amount. Why should they decline in market value? The reason is changing interest rates. As interest rates move in one direction, either up or down, bond prices will generally move in the opposite direction. Since interest rates in recent years have been at such high levels, there are many bonds selling below their original issue price of $1000 per bond.

A 20-year bond which originally sold for $1000 and yielded 8% will have to sell for $828.40 when newly issued bonds offer 10%. By selecting carefully from among these "bargain bonds" you can substantially increase your current return and protect yourself against erosion of capital due to inflation. Let's see just how this might work for you.

Put yourself in the place of Frank Stevens, a retired production worker. Through careful planning and regular contributions he has built up a retirement fund of $100,000. Frank now wants to invest this money so that it will provide a secure income for him and his wife during the next 20 years. His pension is fixed in its amount and Frank is somewhat concerned that his retirement fund provide income that keeps up with inflation. He also would like to preserve the real value of their capital so that it can be passed on to his children and grandchildren.

Frank has decided to invest a part of his retirement fund in a portfolio of discount bonds. With the advice of his broker he has selected a number of bonds so that he will receive some income in each month of the year. He has also varied the maturity dates of the bonds so that some mature in a year or two, others in three to five years, and the balance in about 10 years.

All of the bonds were purchased at prices below their par or maturity value of $1000. For example, one bond with a coupon rate of 9% (meaning it pays $90 per year on each bond) was purchased for $785.00. The actual yield for Frank Stevens is just about 11½% on a current-income basis. But Frank will do even better when this bond matures in 10 years. At that time he will receive the full face value of $1000, not just the $785.00 which he paid. The "extra" $215 he will receive *at the end of 10 years* will push his overall return closer to 12%!

Another bond, a relatively low-rated one, is selling for $550.00 and has a return of $50 per year on each bond. This means a current yield of about 9%, but a "yield to maturity" (which accounts for interest and capital gain) of more than 15% when the bond matures in about eight years! By purchasing these bonds at the present time, Frank has locked in a good current yield and assured himself of additional capital gain (taxable) when each bond matures.

You might even purchase some discount bonds during the accumulation period before your retirement. If you do, select maturity dates shortly after your retirement so that the capital gains on the bonds will fall into your retirement period when your taxes will be lower. You should not commit too much of your retirement fund in this way, however, as there are better ways to invest before you reach retirement age. After retirement, discount bonds can provide a steady stream of income and provide low-risk capital gains to help offset the impact of inflation.

CONVERTIBLE BONDS

Another attractive way to use bonds in your retirement portfolio is to purchase *convertible bonds* which may be exchanged for shares of a company's common stock. For example, a bond originally purchased for $1000 may be convertible into 40 shares of a firm's common stock. In effect, you would have paid $25 per share for the stock, and you would have a profit once the market price of the common stock went above the $25 level.

Convertible bonds generally pay lower rates of interest than similar quality bonds that are not convertible ("straight bonds"), but their yield is often much higher than the dividend yield of the related common stock. Another advantage to owning convertible bonds is the fact that their price is generally more stable than common stocks. Even if the market price of the stock does not increase you will have the safety of a bond and the income from interest payments.

When selecting convertible bonds look first for companies with good future growth prospects. The common stocks of such companies should increase in price and take your convertible bonds along with them. Secondly, try to buy when the conversion price of your bonds is not more than 20% above the present market price of the stock. In the example we used above where the conversion price was $25 per share, you should buy the convertible only when the stock price is at least $20 per share. You don't want to wait too long for the market price to catch up to your conversion price.

Finally, don't make too much of a sacrifice in the way of yield when buying a convertible bond. If a convertible bond yields two percentage points less than other bonds of similar quality, don't buy it! There are many convertible issues each year that meet these criteria. Look for them and consider adding them to your retirement portfolio. They will provide income and the convertible "kicker" will give you some protection against inflation as well.

Preferred Stock

Issues of preferred stock share some of the features of bonds and some of common stock. In general, the negative qualities inherited from bonds outweigh the better features shared with stocks. Because of this judgment we will only touch on them here as they are generally not recommended for a retirement portfolio. This is particularly true during the accumulation period.

Preferred stocks are "preferred" in a number of important ways. They normally are entitled to dividend payments before any dividends can be paid to common stockholders. Also, in the event of liquidation of a company, holders of preferred stock would be paid off before holders of common stock. Most issues of preferred stock are "cumulative" in that if the company fails to make a dividend payment it must make it up at some time before anything can be paid to common stockholders.

The disadvantage of preferred stocks is that they typically pay a fixed dividend that will not increase over time. Thus the income from preferred stocks is bound to lose some of its purchasing power because of inflation. Because of the fixed nature of their income, preferred stocks are quite stable in value. While this may be attractive for some persons concerned with the preservation of capital it is not suitable for anyone planning for retirement. Again, you need to focus on investments that will maintain your ability to purchase what you want when you want it.

The only redeeming quality of some preferreds is a conversion feature similar to that discussed for bonds. With the opportunity to benefit from conversion into common stock, some high-quality preferred shares could be a worthwhile addition to your portfolio. In general, however, preferred stocks are not attractive.

Common Stocks

Common stocks represent an ownership interest in a corporation. This is in contrast to the position of a bondholder, whom we saw involved making a loan to the corporation which was to be paid off at some future date. There is no maturity date on common stock. If you want to recover your investment you must sell your shares at the going market price. This may be more or less than you paid for the stock originally and involves some degree of risk. The corporation makes no guarantees to you as it does to the bondholder.

Another uncertainty involved with common stock is the amount of income you may receive. Most stocks pay some amount of dividend, but it is not guaranteed in the same way that a bond pays interest. A firm may reduce its common-stock dividend or eliminate it altogether without any legal obligation. What a firm pays in dividends is generally a function of its earnings, which may be very good in some years and not so good in others. In recent years the U.S. auto industry has been a good example of the wide swings in earnings which can take place and which will have an impact on the dividends that a company can pay.

Despite these uncertainties concerning price and dividends, common stocks remain one of the best investment vehicles for funding your retirement program. Why? Because stock prices *can* go up, and because firms *do* increase their dividends from time to time as their earnings go up. Now, not *all* stocks experience these results all the time. Yet it is this potential for increased income and for capital gain that makes common stock a "necessary" investment for your retirement plan.

Keep in mind that you are probably planning for a time horizon that extends for 30 to 40 years, maybe longer. Inflation is not going to stop and you must have some investments that will keep up with inflation. Common stock not only provides a vehicle to do so, but may even benefit from the overall impact of inflation. Firms that are able to pass along cost increases and raise their prices to customers will increase their earnings even during inflationary periods. Increased earnings are generally accompanied by rising dividends and share prices.

For example, the common stock of Proctor and Gamble has been an effective hedge against inflation. During the past 10 years the company has regularly increased its dividend from $1.33 per share in 1970 to $3.70 in 1980. Thus dividends have increased at more than 10% per year, faster than inflation over the period of the 1970s. Many companies have a record of increasing their dividends annually that stretches back over many years.

Stock prices, while subject to some rather wide swings, have shown a long-term upward trend. Measured over many years and several business cycles, the average return on all common stocks has been approximately 9% compounded annually. Not much, you may say! But keep in mind that for many of those years the inflation rate in the United States was as low as one, two, or three percent.

Common stocks may not *guarantee* that you will keep ahead of inflation, but at least you will have a fighting chance! A diversified portfolio of common stocks should enable you to keep pace with inflation through reasonable capital gains and regular increases in dividend income. Remember, you are planning for the long-run, and over the long-run common stocks have been a good investment.

There are many ways to invest in common stocks, even if you do not like selecting them and managing your own portfolio. A stock broker, your bank, or a mutual fund which invests in common stocks are all worthwhile alternatives to doing the work yourself. And with the "family of funds" concept so easy to implement, you can switch from stocks to more conservative investments in the time it takes to make a phone call.

What kinds of stocks should you look for? This will depend somewhat on your age, the amount of money you have to invest, your personal risk attitudes, need for current income, other assets you own, and your tax bracket. It is not a simple matter, but it is an important one. Perhaps one way to approach the problem is to determine your needs first and then begin to seek stocks that suit those needs.

First, how long will it be until you retire? If you are more than a few years from retirement you should be stressing capital growth and possibly tax deferral, rather than income. Companies that reinvest most of their earnings and that pay out little in the way of dividends would fit your needs at the moment. Look for firms that have a good record of earnings growth along with a substantial investment in research and development. They should continue to develop new products that will generate higher earnings in the years to come.

If you are in a relatively high tax bracket, companies that pay low dividends or no dividends at all offer another advantage. By reinvesting their earnings they should grow and increase in share price. Selling your shares at some future date for a capital gain will result in a lower tax than you would pay today on dividends. At the present time, 60% of long-term capital gains are excluded from calculation of federal income taxes. At younger ages stress growth, and reinvest any dividends that you do receive!

If you are about to retire you may have to look to your investment portfolio for additional income. This would be the time to consider selling stocks that do not pay substantial dividends and reinvesting in those that will offer a higher yield. Look for stocks that have increased their dividends on a regular basis, and that have provided stable share prices as well. This is no time to be speculating.

Brokerage firms commonly publish lists of companies that have paid regular quarterly dividends for many years. By selecting from this list you can put together a portfolio of stocks that will provide you with a regular monthly income. Choosing those firms which have continually increased their earnings and dividends can go a long way toward providing the financial security you desire for your retirement years.

If you elect to invest through a mutual fund organization, take a look at its record over the years. How does it compare with the performance of the market in general? Also, what are its investment advisory fees and other charges. In general you should select from among the many "no-load" funds that are available so as to avoid any sales charge. Invest in a fund that is part of a fund group that provides not only a common stock fund but also a bond fund, a tax-free fund, and a money-market fund. You may want to use all of them someday!

Real Estate

Investments in real estate have traditionally been considered one of the best ways to offset inflation. Increasing property values and the opportunity to raise rents have been attractive features of income-producing property for years. These advantages are likely to continue in the future, and you may want to consider the purchase of investment real estate as a part of your retirement portfolio.

Despite its obvious advantages, real estate does not lend itself very well to the normal pattern of retirement investments. This is particularly true for the early years of a program when you are trying to build your retirement fund. Real estate investments generally require a substantial sum of capital, at least in comparison with assets such as mutual funds and money-market funds. You'll have a hard time putting $100 a month into any real estate investment!

Once you have accumulated some capital you may want to think about real estate, but there are other problems as well. It is difficult to diversify with real estate unless you have really large amounts of capital and are willing to leverage your investments by borrowing large amounts of additional money. This introduces a degree of risk that is not appropriate for your retirement fund. Also, along with the territory comes the management problem. Are you interested in maintaining the property yourself, advertising it, and looking for new tenants? If not, you may want to look elsewhere to invest your money. This is particularly true once you retire. You may want to do a great many other things instead of keeping up your property.

So far as real estate is concerned, a great deal depends on you and your personality. If you have the time, money, and inclination, large profits can be made and you can offset inflation as well. On the other hand, a good deal of work is involved, the risks are substantial, and not everyone makes money!

Tax-Sheltered Investments

Around April 15 of each year most of us start to think about tax-sheltered investments. When we see the amount of income taxes that we pay it is natural to say, "There must be a better way!" You may be lured by some of the exotic advertising that exists in this area, and that promises to cut your taxes to practically nothing. Be cautious! Any deal that sounds too good to be true probably is. This section will discuss some of the objectives of tax-sheltered investments and also some of the very real pitfalls that exist.

Shelter programs exist because the tax laws have been written in such a way as to encourage investment in certain areas. There is nothing shady, shaky, or illegal about the laws that regulate tax-advantaged investments. The term "loophole" seems to imply something improper, but this is definitely not the case. You can take advantage of these laws, and earn some real benefits, but there are potential problems that you should be aware of.

In the first place, you should never be interested in a particular investment *only* because it is described as a "tax shelter." A tax-sheltered investment should make sense as an investment first and a tax shelter second. If it doesn't make sense economically, it probably won't hold up very well as a tax shelter either. Always remember that nobody is in a 100% tax bracket. You're always ahead to pay your taxes and keep some of your money as opposed to losing all of it on a rotten investment.

If you follow the guidelines noted here you will have a much better chance not only of selecting a good shelter, but of making a basically good investment as well. Depending on your own financial situation a tax shelter may be more or less attractive than it would be to someone else. The principal factor, of course, is your income and the related tax bracket. Your feelings about risk and your personal investment objectives will also have an impact on whether or not tax shelters make sense for you. With these reservations, the following guidelines should be helpful:

1. Look for tax-sheltered investments that are economically sound and able to withstand varying economic conditions.

2. Be aware of changing tax laws that may eliminate the advantage of a particular shelter.

3. The investment should permit you to obtain a high degree of leverage through borrowing.

4. The investment should produce some tax-sheltered income that can be reinvested to accumulate for your retirement.

5. In order to hedge against inflation the investment should have good potential for an increase in value (capital gain) or for increasing income.

6. The investment should be consistent with your long-run financial goals.

In addition to evaluating tax shelters according to the guidelines above, there are other considerations. Before investing you should be provided with a detailed description of the tax shelter. If you do not feel comfortable in analyzing it, contact your broker or banker and ask for their opinion. If one of them is recommending it to you, see the other for a second opinion! Don't buy it unless you understand it.

One drawback to many shelter programs is the need to make additional investments in the future. You may not be able to do so, and may lose not only the tax advantage you hoped for but your original investment as well. How much time is involved with the program? Do you receive any benefits immediately, or are they all somewhere down the road? What is the expected rate of return on the investment as well as the write-off promised for the first year?

It is generally very easy to get *into* a tax shelter, but often much more difficult to get *out*! How will you recover your principal, and when will this occur? Do *you* have to find someone who will buy out your interest, or is this provided for in the shelter agreement? Finally, how much is in it for the other guy; how much are the promoters of the shelter going to make, and how much are they willing to invest in the project? Try to find out the answers to these and any other questions you may have before you make a commitment on the deal. Tax shelters can provide substantial long-run benefits, but they can also involve a very high degree of investment risk that may make them inappropriate for your retirement program.

Once you actually do retire there will probably not be as much incentive for you to invest in any tax-sheltered investments. This will depend on your personal situation, but you are likely to be in a considerably lower tax bracket. Also, at that point you will probably not want to speculate quite as much with your capital as when you were younger. You may also be after a higher rate of income return than is offered by most tax shelters.

CONCLUSION

Investing for your retirement may seem like an immensely complex and difficult problem. While it can be, it does not necessarily have to be so. *You* are the one in control of your retirement program and it should never become so complex that you lose control over it. Keep it simple enough for you to understand it. This does not mean that you should not involve advisers such as a banker, broker, or financial planner, but remember that it is *your* money and nobody is going to be as concerned about it as you will be.

As this chapter has illustrated, there are many different types of investments to select from. We have covered only the major ones and there are dozens of others that run the gamut from gold to scotch whiskey! Which ones are best for you and for your retirement plan will depend on your personal situation, your income, how much time you have until retirement, your pension and Social Security benefits, and a host of other factors.

It is far more important to start planning for your retirement now and to keep at it than to worry about constructing the most sophisticated plan in the world. You have time on your side, and, as we have said many times, the benefit of compound interest that will make your investments grow steadily. It is better to start a conservative plan immediately and then develop new investments as you become more knowledgeable and as your capital grows.

If you haven't done anything so far to begin a financial planning program, start now! Open an account with a money-market fund and begin to put something into that account each month. Don't skip a month here and there and expect to make up for it later. You won't be able to skip eating any months after you retire. Put something aside now and you'll be amazed at how it will grow over time.

Once you have made a habit of regular contributions to your retirement plan you can begin to think about how this fund should be invested. But, don't be in any hurry to get there. The money-market fund will do nicely until you are sure of where you are headed and how you want to get there. Good luck!

6

LIFE INSURANCE

*A policy of life insurance is the oldest
and safest mode of making certain provision for one's family. It is a strange
anomaly that men should be careful to
insure their houses, their ships, their
merchandise and yet neglect to insure
their lives, surely the most important
of all to their families, and more subject
to loss.*

Benjamin Franklin

The purchase of life insurance is one of a person's most unselfish acts. The reason, simply stated, is that the fruits of the purchase of life insurance cannot be harvested until the insured is dead. Comedian Robert Klein explains how he has avoided buying large amounts of life insurance. He envisions himself on his deathbed suffering pangs of guilt resulting from the failure to provide for the future of his family and not meeting his obligations to his creditors when suddenly he is dead and, as he puts it, "I don't care anymore."

Such a mental maneuver may work for Robert Klein, but fortunately he is in the minority. People buy life insurance despite the fact that once the risk occurs against which it protects, the insured can no longer be held to account for any of his or her obligations. It is the thought, while living, of the consequences of dying without proper amounts of life insurance that motivates its purchase.

Adequate amounts of life insurance provide a hedge against the uncertainty of *when* death will occur, permitting the insured to take greater risks in the present to secure a lifetime of freedom from financial wants. Put an-

105

other way, life insurance is the foundation upon which a financial plan should be built. This advice is generally given by all financial planners, regardless of whether they market life insurance.

Reaching a positive decision about the purchase of life insurance leads to a host of questions that must be answered—questions like: What type of life insurance? What do all those provisions in the contract really mean? How much life insurance should I purchase? From whom should I buy my life insurance? How do I know if I'm getting the most for my premium dollar? These are some of the questions that this chapter will attempt to answer.

HOW MUCH LIFE INSURANCE DO YOU NEED?

What are you purchasing when you buy life insurance? Basically, you are buying dollars for delivery upon the happening of a future event whose time of occurrence is uncertain. If you are like most people, the purchase of life insurance is about the only way to adequately provide for the financial security of your dependents after your death. For those with enough accumulated wealth to provide for the needs of their dependents, life insurance may still be purchased because it's the most inexpensive source of dollars to meet certain cash demands. These include estate administration expenses and death taxes that must be paid within a short time after death occurs. Whether you are in the market for life insurance to create an estate or to preserve an estate which you have created during your lifetime, there are certain factors that should be considered when determining how much life insurance you need.

Life Insurance To Create an Estate

Virtually everyone has accumulated some assets during his or her lifetime. These may take the form of cash, tangible personal property such as jewelry, cars, clothing, household furnishings, etc. They may take the form of intangible personal property such as savings certificates, stocks, bonds, mutual funds, annuities and the cash value of life insurance. Some assets may be in the form of real property such as a house, condominium, vacation home, or commercial real estate. Other assets may be in the form of benefits that will be payable in the future upon the happening of an event such as retirement or death. Examples would be social security benefits, pension benefits, deferred compensation, group and individual life insurance, and other employer-sponsored death benefit plans.

A somewhat different type of asset, but often the most valuable of all assets you possess, is the flow of income that will be produced by your personal work efforts. It is this asset that most of us depend upon to meet the bulk of our financial needs, and it is this asset which death cancels.

In addition to acquiring assets, you have also acquired financial obligations. Just as on the asset side, some of these obligations are current and ongoing, such as food, clothing, shelter, medical expenses, income taxes, entertainment, and travel. Death will someday terminate these obligations for you, but not for your dependents—your spouse, children, parents, or other relatives or friends. For your dependents, your death also creates new financial obligations, such as funeral expenses, estate administration expenses, and death taxes. To meet the immediate demands for cash at your death and for their ongoing needs, your dependents will look to the assets you have accumulated up to the time of your death. To the extent that your assets will fall short in meeting these financial obligations you have a need for additional life insurance.

The Unknowns in the Equation

When trying to estimate your future financial needs you are faced with a series of unknowns. How long will you and your dependents live? Will your spouse remarry and be cared for by someone else? Will your spouse become a wage earner or continue to earn a wage if already working? Will your children go to college? Will your children become wage earners or continue to earn a wage if already working?

Rather than guessing what the future will bring, why not determine what you *want* the future financial status of your dependents to be? Then see to it that the necessary assets and income flow are provided at the time of your death. Assume, however unappealing it may seem, that you were to die tomorrow; then compare the assets and income flow your family would need with the assets and income flow you actually have. The answer will indicate how much additional life insurance, if any, you should carry.

You are often advised that an expense that will not arise until some time in the future can be met by a lesser dollar amount presently on hand. This is because the present amount can be invested and earn interest from today until the time the payment becomes due (e.g., the college tuition payable

10 years from now for a child who is presently eight years old requires less on hand today than the actual tuition cost). You are also advised that in estimating the cost of future expenses, such as college tuition, the effects of inflation should be taken into account. Both of these items of advice are good ones. However, future interest rates and inflation rates can only be estimated. If you believe that the two will be significantly different, then it pays to factor both into your calculation of the assets and income that will be needed in the future. If you believe that interest rates and inflation will be comparable, then the procedure can be simplified by assuming these two factors cancel each other. The latter approach should work satisfactorily in most cases. For example, when estimating the amount you must have on hand to pay college tuition 10 years from now, simply use the present cost of a college education.

WILL MY FAMILY BE SHORT OF INCOME?

Ascertaining the extent of your family's assets, income flow, cash needs, and income needs is often best accomplished with the aide of a professional financial planner. However, you should become as familiar as you can with the process. This will enhance your ability to do it alone. It will also enable you to work more efficiently with a professional if one is used. In addition, since planning for your family's financial security involves the use of legal documents such as wills and perhaps trusts, as well as the need for tax planning, the services of a lawyer skilled in what is generally termed estate planning should be sought. The ultimate cost of doing it yourself may be far greater than the cost of professional advice.

To get a true picture of your family's financial condition your advisor should conduct a hypothetical probate of your estate. That is, assuming that you were to die today, what would be your family's needs for capital and income and how would those needs be met? You must play an active role in this process by deciding which of your assets should be disposed of to meet the demands for cash. Once you have determined the assets to be sold, the next step is to determine which family members will receive the remaining assets and how much income can be expected to be produced by these assets.

Often the assets that are good income producers—such as savings certificates, bonds, and stocks—are also the ones sold at the time of death because they are easily turned into cash. This may leave your family with assets that have substantial value but do not produce income. Examples would include a personal residence, cars, household effects, jewelry, art work, etc. What may also come to light from this analysis is that a particular family member who needs substantial income will not end up with the property which can produce that income because of a poorly drafted will or perhaps no will at all. For example, if you have no will, depending on your state's law and the number of children you have, your spouse may receive only one-third to one-half of your property. The balance would go to your children. (For a more detailed discussion of this area see Chapter 8, Estate Planning.)

Once you determine the income from assets remaining after all demands for cash at death are met, then compute the income from other sources. These would include Social-Security benefits, private pension-plan benefits, disability income benefits, and earnings from employment. When calculating the amounts available from these other sources of income, keep in mind that a dependent's earnings from employment may reduce or perhaps eliminate any Social-Security benefits.

After the income that will be available to dependents during various periods of time has been calculated, it must be compared with the needs for income that will exist at different times. To the extent that the needs for income exceed the income available, there is a demonstrated requirement for additional assets that can be invested or liquidated systematically to make up for the income deficit. Worksheets that can be used to determine whether or not there will be any income shortages will be found at the end of this chapter (Figs. 6.2 through 6.4). The most practical way to guarantee that these additional assets will be available whenever death occurs is to purchase additional life insurance. The remainder of this chapter provides you with a wealth of information to enable you to become familiar with the variety of life insurance products. As an informed consumer you will be able to decide on the best life insurance for your needs.

ALL ABOUT TERM INSURANCE

Term insurance may be thought of as the "no frills" life insurance contract. The premium for each $1000 of death benefit at a given age is substantially less than it would be for a new permanent type life policy which includes several options and guarantees, including living benefits, in addition to providing life insurance protection. For example, at age 35 the premium for one year of term insurance is about $3 per $1000 of death benefit. At the same age the premium for one year of permanent insurance is about $18 per $1000 of death benefit. But this is like comparing apples and pears, as you will see.

Level Term Insurance

A level term insurance policy provides a fixed amount of life insurance protection at a guaranteed level premium rate for a specified term of years. Typical terms are one year, five years, 10 years, 20 years or until some specified age, such as 65. In order for the beneficiary to collect on the policy, your death must occur during the term. If the term expires while you are still alive, you may apply for a new policy for another term of years, with the premium rate based on your age at the time the new policy is issued.

EFFECT OF LENGTH OF TERM ON AMOUNT OF LEVEL PREMIUM

The cost of life insurance protection varies directly with increased age. Therefore, if an insurance company issues a level premium policy for a term of five years, the annual premium will be, generally speaking, an average of what the sum of the annual premiums would be for five consecutive one-year term policies. Thus, if you are willing to forego the guarantee of a level premium beyond one year, you can acquire coverage for that year alone at the lowest premium possible for each $1000 of protection by purchasing one-year term insurance. One problem with this pure annual term insurance approach is that it requires new evidence of insurability each year.

GUARANTEED RENEWABLE FEATURE

To overcome the problem of the year ending with you seriously ill and not eligible for insurance the following year, the guaranteed renewable option may be added to the pure annual term policy. This option permits you to renew the policy for another year without passing a medical exam or presenting any other evidence of insurability. *Even though the acquisition of the guaranteed renewable option will increase the annual premium, it is a "must" for any sound insurance plan.* Of course, the premium rate for the new term will be based upon your attained age and not upon your age when the policy was originally issued. The guaranteed renewable option is also available with policies whose term is more than one year (e.g., five-year renewable term).

Decreasing Term Insurance

Most term insurance provides a level death benefit for the period of the term. However, it is possible to purchase term insurance with a death benefit that decreases annually over the period of the contract. Such a policy is attractive where the need for protection decreases over time. A good example is what is commonly called mortgage insurance. Mortgage insurance is no more than a decreasing term policy with a term period equal to the period of the mortgage and a face amount that decreases each year at approximately the same rate as the principal of the mortgage decreases. The annual premium for decreasing term generally remains level throughout the term at a rate which takes into account the decreasing coverage.

"Fresh Start" Term Insurance

Where term insurance is guaranteed renewable, the premium rate for each renewal term is also guaranteed at the time the policy is first acquired. Since this rate is guaranteed well into the future and no evidence of insurability is required to renew the term, the renewal premium rate is generally higher than the insurance company's premium rate for a new term policy at the same age where evidence of insurability is required. To give old policyholders the opportunity to qualify for the lower rate, some renewable term policies provide that if you present satisfactory evidence of insurability, you will be granted a "fresh start." The premium rate will be the same as that charged to a new policyholder. *Therefore, if you are in good health, you should not merely renew your existing term contract, but instead, present evidence of insurability and qualify for the lower rate applicable to new contracts.* This is also sometimes referred to as "reentry" term insurance.

Convertible Term Insurance

As you grow older, the annual premium rate for renewal of a term policy increases until it becomes prohibitive. Now the fact that you have not selected a longer term or some form of permanent life insurance protection works to your detriment, since you cannot average in the lower premium rates that applied to your younger years. Instead, the rate will be based on the current year for annual renewable term and an average of the current and future years for longer period term.

The guaranteed renewable feature for most term policies terminates at age 65 or 70. However, there are some term policies that are guaranteed renewable to age 100. The problem is that at more advanced ages the annual premium rate for term insurance increases dramatically. Table 6.1 gives examples of the yearly premium rate for a minimum of $100,000 of annual renewable term to age 100 every fifth year beginning at age 55. A look at this table makes readily apparent the fact that the right to continue annual renewable term insurance much beyond age 70 is of questionable value because of the enormous premium each year.

There are instances, however, when individuals have a need for cash at death no matter what their age, and life insurance is an ideal vehicle for providing that cash. For example, wealthy persons whose assets are tied up in nonliquid investments (such as real estate and closely held businesses) will need to leave a source of cash at death—at whatever age that occurs—so that their beneficiaries can meet the administrative costs and death taxes associated with the settlement of their estates.

Convertible term insurance may be the answer. That is, a term insurance policy which gives you the privilege of converting to a permanent life insurance policy, up to a stated age such as 65, without presenting evidence of insurability. For example, the same company that sells the term-to-age-100 policy mentioned above will also permit its term contract to be converted to a whole life policy (permanent insurance with premiums payable for the whole of life) at age 55 with an annual premium of $35 per $1000, age 60 for $46 per $1000, and age 65 for $59 per $1000.

TABLE 6.1 RENEWABLE TERM INSURANCE PREMIUMS

AGE	ANNUAL PREMIUM PER $1,000 OF PROTECTION	ANNUAL PREMIUM FOR $100,000 OF PROTECTION
55	$ 12	$ 1,200
60	18	1,800
65	28	2,800
70	50	5,000
75	81	8,100
80	142	14,200
85	233	23,300
90	369	36,900
95	568	56,800
99	772	77,200

These rates would thereafter be guaranteed for as long as you lived and the whole life policy would generate substantial cash values available during your lifetime, reducing the net cost. (Whole life insurance will be discussed in more detail later in this chapter.) *Thus, the right to convert term insurance to whole life insurance is an important feature which should be included in most term policies.*

In addition to an "attained age" conversion (i.e., converting to a permanent policy with the premium based on your age at the time of the conversion), many term policies permit you to convert to a permanent contract with a premium based on your age at the time the *original* term policy was acquired, a so-called "original-age" conversion. This will result in a lower annual premium for the permanent policy. However, to exercise an original age conversion you must pay an additional charge equal to the difference between premiums paid on the term insurance and the premiums that would have been paid if the permanent insurance had been purchased originally. Interest will be charged on the yearly differences in the two premium rates.

The additional charge associated with an original-age conversion makes it expensive initially; therefore this privilege is rarely used except where the conversion is being made only a short time after the purchase of the original term policy. Another reason for the original-age conversion's lack of popularity is that the payment of the interest charge is not deductible for income-tax purposes since it is not associated with an existing indebtedness.

Deposit Term Insurance

Deposit term insurance may be described as a form of level term insurance which, for an additional first year premium (the deposit), provides a living benefit that is available at the end of the initial term period. Typically, if the policy is terminated for any reason other than your death during the initial term period, all or a portion of the "deposit" is forfeited. If the policy is maintained at least until the end of the initial term period (e.g., 10 years), then you will receive an amount equal to the deposit plus interest at a rate which is generally higher than that paid on the cash value portion of a typical permanent life insurance contract.

At the end of the initial term period, the typical deposit term policy automatically converts into a permanent life insurance contract such as whole life. However, by notifying the insurance company prior to the end of the initial term you may avoid the automatic conversion to permanent insurance and instead elect to continue the term insurance coverage.

Deposit term insurance is labeled a good buy by its proponents because the insurance company will be able to pass on substantial administrative cost savings to the policyholders. This results from the fact that very few deposit term policyholders allow their policies to lapse prior to the end of the initial term, since doing so results in a forfeiture of all or most of the additional first year premium (deposit). However, this cost savings is somewhat offset by the fact that the first year sales commission typically paid by the insurance company on deposit term insurance is higher than the sales commissions paid on term insurance without the deposit feature. The higher commissions on deposit term are made possible as a result of the additional first year premium.

The cash benefit equal to the first year additional premium plus the amount which has been credited to it over the initial term period is received by the insured free of income tax. This tax benefit is based on the treatment of the cash benefit as a return of an overcharge for the insurance protection rather than as taxable interest during the initial 10 year period. Thus, the income tax treatment is the same as that accorded to a dividend on a participating life insurance contract. (Participating and nonparticipating life insurance contracts are discussed later in this chapter.)

Although the interest earned on the first year additional premium deposit taken by itself may be at a relatively high rate, such as 10%, this is frequently offset by the fact that the *annual* premium for the term insurance coverage is often higher than it is for a level term policy without the deposit feature. If the extra amount of *annual* term premium is added to the first year additional premium deposit, the rate of return applied to the total may be substantially reduced.

For example, one study compared the deposit term policy of 10 insurance companies to the same companies' level term policies without the deposit feature. The comparisons were for a male age 25 and a male age 45, using a $100,000 policy. The results indicated that if the male age 25 purchased a level term policy without the deposit feature he would need to earn only a 1.24% rate of return on the difference between the lower premium cost without the deposit feature and the higher total premium cost with the deposit feature to be better off without the deposit feature. The same result occurred at age 45 if earnings on the difference in premium were at least 0.44% (less than one-half of one percent).

From the above study it is clear that deposit term is no panacea when it comes to life insurance protection. *Where term insurance is your objective, even where you are sure that the policy will stay in force for the entire initial term, a cost comparison should be made between level term policies with and without the deposit feature.*

PERMANENT LIFE INSURANCE

Unlike term insurance, which provides a death benefit only if death occurs within a specified time, permanent insurance provides a death benefit no matter when death occurs; and it does so in return for the payment of a level premium either throughout your lifetime (whole life or straight life) or over a limited period, such as 10 or 20 years, or until you reach a specified age, such as 65 (limited payment life insurance).

Living Benefits

The other significant distinction between term insurance and permanent insurance is that permanent insurance contains a lifetime benefit (cash value). This cash value stems from the fact that in the early years of a permanent life insurance contract, the annual premium is greater than the annual cost of insurance protection.

In arriving at its level premium charge, the insurance company anticipates that it will have these excess funds to invest on its own behalf. A portion of this fund is used to make up the deficiency of the level premium in later years when the annual cost of insurance protection actually exceeds the level premium. The balance of this fund is held by the insurance company for the benefit of the policyholder in the form of a cash value or savings portion of the policy.

The cash value of the policy increases each year in accordance with a guaranteed schedule contained in the contract. (A sample schedule is shown in Fig. 6.1) The guaranteed annual increase in cash value differs substantially with the policies of various life insurance companies. With some exceptions, however, most policies have relatively small annual increases in cash value during the first year or two of the policy. This is to protect the insurance company against the substantial loss it could incur if the policy is surrendered for its cash value in the first few years after its purchase. This loss would re-

Plan and Additional Benefits	Amount	Premium	Years Payable
Whole Life (Premiums payable to age 90)	$10,000	$229.50	55
Waiver of Premium (To age 65)		4.30	30
Accidental Death (To age 70)	10,000	7.80	35

A premium is payable on the policy date and every 12 policy months thereafter. The first premium is $241.60.

TABLE OF GUARANTEED VALUES

End of Policy Year	Cash or Loan Value	Paid-up Insurance	Extended Term Insurance Years	Days
1	14	30	0	152
2	174	450	4	182
3	338	860	8	65
4	506	1250	10	344
5	676	1640	12	360
6	879	2070	14	335
7	1084	2500	16	147
8	1293	2910	17	207
9	1504	3300	18	177
10	1719	3690	19	78
11	1908	4000	19	209
12	2099	4300	19	306
13	2294	4590	20	8
14	2490	4870	20	47
15	2690	5140	20	65
16	2891	5410	20	66
17	3095	5660	20	52
18	3301	5910	20	27
19	3508	6150	19	358
20	3718	6390	19	317
AGE 60	4620	7200	18	111
AGE 65	5504	7860	16	147

Paid-up additions and dividend accumulations increase the cash values; indebtedness decreases them.

Direct Beneficiary	Helen M. Benson, wife of the insured
Owner	Thomas A. Benson, the insured

Insured	Thomas A. Benson	**Age and Sex**	35 Male
Policy Date	May 1, 1980	**Policy Number**	000/00
Date of Issue	May 1, 1980		

FIG. 6.1 SAMPLE SPECIFICATIONS PAGE FROM A LIFE INSURANCE CONTRACT

sult from the high fixed costs of issuing a new policy, such as payments for medical examinations and agents' commissions which are typically 55% of the first year's premium.

The longer the policy stays in force, the greater will be the annual increases in cash value. Eventually, the guaranteed cash value will be equal in amount to the face of the policy (i.e., the amount payable on account of death) and at that time the entire cash value will be payable despite the fact that you are still living. In most permanent contracts this occurs at the insured's age 100. In effect, a permanent life insurance contract is really an "endowment at age 100" contract. An endowment contract is one which pays the policyowner the face amount of the contract after a stipulated number of years (e.g., 20 years) or when the insured reaches a specified age (e.g., age 65) or in the event of the prior death of the insured.

Nonforfeiture Options

Most insureds either die or cancel their permanent insurance policies long before they reach age 100. If you cancel a permanent life insurance contract, the cash value of the policy accumulated to that date belongs to you. You may receive this amount in cash or elect to have it applied under one of the other so-called nonforfeiture options. When you elect to receive cash, all life insurance protection ceases.

In some cases the policy is being canceled not because you no longer have a need for insurance protection, but because you can no longer afford to pay the premiums. Where there is still a need for insurance protection, you may elect either "reduced paid-up" life insurance or "extended term" life insurance in lieu of receiving cash. If "reduced paid-up" life insurance is selected, the cash value will be applied as a single premium to purchase as much permanent life insurance of the same type as the original policy as can be purchased on a paid-up basis at your attained age. For example, as shown by the Guaranteed Values Schedule in Fig. 6.1, for a $10,000 whole life policy issued at age 35 that is terminated after 15 years, a fully paid-up whole life policy with a face amount (death benefit) of $5140 can be acquired. This results in a smaller death benefit but preserves the cash value for later use during lifetime. This option would be appropriate where your need for insurance has diminished but has not been entirely eliminated.

Where you can no longer afford to pay premiums but the need for life insurance protection has not diminished, it may be appropriate to elect the extended term life insurance nonforfeiture option. Here, the cash value is applied as a single premium to purchase an amount of level term insurance equal to the face of the original policy for as long a term as can be purchased at your attained age. For example, referring again to Fig. 6.1, for a $10,000 whole life policy issued at age 35 that is terminated 15 years later, a fully paid-up term policy with a face amount (death benefit) of $10,000 can be acquired for a term of 20 years and 65 days.

The premium rates that are applicable under the nonforfeiture options are lower than they would be for the purchase of a new policy of the same type because there is no expense associated with underwriting this insurance protection and no agents' commissions are paid.

Policy Loan Provision

A typical permanent life insurance contract obligates the insurance company to pay the entire cash value (which will equal the face amount of the policy) when you reach age 100. In addition, the insurance company agrees to give you, upon request, an amount equal to the cash value that has accrued in the policy at any point in time even though you have not yet attained age 100. The receipt of these funds is commonly referred to as a policy loan, but it is actually an advance payment of the cash value which is due at age 100. This is evidenced by the fact that the "loan" need not be repaid until you die or reach age 100. At that time the amount that has been advanced and not repaid will be subtracted from the face amount of the policy which is then payable.

When structuring its premium rates, the insurance company assumes that it will have the cash values to invest on its own behalf until you reach age 100 or die. Therefore, when a portion of the cash value is loaned to you, you must pay interest to the life insurance company to make up the loss of investment income that results from the company's not having these funds to invest itself. The policy loan interest rate is guaranteed in the contract.

At the time of this writing, the policy loan interest rate for most new contracts is 8%. Older policies contain a 5% or 6% interest rate. A growing number of new policies now contain a policy loan interest rate that varies from year to year based on stated criteria. The relatively low interest rate, together with the fact that the policy loan and even the interest due on the policy loan need not be repaid (except from the policy proceeds) make the policy loan provision an attractive one when you have a temporary need for funds but do not want to terminate your life insurance policy. Note that if interest is allowed to accrue on the policy loan and the two together equal the entire cash value of the policy at any time, the policy will be automatically terminated, and the cash value will be retained by the company in repayment of the loan and interest.

Any interest that is paid on a policy loan generally will be deductible for income-tax purposes. The one major exception is where you entered into a systematic plan of borrowing in order to finance the purchase of the policy.

However, there will not be a "systematic plan of borrowing" if you pay at least four of the first seven annual premiums without borrowing. During the first seven years after the purchase of a new policy, if you borrow an amount in one year that is in excess of the annual premium for that year, such excess will be treated as if it were borrowed in the previous year for purposes of applying the "four out of seven" test. However, if the test has been met by the end of the seventh year, then in the eighth year and thereafter you can borrow as much as the policy will permit without jeopardizing the interest deduction for income-tax purposes.

By making the minimum out-of-pocket premium contribution required to qualify for the interest deduction, with the balance of the premium being paid by policy loans, you may be able to acquire life insurance protection through the purchase of permanent insurance with a net after-tax cost that is less than if you purchased a term insurance policy. This is one reason why many life insurance agents recommend so-called "minimum deposit" permanent life insurance plans as alternatives to term insurance.

Automatic Premium Loan Provision

All insurance policies (term and permanent) provide for a limited time period during which a policy will remain in force even though the premium is overdue. This so-called grace period is usually 31 days. As long as the premium is paid prior to the expiration of the grace period the policy will not be canceled. If the grace period expires without payment of the premium, the policy will be canceled. If it is a permanent policy having a cash value, one of the nonforfeiture options previously described will become applicable.

To prevent a permanent policy from being canceled when the premium has not been paid within the grace period, you may elect the "A.P.L.," the "automatic premium loan provision." Under this provision if a premium has not been paid by the expiration of the grace period the insurance company will pay the premium out of the policy loan value. This loan is then treated in the same manner as any other policy loan. *Since the election of the automatic premium loan provision can prevent an unintentional lapse of the policy and is available at no additional cost, it should be elected whenever available.* If the automatic premium loan provision is not elected and the grace period on a permanent policy passes, the coverage will be canceled; but the policy can be reinstated if certain conditions are met. Reinstatement must take place within a specified number of years; e.g., three years from the date of cancellation. Furthermore, new evidence of insurability must be presented, and premiums that have not been paid since the cancellation must be paid, together with interest from their due dates.

Why would you choose to pay back premiums plus interest to reinstate an old policy for which you would have to present evidence of insurability when you could simply purchase a new policy? One reason is to avoid the high first-year costs associated with putting a new life insurance policy into force which generally results in only a modest amount of cash value and dividends for the first one or two years. Second, older life insurance policies are likely to have a lower policy loan interest rate. Third, a new policy would require payment of a higher annual premium based on your attained age.

Incontestable and Suicide Clauses

Another reason for reinstating a lapsed life insurance policy rather than purchasing a new one has to do with the operation of the incontestable and suicide clauses.

The incontestable clause provides that after a life insurance contract has been in force for a stated period of time, usually two years (one year in some contracts), the insurance company agrees not to deny a claim because of any error, concealment, or misstatement, even if willfully made. Thus, once the contestable period has expired the insurance company will not challenge a claim on the above grounds. This clause is particularly important to a beneficiary after your death, when it might be difficult to prove that a policy was not acquired through some form of deception.

The suicide clause provides that if you commit suicide within a certain period of time after the purchase of the insurance, generally two years (some policies contain a one-year suicide clause), the insurance company will have to pay the beneficiary only an amount equal to the premiums paid, sometimes with interest. Once the policy has been in effect for the stated time period, the insurer must pay the full fact amount even if death is a result of suicide.

It is to prevent reactivating the contestable period and the suicide period that reinstatement of an old policy may be preferable to purchasing a new one. These two provisions will be found in term as well as permanent life insurance policies.

Participating versus Nonparticipating Life Insurance

Life insurance, either term or permanent, may be "participating" or "nonparticipating." Participating policies refund a portion of the gross premium to the policyholder. These refunds are referred to as "policy dividends" and are paid after the insurer's actual costs for the year have been determined. Premiums on participating policies are set at a higher rate than would normally be required in order to provide funds which might be needed by the insurer in the event of an unexpected emergency. At the end of each year, an amount is returned to you in the form of a policy dividend which is determined by the insurance company's death claims, operating expenses, and investment income.

The amount of each policy dividend is not guranteed in advance by the insurer; instead, the amount you receive will be determined by the actual experience of the insurance company. When determining the true cost of participating life insurance, policy dividends must be taken into account. Illustrations provided by the insurance company indicate what the insurer believes the dividends will be for each year in the future. However, this is only an estimate and not a guarantee of the amount of money the insurer will return to you as an overcharge, i.e., a dividend each year.

Most insurance companies, particularly the larger ones, tend to be conservative in their estimate of future policy dividends. As a result, actual dividends are often higher than those that are estimated. *To determine the reliability of a particular insurance company's dividend estimates, request that the company provide you with a comparison of the dividends that were estimated over the previous five or 10 years and the actual dividends that were paid during the same period. If actual dividends have equaled or exceeded the estimated dividends in the past, that is some indication that future estimates will be trustworthy.*

Policy Dividend Options

You have several options when it comes to choosing what to do with policy dividends. You can request that policy dividends be paid in cash or applied to reduce future premiums due on the policy. Alternatively, you may elect to have policy dividends held by the insurance company at interest. In this case, the insurance company acts much like a bank or savings and loan, paying accumulated dividends to the policyowner upon demand. Interest earned on dividend accumulations is taxable as income to you in the year earned even if not withdrawn in that year. The interest rate paid on dividend accumulations is comparable to that offered on savings accounts.

The two remaining dividend options involve the use of policy dividends to purchase more life insurance. Under one, the dividend is used as a single premium to purchase an additional amount of paid-up life insurance of the same type as the policy that pays the dividend. The single premium is based on your attained age but is lower than it would be if a new policy were purchased because there is no charge for underwriting expenses or commissions.

For example, if your policy is a whole life contract and the "paid-up additions" dividend option is elected, the annual dividend will be applied to purchase more paid-up whole life insurance based on the single premium cost for such insurance at your attained age.

The final dividend option available in most policies is the application of the dividend to purchase one-year term insurance with the premium based on your attained age. Here, too, the premium will be lower than it would be for a new policy because there is no charge for underwriting expenses or commissions.

Some insurance companies put a limit on how much one-year term insurance you can purchase through application of policy dividends. For example, the maximum amount of one-year term insurance may not exceed the policy's total cash value at the end of the preceding year. In this case, if the entire dividend cannot be used to purchase one-year term insurance, one of the other options must be selected for the balance.

If a life insurance policy is nonparticipating, then regardless of the actual cost to the insurer of providing insurance protection based on its experience, no portion of your premium is refunded in the form of policy dividends. To reflect this fact, the premium for a nonparticipating or "nonpar" policy will generally be less than the gross premium for a participating or "par" policy of the same type and amount. Of course, when determining which is a better buy for you, policy dividends paid on the par contract must be taken into account. Generally, most par policies pay dividends that increase each year with policy duration.

As long as investment income of insurance companies continues to increase as a result of inflation, and life expectancies continue to increase, reducing mortality costs, it is likely that future policy dividends on contracts purchased today will increase each year. Thus, *in determining which is a better buy, par or nonpar insurance, it is necessary to estimate how long the insurance is likely to stay in force. The average annual cost for the par policy usually decreases each additional year it stays in force, while the average annual cost for the nonpar policy remains constant. Hence, good health plus a financial situation that is not likely to require an involuntary cancellation of the policy are factors that favor the purchase of par over nonpar life insurance.*

Mutual and Stock Life Insurance Companies

In general, mutual life insurance companies sell only participating life insurance policies while stock life insurance companies sell nonparticipating policies and, in many cases, participating policies as well. The reason a mutual life insurance company issues only participating policies results from its ownership structure. Ownership is not based on shares of stock; there are no stockholders in a mutual life insurance company. Technically, a mutual life insurance company is owned by the persons who have policies with the company. Thus, when a mutual life insurance company takes in more money during a year than it needs for expenses and claims, it returns some of this excess money to the policyowners (the owners of the company) in the form of policy dividends because the policy owners have been charged more than was necessary to provide insurance protection.

A stock life insurance company is owned by stockholders and is managed for the benefit of its stockholders, rather than its policyholders, just as most other publicly-owned corporations are run for the benefit of their stockholders, rather than their customers. Thus, when a stock life insurance company issues nonparticipating policies and takes in more money during the year than it needs to cover its expenses and claims associated with those policies, a portion of its excess monies are paid to the stockholders in the form of dividends on their stock.

To better compete with mutual life insurance companies, many stock companies also issue a separate line of participating policies. These policies are accounted for separately from the nonpar contracts. A portion of the money received from these par policies that exceeds expenses and claims allocated to them is returned to the policyholders as reimbursement for an overcharge just as with the par policies issued by a mutual company.

OPTIONAL ADDITIONAL BENEFITS

Several optional benefits (often called "riders") can be added to an individual life insurance policy regardless of whether it is a term or permanent contract. Since these benefits are not built into the basic policy, there is an additional charge if they are selected.

Accidental Death Benefit

For an additional annual premium of about $1 per $1000 of coverage regardless of age you may purchase an accidental death benefit as a rider to your individual life insurance policy. In most cases the accidental death benefit is equal to the face amount of the underlying policy. This is known under the popular term of "double indemnity" since the beneficiary of—for example—a $100,000 policy would receive $200,000 if death occurred in the specified manner. In some cases twice the face amount of the underlying policy ("triple indemnity") is payable under the accidental death benefit rider.

To collect under accidental death benefit coverage, death must be the direct result of bodily injuries caused by "accidental means." Most policies also read that death must occur within 90 or 120 days of the accident. The cost of accidental death benefit protection is relatively low because the chances of dying as the result of an accident are remote.

Accidental death does not result in greater financial need for your dependents than would death caused by sickness. In fact, the absence of a prolonged illness may reduce the financial burden associated with death. Why then should anyone purchase accidental death insurance? If you can afford to purchase as much regular life insurance protection as you need, then you probably should not bother with accidental death benefit insurance. However, many individuals, particularly at younger ages, cannot afford the amount of life insurance required to make their families financially secure in the event of their early death. Although death by accident is statistically infrequent overall, it is more often the cause of death for people from 25 to 45 years old than for people over 45. More persons in that age range engage in potentially dangerous activities, such as scuba diving, motorcycling, mountain climbing, sky diving, hang gliding, etc. Therefore, to be sure that your family is fully protected in the event of an early death, accidental death benefit protection may be prudent at these ages.

Waiver-of-Premium Benefit

If the "waiver-of-premium" provision is in force and a disability occurs that meets the definition contained in the provision, your obligation to pay future premiums for the underlying life insurance policy will cease. Nevertheless, the cash values, dividends, and other benefits of the policy will continue to grow just as if you continued to pay premiums. Thus, the waiver-of-premium benefit is really disability income insurance with the disability benefit equal to the life insurance premium that is waived in the event of disability. Some life insurance contracts include the cost of the waiver-of-premium benefit in the basic policy premium, but most provide it as an additional optional benefit for an extra premium.

The typical definition of disability found in a waiver-of-premium provision requires that you be totally disabled as a result of accident or illness and unable to engage in any business or occupation, or perform any work for compensation or profit. The disability must continue for a minimum period, usually six months. In addition, the disability must occur before a stated age, typically 60 or 65. A six-month period of total and continuous disability is generally required before the waiver-of-premium provision takes effect. But once the six months have elapsed, premiums that you paid during the six-month waiting period will be returned to you and the policy will continue as if you were still paying premiums.

The waiver-of-premium rider may be added to a permanent policy or a term policy. Where a term policy is involved, the effect of a disability on the subsequent right to convert to a permanent policy differs from company to company. *Some policies will not allow conversion to a permanent policy once a total disability has occurred, but others will. After a disability has occurred, it is obviously advantageous to be able to convert to a permanent contract that will build cash values with all future premiums waived. This is a substantial advantage and should be considered whenever comparing term policies.*

An alternative to the purchase of a waiver-of-premium benefit is the purchase of additional disability insurance that will pay you income if you are disabled as defined in the disability policy. This would be separate and apart from any life insurance with the benefits sufficient to cover your life insurance premiums. The additional premium for the waiver-of-premium rider varies considerably from company to company and should be compared with the premium for separate disability income insurance to determine which is the better buy from a cost standpoint. In addition, the definition of "total disability" in disability income insurance is often more liberal than that found in the waiver-of-premium rider.

For example, a typical disability income insurance policy will pay disability income benefits for the first two years (or even longer) following a disability if you are unable to perform your *present job*. It is only thereafter that you will have to demonstrate that you are unable to perform in *any* occupation for which you are reasonably fit by virtue of education, training, or experience in order to continue to receive benefits. Thus, disability benefits may be payable under a disability income policy when they would not be payable under a waiver-of-premium rider.

Guaranteed Insurability Option

Would you be willing to pay a small additional premium now to guarantee your insurability for a specified time in the future? If so, you will want to add the guaranteed insurability (purchase) option rider to the policy you are purchasing. This rider permits you to purchase specified amounts of additional permanent or term insurance without evidence of insurability. The new insurance is issued at standard rates on the basis of your attained age when the option is exercised.

While provisions of the guaranteed insurability rider vary from company to company, the typical rider permits you to purchase additional insurance three years after the date of the original purchase and every three years thereafter until age 40. Some riders provide for additional purchase dates at the time of your marriage or the birth or adoption of a child. The amount of insurance that can be purchased on each option date generally cannot exceed the face amount of the original policy or some specified dollar amount, whichever is less.

If you become disabled and the waiver-of-premium provision is opera-tive under the original policy, some policies provide that premiums on any new insurance purchased under the guaranteed insurability option will also be waived from the beginning. When comparing policies, this is an im-portant feature to consider.

Even without the guaranteed insurability option, most persons will be able to acquire additional amounts of life insurance in the future de-spite impaired health. However, the premium for such insurance may be considerably higher than the standard rate. *Thus, if you have a family history of serious illness prior to age 40, and it is likely that you will need more life insurance in the future, the guaranteed insurability option rider is a good buy.*

Payment of Premiums

Insurance companies calculate premium rates on the basis of the assump-tion that you will pay each year's premium at the beginning of the policy year so that they will have those premium dollars to invest for the entire year. When premiums are paid semiannually, quarterly, or monthly instead of annually at the beginning of each policy year, the insurer levies an ad-ditional charge to make up for the loss of the use of those premium dollars for the entire year. In addition, there is a charge for the extra administra-tion expense associated with the collection of multiple premium payments during any one year.

When the insured authorizes his or her bank to pay the insurance com-pany monthly with funds from the insured's account, the savings in expense to the insurance company reduce the additional charge to approximately what it would be if premiums were paid semiannually. Table 6.2 illustrates

TABLE 6.2 INSURANCE PREMIUM PAYMENT OPTIONS

		TOTAL ANNUAL COST			
Life Insurance Company	Annual Premium Payment	Semi-annual Premium Payments	Quarterly Premium Payments	Monthly Premium Payments	Automatic Monthly Bank Plan
Company A	$100.00	$101.60	$102.40	$104.40	$102.00
Company B	$100.00	$102.00	$104.00	$106.80	$103.00
Company C	$100.00	$103.00	$106.00	$114.00	$105.00

what the *total* yearly premium cost would be for each $100 of *annual* premium under the various premium payment options quoted by three different life insurance companies.

From this table it can readily be seen that companies differ widely with regard to the charge made for the privilege of paying each annual premium in periodic installments. Furthermore, the charge can be substantial, particularly where premiums are paid monthly. Of course, where premiums are paid in installments rather than annually at the beginning of each year, you retain possession of a portion of your premium dollars for a part of the year and can invest that portion yourself during that time. The annual return you would have to earn on the amounts that remain in your possession during the year to make up for the additional charge levied by companies A, B, and C if premiums are paid monthly would be 8%, 13% and 25.5%, respectively.

The amount you would have to earn to offset the insurance company's charge drops substantially if the automatic monthly bank plan is selected. Where the automatic bank plan is not selected, the length of time during which you retain a portion of the year's premium to invest can be increased by delaying the periodic payment until near the end of the 31-day grace period. This can be done at no additional cost since most insurance companies do not charge interest for premiums that are paid during the grace period.

ADJUSTABLE LIFE INSURANCE

In recognition of the fact that the amount of insurance a person needs changes during his or her lifetime and the type of insurance (term or permanent) that is best for an individual changes from time to time, the Minnesota Mutual Life Insurance Company created adjustable life insurance in 1971. Since then, Bankers Life of Iowa, The College Life Insurance Company of America, and a few others have begun to offer adjustable life, and other companies are sure to follow.

An adjustable life policy allows you to purchase all term insurance, all permanent insurance, or some combination of the two. The proportion of term insurance to permanent insurance may be adjusted periodically in accordance with your needs. Furthermore, the amount of insurance coverage can be decreased without canceling the entire policy. (With a conventional life insurance policy a partial termination is not permitted. In order to decrease the amount of coverage under a conventional policy, the policy must first be split into two smaller ones and then one of these smaller contracts canceled.)

Adjustable life also acts as an inflation hedge by allowing you to increase the amount of insurance protection without evidence of insurability. The insurance acquired may be term insurance, permanent insurance, or a combination of the two. There is no additional premium charge for the "cost-of-living" feature; however, there is a charge for any new insurance actually acquired. Few conventional policies have this cost-of-living feature and those that do generally allow for the purchase of additional permanent insurance but not term insurance.

Typically, the cost-of-living option must be exercised every three years or the right to use it will be forfeited. Generally, any one cost-of-living increase cannot exceed the percentage of existing face amount equal to the total Consumer Price Index (CPI) change over the last three years, or 20% of the existing face amount of the policy, whichever is less. There is also an absolute dollar limit, which is relatively low, for any one increase. However, despite its policy limitations, Bankers Life recently permitted a 31.9% increase—since that was the CPI change over a three-year period—to a $30,000 maximum, rather than $20,000 as contained in the policy.

In addition to cost-of-living increases, a guaranteed insurability rider can be added to an adjustable life contract just as with a conventional life insurance policy. The operation of the guaranteed insurability rider for adjustable life is similar to that previously discussed for conventional policies; however, the additional premium appears to be slightly higher under the adjustable life contract.

Designing the Adjustable Life Coverage

Once you have determined how much life insurance protection you need and how many dollars you have available for premium payments, this information is fed into the insurance company's computer. The computer will tell you whether the amount of premium dollars is sufficient to purchase all the protection needed, using the lowest premium plan available (e.g., five-year term with Minnesota Mutual and 10-year term with Bankers Life of Iowa).

If the premium is not sufficient, the insurance protection will be decreased, and only the lowest premium policy would be purchased.

If the amount of premium dollars available is greater than the cost of the desired protection using the lowest premium policy, the computer will automatically adjust the coverage to some combination of term insurance and permanent insurance that will provide the insurance protection desired for the premium dollars that are available. Using this approach, if the premium dollars available are at least sufficient to purchase the needed amount of insurance coverage using the lowest premium policy, the insured will be fully protected.

If there are additional premium dollars available, then some or all of that protection may be in the form of permanent insurance. This is the typical method used to illustrate how the adjustable life policy coverage is designed. Of course, you are free to purchase some other combination of term and permanent insurance or all term or all permanent insurance by changing the amount of the premium. In the future, as the number of premium dollars available and the amount of insurance protection vary up or down, the proportion of term insurance to permanent insurance will be adjusted to accommodate the changes.

Drawbacks to Adjustable Life Insurance

Although there is a great variety in the types of insurance coverage that can be acquired under an adjustable life policy, the selection does not run the full gamut. For example, annual renewable term insurance, which is exceedingly popular in an inflationary economy because of its relatively low cost, is not available under the adjustable life contracts. Also, one of the justifications for purchasing traditional permanent insurance is that it provides a method of forced savings that will be available for dire emergencies. That is, the cash value will continue to increase each year with the payment of the level premium. With adjustable life the compulsion to save is diminished substantially by the fact that if there is any squeeze at all on your current cash flow, the premium can be reduced with the amount of insurance coverage remaining level by adjusting the proportion of term to permanent insurance in favor of the term insurance, thereby reducing the amount of future savings.

When Adjustable Life Insurance Is Most Attractive

Nevertheless, adjustable life's unique features make it worthy of consideration as an alternative to either the traditional term or permanent policy.
It would seem to be particularly attractive for the relatively young insured
whose present financial picture and need for insurance point to term
insurance, but who is likely to have a continuing need for insurance protection in later years. The premium for yearly renewable term insurance becomes prohibitive at the older ages. Likewise, conversion of term insurance
to permanent coverage at attained age results in a relatively high annual
outlay when conversion takes place at the older ages.

　　With a conventional term policy it is possible to convert as of issue
age to get a lower annual premium for permanent insurance, but to do
so requires the payment of a substantial lump sum to make up the difference between what the permanent premiums would have been and what
the term premiums actually were, plus interest on that difference. Under
adjustable life, when the insured reaches the age when conversion to
permanent coverage seems desirable, the new annual premium will be somewhere between an attained age and an original age conversion to permanent
coverage. The exact amount of premium will depend upon how much
policy improvement has taken place through the application of policy
dividends. Thereafter the policy will be treated as permanent insurance, with
the increased premium generating future cash values. The policy is not
credited with cash values that would have been earned if the insurance were
permanent from the beginning, and therefore, unlike an original age conversion of a traditional policy, no back premiums or other retroactive adjustments are required. Thus, permanent protection can be provided when
needed at a reasonable price.

INFLATION-FIGHTING POLICIES

Under the terms of a life insurance policy, the insurance company promises
to pay dollars upon the happening of an event at some time in the future.
The effect of double-digit inflation on the value of this promise is easily
demonstrated. For example, with a 10% annual inflation rate, if death occurs
20 years from now, a promise made today to pay $100,000 will actually

result in the payment of only $14,860 of buying power (although the gross sum paid will still be $100,000). Put another way, to be assured that your family will receive $100,000 of buying power at today's prices, should you die 20 years from now, and assuming inflation continues at an annual 10% rate, you will have to purchase $611,000 of life insurance.

On the positive side, inflation also means that in the future, level premiums will be paid with less expensive dollars. For example, assume the gross annual premium for a $100,000 whole life policy is $2500. If death occurs in 20 years, with a 10% annual inflation rate the payment of total gross premiums of $50,000 will actually result in the payment of only $21,280 of buying power. Of course, the receipt of policy dividends would reduce both the gross premium cost and the cost in terms of buying power. Furthermore, the premium charge for new life insurance at a given age is likely to decrease in the future as a result of insurance company investment gains. Reacting to these facts, many life insurance companies are developing specially designed products to put the insured in a more favorable position to combat future inflation.

Adjustable-Premium Feature

For example, one life insurance company has developed a product which is designed to capture the best characteristics of both a nonparticipating policy and a participating policy. Under this contract, the initial premium is guaranteed for the first two policy years. Thereafter, there is a guaranteed maximum to which the premium may increase, but if actual experience of the company is better than that upon which the guaranteed maximum is based, the premium will be reduced, perhaps even below the initial premium for the first two years. Although this approach is similar to a par policy, it differs in that the initial premium rate and the guaranteed maximum premium will generally be less than the gross premium charged under a par contract. Of course, the dividends paid under the par contract must be taken into account in making a true cost comparison.

Also, the savings that result from good experience under this contract are automatically applied to reduce further premiums. Under the typical par policy these savings, paid in the form of dividends, can be used in a variety of ways, including the purchase of additional insurance as previously explained. This company makes the adjustable premium feature available on either whole life insurance or one-year renewable term insurance. The minimum face amounts are $25,000 and $100,000 respectively.

Automatically Increasing Whole Life Insurance

Some life insurance companies have responded to the effects of inflation by offering a whole life policy with a face amount that automatically increases at a given rate each year. One example is an increasing whole life policy that grows at a compound rate of 3.5% annually for the 20-year period following issue of the policy, at which time the face amount will be double the original face amount and remain level thereafter. During the first 20 years of this contract the premium is increased every 5 years, with each increase being 25% of the original premium. Thus, the last increase in premium occurs in the sixteenth year with the premium remaining level thereafter. To the extent that the inflation rate exceeds 3.5% compounded annually, this policy will provide only a partial offset to inflation. However, it is a step in the right direction.

If a given face amount of permanent life insurance protection is needed but the premium would be too high for your present financial situation, increasing whole life can be combined with a decreasing term rider. This provides what is effectively permanent protection equal to the needed face amount but with a much lower annual premium outlay. For example, if $100,000 of permanent protection is needed, a $50,000 increasing whole life policy combined with a $50,000 decreasing term rider that decreases at exactly the same rate as the whole life policy increases will provide a level death benefit of $100,000 permanently with the premium level from the sixteenth year and after.

Combination of Term and Whole Life insurance

There are other ways to provide permanent protection equal to a given face amount at a level premium that is less than it would be for a regular permanent policy. One is to combine a smaller permanent policy with a term policy and use policy dividends to provide insurance protection when the term insurance expires. For example, one company markets a policy that is one-half term to age 65 and one-half whole life. The premium is a level amount and is payable for life. To maintain the death benefit at a level amount beyond age 65 (when the term insurance has expired), the policy uses a unique dividend option. Prior to age 65 dividends are used to purchase paid-up additional amounts of permanent insurance, but if death occurs prior to age 65, only the cash value of the paid-up additions will be payable; you forfeit your right to the pure insurance portion of the paid-up additions. After age 65, the full fact amount of the paid-up additions is payable as a death benefit. By this approach, a greater death benefit is provided by the dividends after age 65 than would otherwise be possible.

On the basis of the insurance company's present dividend projections, the face amount of the paid-up additions payable after age 65 will at least equal the death benefit up to age 65 that was provided by the term insurance portion of the policy.

Where the need for life insurance protection is likely to be permanent throughout your lifetime, these combination term and permanent contracts offer a happy medium between the high initial cost of all permanent protection and the very high premium cost of annual renewable term insurance at the older ages.

Universal Life Insurance

In a direct effort to provide a better rate of return than on the cash values of traditional permanent life insurance, a growing number of insurance companies are now offering a policy popularly called "universal life."

The cash values of universal life insurance generally are invested in a variety of high-yield (currently in excess of 10%) government securities. A recently issued Internal Revenue Service Private Letter Ruling provides that universal life will be accorded the same tax treatment as a traditional permanent life policy. This means that the tax on earnings during lifetime will be deferred until the policy is surrendered. Furthermore, if the policy is retained until the death of the insured, the proceeds will be received by the beneficiary entirely tax free.

Universal Life also contains many flexible features not found in traditional permanent life insurance. Examples include the following:

· After payment of the first premium, subsequent premiums may be paid at any time and in any amount. If the payments are insufficient to meet the cost of the year's insurance protection, the balance is charged against the cash value.

- The amount of death protection can be adjusted up or down in the same policy; however, increases will require new evidence of insurability.

- Partial surrenders, releasing a portion of the cash value, can be made without surrendering the entire policy.

Inflation has driven many purchasers away from traditional permanent life insurance with its relatively low rates of return on cash values. Instead, purchasers are buying low-cost term insurance and putting the balance of what they would have paid for permanent insurance into other investments, such as money market mutual funds. Universal life presents another viable alternative that can meet your investment objectives without sacrificing the permanency of your life insurance protection.

Meeting the Demands for Cash

Case # _____

(Husband's) (Wife's) Estate When (He) (She) Dies (First) (Second)

☞ _____ for Funeral and Administration Expenses

☞ +_____ for Debts and Taxes

☞ +_____ for Federal Estate Taxes

☞ +_____ for State Death Taxes Payable

☞ +_____ for Charitable and Cash Bequests or other Needs

		Sources of Meeting	Future Income
_____ TOTAL CASH REQUIRED		Cash Demands†	Loss‡
‗_____	Source - Item ( )_____		_____
_____ Balance needed			
‗_____	Source - Item ( )_____		_____
_____ Balance needed			
‗_____	Source - Item ( )_____		_____
_____ Balance needed			
‗_____	Source - Item ( )_____		_____
_____ Balance needed			
‗_____	Source - Item ( )_____		_____
_____ Balance needed			
‗_____	Source - Item ( )_____		_____
_____ Balance needed			
‗_____	Source - Item ( )_____		_____
_____ Balance needed			
‗_____	Source - Item ( )_____		_____

Paid in Full
_____

Total Capital	Total Annual
_____ Loss	Loss of Income _____

†Specify each asset used and indicate if it has been loaned to the estate or represents purchase money for assets sold to family members or a trust.

‡Use actual income if known or _____ % interest per year.

©1981 by The American College as part of **Advanced Estate Planning Casebook**

FIG. 6.2 (This form can be used to list the assets that will have to be liquidated in order to meet the demands for cash.)

Assets Available for Survivors

Case # _____

Asset*	Fair Market Value	Income † (%) Annually	Successor in Interest
Item Number			
( )			
( )			
( )			
( )			
( )			
( )			
( )			
( )			
( )			
( )			
( )			
( )			
( )			
( )			
( )			
( )			
Totals			

*Indicate Surviving Spouse's Own Assets with ✓

†Use actual income produced if known or _____% interest per year.

© 1981 by The American College as part of **Advanced Estate Planning Casebook**

FIG. 6.3 (This form can be used to list the remaining assets that will pass to various dependents and the amount of income that can be expected to be produced from those assets.)

Income Needs of Survivors

Case # _____

Income Needs After (Husband's) (Wife's) Estate Settled

(Husband's) (Wife) Dies (First) (Second)

Period of Time (in years)	Annual Need	Annual Income	Annual (Deficit) or Surplus	Total (Deficit) or Surplus for Period

Other Information

FIG. 6.4 (This form can be used to record whether there will be a deficit or surplus of income during various periods in the future.)

7
PERSONAL RETIREMENT PLANS

It doesn't matter if you're rich or poor,
as long as you've got money.

Joe E. Lewis

In Chapter 3, Social Security, we discussed what many persons have called "the world's largest retirement plan." In this chapter we will consider some of the smallest. For the millions of workers in covered employment, Social Security is the foundation of their future financial security. Probably the largest part of their retirement income will come from these federal benefits. In addition, many of those receiving Social Security payments will also receive income from a pension plan provided by their employer. In some cases the employee will have contributed to such a plan and in others it will be a noncontributory plan funded solely by the employer. In either case, pension benefits provide another important source of retirement income.

However, many individuals are not participants in a pension plan. Small employers often do not provide such benefits for their employees. Even where a plan is offered employees may not qualify for benefits when they retire. This is particularly true for persons who change jobs frequently throughout their working careers. They may never be covered by one employer long enough to accumulate adequate benefits or to become fully "vested" in the program. Vesting refers to the ownership interest an employee acquires in the employer's contributions to the pension plan. The rights of a retiring employee, or one who withdraws from the plan for various reasons, depend upon the vesting provisions in the pension agreement. Of course, you are always entitled to the return of your own contributions to your pension plan.

Some of the most severe problems in the area of pensions were corrected by passage of the Employee Retirement Income Security Act (ERISA) in 1974. This legislation established requirements which must be met by all pension plans. Among the requirements were conditions for eligibility, retirement age, and benefit formulas. These requirements should reduce the number of situations in which persons work for many years but end up without any pension benefits, or only inadequate coverage.

Still, millions of persons simply are not covered by any pension plan. In addition to employees who lack pension coverage, there are large numbers of self-employed persons who do not have a plan available. Both of these groups have a unique opportunity, however, to create their own "personal pension plans." We will discuss the two most common types of such plans: Individual Retirement Accounts (IRA) and Keogh, or HR–10, plans. Used properly, these plans can add greatly to your financial security in retirement if you are not covered by a regular pension plan.

INDIVIDUAL RETIREMENT ACCOUNTS (IRA)

Individual Retirement Accounts were authorized as part of the ERISA legislation passed by Congress on September 2, 1974. Since that date many millions of plans have been started by eligible persons of all ages and occupations. Even so, it is estimated that some 36 million persons who could be eligible for an IRA have not taken advantage of this preretirement planning opportunity. If you are one of these persons, you are passing up an excellent opportunity not only to reduce your current Federal income taxes, but also to provide additional security for your future.

IRAs permit individuals who are eligible to subtract a portion of their earnings from taxable income and to contribute these amounts to special IRA accounts offered by banks, savings institutions, insurance companies, and mutual fund organizations. These funds, plus the income earned on their investment, will not be subject to Federal income taxes until benefits are withdrawn from the account, usually after age 59½. An IRA may also be used to postpone taxes on a lump-sum distribution from a company pension or profit-sharing plan.

Who Is Eligible?

You may establish an IRA if you are *not* currently a participant, or eligible to be a participant, in any other retirement plan: These include corporate pension, profit-sharing, stock bonus, or employee stock purchase plans, tax-deferred annuities, or any type of governmental plan, excluding Social Security. In addition, you must be less than 70½ years of age before the close of the tax year.

Finally, if you are married, you *may* be eligible to set up a Spouse Individual Retirement Account (SPIRA) as well as one for yourself. This would be possible where one partner qualifies for an IRA and is a wage earner, while the other spouse has *no* earned income at any time during the tax year. In order to qualify as a married couple, you must be legally married on the last day of the tax year.

Contributions

Even if you do qualify for an IRA there are certain limitations on how much you can contribute each year. You may set aside in an IRA up to $1500 or 15% of your *earned income*, whichever is less. The earned income must be produced from personal services. Such income would include wages, salaries, professional fees, sales commissions, tips, and bonuses. Unearned income such as dividends, interest, or rent cannot be used in determining the amount of your IRA contribution.

For example, if you had wages of $10,000 during the year and were eligible to set up an IRA, you could contribute $1500, or 15% of your earned income. If your earnings were $20,000 you would still be limited to a $1500 contribution. If you had earned income of $8000, you could make a contribution to your IRA of $1200. The 15% limitation is applied to net earned income, an individual's gross earnings less any business deductions which are allowed.

Using the example mentioned above—wages of $10,000 per year—Table 7.1 compares a savings plan ($1500 annually earning 8% compounded

TABLE 7.1 IRA VERSUS A SAVINGS ACCOUNT		
AFTER	SAVINGS ACCOUNT	IRA
10 years	$ 16,314	$ 24,081
20 years	46,724	78,298
30 years	103,406	200,362

daily) with an IRA, assuming that the investor's tax bracket is only 24%. Of course, benefits would be greater for an investor in a higher tax bracket.

If you are eligible to contribute to a SPIRA account, the dollar limit of your total contributions is raised to $1750 but still cannot exceed 15% of your net earned income. Also, an equal amount must be contributed to each account. Separate IRA accounts must be established for each spouse, which means that the maximum contribution to each account would be $875 per year. Neither spouse can be an active participant in a corporate retirement plan, a Keogh arrangement, a tax-deferred annuity, or a government retirement plan at *any* time during the tax year.

Establishing an IRA Account

Creating an IRA account for yourself and/or your spouse is a simple and easy thing to do. Application forms are not complicated and are readily available from a wide variety of financial institutions. Almost all banks, savings and loan associations, mutual savings banks, insurance companies, and mutual funds offer IRA services. Your IRA may be in the form of a savings account, a retirement insurance policy, or shares in a mutual fund. In addition, the federal government issues Individual Retirement Bonds which can be purchased directly from the government in denominations of $50, $100, and $500.

Your may establish an IRA account and claim the tax deduction any time prior to the due date of your tax return. For most persons this will be April 15th. However, since earnings on your account accumulate tax-free, you may want to make your contributions early in the tax year. Any extension of the due date for your return also extends the deadline for establishing and contributing to an IRA.

Withdrawal of IRA Benefits

IRAs provide an incentive for you to build up, over a period of time, assets which will provide you with additional income during your retirement years. In addition to offering tax incentives for contributions, the government penalizes withdrawals from IRAs prior to age 59½. The penalty is in the form of a Premature Distribution Tax of 10% of the amount that is withdrawn. Therefore, you should only contribute funds which you are confident can be left in the account until you are ready to retire, or at least until you reach age 59½. Even then you are not *required* to make withdrawals from the IRA account. If you wish to continue the tax sheltering effect until a later date you are not required to begin receiving benefits until age 70½. The age restrictions apply only to amounts actually removed from an IRA and used as spendable income. The age rules do not apply to transfers between IRA accounts or sponsoring organizations. Such transfers may be made once a year without any tax penalty. The penalty tax is also waived if withdrawal is due to the death of the participant or to their disability.

After you reach age 59½ you may begin to make withdrawals from your IRA account without a *penalty* tax, but the distributions will be included in your regular taxable income. You may withdraw any amount from the account, at any time, and you may do so even if you continue to work. Distributions are not eligible for capital gains tax treatment or the special 10-year averaging rules that apply to lump-sum distributions from qualified employer plans. However, they do qualify for regular income averaging.

Distributions must begin before the end of the tax year in which you reach age 70½. You can receive your entire interest in your IRA, or, if you prefer, one of a number of other payment options. You can receive periodic payments over your life and the life of your spouse, a fixed period not longer than your life expectancy, or a fixed period not longer than the life expectancy of you and your spouse. Your actual life expectancy is determined from tables provided by the Internal Revenue Service (IRS).

If after reaching age 70½ you do *not* withdraw sufficient amounts from your program, you may be liable for a 50% excise tax on the underdistribution. An underdistribution is the difference between the minimum payout required for the tax year and the amount actually paid to you.

As we noted earlier, one of the key advantages of an IRA account is the ability to deduct contributions from your taxable income each year. In addition to lowering your annual tax bill, the earnings from your account will accumulate tax-free until they are withdrawn. Even then, you can expect to pay substantially less in taxes on your withdrawals than you would have during your working years. First, you will likely be in a lower tax bracket after you retire. And, after age 65, you and your spouse will be entitled to double personal tax exemptions.

With all of its desirable features an IRA provides a useful means of accumulating important assets for your future financial security. While there are some disadvantages, such as the 10% penalty tax and possible commissions and fees, you should probably give serious consideration to establishing a plan if you are eligible.

Rollover IRAs

Even if you are not eligible for an IRA account during your working years you may find one useful when you do retire. A Special IRA account may be created by persons who receive a complete distribution of benefits from an employer-sponsored retirement plan. The distribution must be paid as a result of termination of your services, retirement, disability, or elimination of the employer's plan. Only the amount representing employer contributions and investment earnings can be "rolled over" from the employer plan to the IRA account. Your contributions are not eligible. Death benefits which are paid in a qualified lump sum to a surviving spouse can also be placed in a Special IRA. You must make the deposit to a Special IRA within 60 days of receipt of the distribution to take advantage of the tax deferral.

Once you have created an IRA rollover account from a lump-sum distribution it becomes a fixed account in that no further contributions can be made to that specific IRA account. The Special IRA becomes a "holding trust" used to preserve the tax-sheltered status of any present and future employer-paid retirement benefits. If you are eligible to make regular IRA contributions each year, they must be made to a separate IRA account.

KEOGH PLANS

Keogh plans, sometimes referred to as HR–10 plans, provide the same, if not better, retirement planning opportunities for *self-employed* persons as IRAs do for eligible employees. These plans have been used by doctors, dentists, and other unincorporated professionals for a number of years.

In more recent years, however, such plans have come into more frequent use among eligible persons at considerably lower income levels. Increasing concern over future financial security, combined with the bigger bite taken by higher federal taxes, have prompted many more persons to seek refuge for at least part of their income in a Keogh plan.

Even persons who are basically employees, and who are covered by a qualified pension plan, may be able to take advantage of Keogh plan benefits. If you have a second income from "moonlighting"—consulting, director's fees, writing, or other sources—you can start a Keogh plan.

For example, John McFadden, a lawyer, teaches at a college where he is covered by a retirement plan. In addition, John also does some outside legal work for which he was paid $8000 during 1981. Even though he is covered by a qualified retirement plan, John can still put away 15% of his outside income, or $1200, in a Keogh plan. He can deduct this $1200 from his taxable income for 1981, and the income he earns on contributions to his Keogh plan will not be taxed until it is withdrawn from the plan.

Don't feel that the relatively small amounts of income you may earn from any of these outside sources are unimportant to your retirement planning. Even small contributions, made on a regular basis and sheltered from income taxes until paid to you, can add up to large sums over the years. They can provide a real bonus to your retirement income.

The Keogh Plan Calculator shown in Figure 7.1 provides examples based on the maximum contribution for a varying number of years. As you can see, the tax-deferred earnings portion of the account will eventually exceed the amount of your annual contributions. This is a strong incentive to start early and continue to make the largest allowable contribution throughout your working years. The bottom portion of the figure shows how to calculate your net tax savings from Keogh contributions.

If you are completely self-employed, a Keogh plan can provide the second most important source of retirement income, after Social Security. And, even though they are easy to start, getting the most out of a Keogh plan requires careful planning and discipline over the years. No one year's contributions will be very significant in building up your assets. A successful Keogh plan depends on: (1) regular contributions during your working career; (2) reinvestment of earnings during the accumulation period; and (3) the tax-sheltered status of earnings until they are distributed.

Like IRAs, Keogh plans may be created through a broad range of financial institutions. These include banks, thrift institutions, insurance

Here is what a $7500 annual Keogh contribution could add up to (earning 8% in a savings account, compounded daily):

Number of years	Contributions	Tax Deferred interest	Total in account
5	$ 37,500	$ 10,645	$ 48,145
10	$ 75,000	45,365	120,365
15	112,500	116,201	228,701
20	150,000	241,213	391,213
25	187,500	447,490	634,990

KEOGH CALCULATOR TO FIGURE ANNUAL TAX SAVINGS

Yourself	Example	Your Figures
Yourself		
1. Earned income	$50,000	$————
2. Contributions for yourself, (up to 15% of Item 1 or $7500, whichever is less)	$ 7,500	$————
3. Your tax bracket	50%	————%
4. Tax saving on your contribution (Item 3 x 2)	$ 3,750	$————
Employees		
5. Total annual salaries of your eligible employees	$15,000	$————
6. Contribution percentage of compensation (Item 2 divided by Item 1)	15%	————%
7. Amount of contribution for employees (Item 6 x Item 5)	$ 2,250	$————
8. Tax saving on contribution for employees (Item 7 x Item 3)	$ 1,125	$————
9. Net cost of employee contribution (Item 7 minus Item 8)	$ 1,125	$————
Summary		
10. Tax saving on your contribution (Item 4)	$ 3,750	$————
11. Net cost of employee contribution (Item 7 minus Item 8)	$ 1,125	$————
12. Your net tax saving (Item 10 minus Item 11)	$ 2,625	$————

FIG. 7.1 KEOGH PLAN CALCULATOR

companies, and mutual fund organizations. Each of these is anxious to increase its retirement plan business, especially in the form of Keogh plans. Such plans generally involve stable, long-term investments that require only a modest degree of customer servicing. Keogh plan arrangements are widely advertised, particularly at the end of the calendar year and near the Federal income tax filing deadline. You should not have any difficulty in obtaining information from a variety of sources concerning these plans.

Eligibility

You are eligible to create a Keogh retirement plan if you are self-employed either as a sole proprietor or as a partnership. Even if you are an employee, you may make Keogh contributions on the basis of any self-employment income earned in addition to your normal wages. Such income must be earned from personal services and cannot include "unearned income" from such sources as dividends, interest, etc.

You may also be eligible to participate in a Keogh plan, even as an employee, if the owner of a business for which you work establishes such a plan. Employees of the business *must* be included as participants in the plan on the same general basis as any owner-employees. The percentage of net income, not net earnings, contributed on behalf of employees may not be less than that contributed on behalf of the owner-employee. However, the employer has the right to select the period of employment that shall be required for eligibility of the owner-employee and any employees. Such a period of eligibility cannot be longer than 36 months.

Contributions

The limits on Keogh plan contributions are more liberal than those applied to Individual Retirement Accounts. (Incidentally, legislation has been introduced in Congress to equalize these two types of private pension plans.) Self-employed persons are still limited to contributing no more than 15% of their income, but the dollar limit on contributions is $7500. Thus, a self-employed person may contribute five times as much to a Keogh plan as a person eligible for an Individual Retirement Account. Keogh plans offer an opportunity, therefore, to accumulate much larger sums during your working years and to provide really significant benefits after retirement.

If you have the option of establishing either a Keogh plan or an IRA, the best choice is almost always the Keogh plan. The higher contribution limits permit larger tax deductions during your working years and the opportunity to accumulate a much larger retirement nest egg. In turn, this will result in a much larger retirement income when the funds are distributed to you. Also, during the accumulation period, the larger capital base will provide more earnings which grow on a tax-deferred basis.

Special contribution rules apply to those persons who are eligible to create a Keogh plan, and whose annual adjusted gross income (income from all sources) is $15,000 or less. Such persons may make a minimum contribution to their plan of $750 or 100% of their earned income, whichever is less.

As an example of these special rules, consider Kathy Doyle, a commercial artist whose salary is $12,000 per year. Kathy also earned $750 this year for some drawings she sold through a local gallery. Because her adjusted gross income is less than $15,000, Kathy can contribute the entire $750 of self-employment income to her Keogh plan. If her regular employment income had been more than $15,000, she would have been subject to the 15% limit, and could have contributed only $112.50 to the Keogh plan.

An employee who participates in a Keogh plan funded by employer contributions may make additional voluntary contributions on his or her own as well. Such personal contributions cannot exceed: (a) the amount that could be contributed on the employee's behalf by the employer, or; (b) $2500, or; (c) 10% of the contributing employee's regular compensation— whichever is *least*.

There is a disadvantage to such voluntary contributions, however, in that they are not tax deductible. While the employer's contributions are deducted from taxable income, participants who make additional voluntary contributions are simply investing money on which they have already paid Federal income tax. However, the income earned on voluntary contributions is still tax-deferred until it is received by the participant as income after retirement.

Withdrawals

Much of what was said previously about withdrawals from an IRA also applies to Keogh plans. Regulations provide a strong incentive to accumulate funds during your working years and not to make any withdrawals until at least age 59½. These provisions emphasize the nature of the Keogh plan as a substitute for an employer's retirement or pension program.

Just as you cannot ask for an advance payment from a pension plan, you should not expect to dip into your Keogh plan to meet unexpected expenses. You should set a regular schedule of payments to the Keogh account, and treat those payments as if they were a bill to be paid. Because the Keogh plan is a voluntary one, there will be a temptation to skip a payment once in a while, particularly when money is tight. Missing your Keogh payments, or, even worse, making early withdrawals, will undermine your future financial security.

Withdrawals from a Keogh plan prior to age 59½ are subject to the same 10% Premature Withdrawal Tax that applies to Individual Retirement Accounts. In addition, whatever amount is withdrawn is considered ordinary income for income tax purposes. Therefore, a dollar withdrawn from your Keogh plan prior to age 59½ receives a double tax penalty and does not actually provide a dollar of disposable income.

Rather than make unnecessary withdrawals from your Keogh plan, it is probably wiser to borrow from a bank, savings and loan, or credit union. Although it is an extreme case, it may well pay to borrow the money to make the Keogh plan payments. This is true particularly for those persons in a high tax bracket. Interest on the borrowed funds will be deductible from Federal income taxes, reducing the "real" cost of borrowing on an after-tax basis. In the meantime the earnings on your Keogh plan will continue to grow on a tax-deferred basis until retirement. Taken together, these two factors may justify "borrowing money to save it."

Regular withdrawals from a Keogh plan may be made after age 59½ without a penalty. Withdrawals must begin by at least age 70½ and are included in your taxable income at that time. Thus, a Keogh plan allows you to *defer* tax on a portion of your self-employment income not to *avoid* it altogether. As we mentioned earlier, however, the tax rate applicable to your income after retirement is likely to be considerably lower than the rate which would apply during your peak earning years. Double deductions and lower taxable income will reduce the actual tax paid on your Keogh withdrawals.

Keogh benefits must be paid out in substantially equal amounts on at least an annual basis. The payout period must be less than or equal to your own life expectancy or the joint and survivor life expectancy of you and your spouse. The appropriate life expectancy period is determined as of the date you actually begin to receive payments from the plan.

Defined-Benefit Keogh Plans

Up to this point we have been talking about the regular type of Keogh plan that has been allowed since 1962. Such plans are more formally called "defined-contribution" plans since they specify the annual contribution that you can make to the plan and deduct from your taxable income. The benefits you will ultimately receive from such a plan are unknown and will depend on the amount and timing of your contributions as well as the rate earned on your investments.

In 1974 the Employee Retirement Income Security Act (ERISA) created a second type of Keogh plan, a "defined-benefit" plan. Rather than specifying a limit on your contributions each year, the new plan lets you tailor your contributions to obtain a specific level of income when you retire. In effect, you decide how much income you want from your plan and for how long you expect to receive it.

The defined-benefit plan allows a self-employed individual to make larger contributions to their plan than are allowed by a regular Keogh plan. You are permitted to make whatever contributions are necessary (within limits) to fund your own life annuity upon retirement. Depending on your present age, current income, and desired benefits, you may be able to put as much as $14,000 or more into a Keogh plan and reduce your taxable income by the same amount.

Let's look at an example to see just how this "maxi-Keogh" plan might work for you. Dr. Welty is a 50-year-old physician who earns $50,000 per year. Using a regular defined-contribution Keogh plan he could put away a maximum of $7500 annually.

If he adopted a defined-benefit plan, however, Dr. Welty would first determine his desired income from the plan during his retirement period. The Internal Revenue Service provides a table showing the maximum allowable income based on an individual's current age and income. A person 50 years of age earning $50,000 per year would be able to set a retirement income target of $22,500. This is found by multiplying his annual earnings (up to a limit of $50,000) by the annual percentage factor defined by the IRS.

Assuming a 6% rate of return on his Keogh retirement fund, Dr. Welty could contribute $9400 annually to his plan, or $1900 more than he could with a regular Keogh plan. Over the 15 years until he starts to receive benefits from the plan, Dr. Welty would be able to contribute $28,500 more to the maxi-Keogh than to a regular plan.

A maxi-Keogh plan is most advantageous to older persons who want to build a large retirement fund in a relatively short period of time. Younger persons, particularly those with incomes in excess of $50,000, will find little real difference in the two plans.

In summary, if you *can* have an IRA or Keogh plan, you *should* have one. Each provides an excellent opportunity for you to put away relatively small amounts on a voluntary, annual basis tax-free. Not only will these plans reduce your current income taxes, but the money will accumulate tax-free until you begin making withdrawals after your retirement.

Answers to some of your most important questions concerning IRAs and Keogh plans can be found in Chapter 10 of this book.

8
ESTATE PLANNING

*The difference between death
and taxes is that death doesn't
get worse every time congress
meets*

Anonymous

ESTATE PLANNING—WHAT IS IT AND WHO NEEDS IT?

Death is inevitable. But death *taxes* are not. Almost everyone can reduce their Federal estate and state death tax burden. Many of us can legitimately avoid taxes altogether. But a large chunk of your estate won't go to your heirs and beneficiaries—if you don't plan. What you do now to accumulate, preserve, and distribute your estate upon death will strongly influence whether or not your lifetime personal financial goals for yourself and your family will be achieved.

Estate planning is a continuous process of accumulating, conserving, and distributing assets in the manner which most effectively accomplishes your objectives. Estate planning is a way to meet personal needs, desires, and objectives through the use of tax minimization tools and techniques.

Estate planning is not only for wealthy people. In fact, estate planning is even more important for individuals of modest or moderate means. A needless loss of assets to pay taxes or estate settlement costs hurts the survivors more when the estate is smaller.

At this point you may be thinking, "What goals do I have that would fall under the category of estate planning?" Typically, most people are motivated to engage in estate planning in order to: (1) provide for a comfortable retirement; (2) take care of themselves and their families in the event of a long-term disability; (3) pay off large debts and mortgages and assure financial security for family members in the event the head of the household should die; (5) secure enough capital to meet college education costs or other special needs; and (6) provide for favorite schools and charitable organizations.

WHO CARES?

Certainly not the IRS or your state's tax authority. In fact, if you don't care, nobody will. But you should know that "planning" occurs in every estate. If you do nothing, the federal government and the government of the state in which you reside will plan your estate. This is often called "uncontrolled" planning, because if you do nothing you forfeit the right to arrange for the disposition of assets and the minimization of tax and other estate settlement costs.

You can control the planning of your estate. You, together with your professional counselors, can measure your needs, establish an order of needs, and give first preference to accomplishing those needs or objectives which you—and not the federal or state government—feel are important.

"PEOPLE-PLANNING" INDICATORS

Do you really *need* to plan your estate? Maybe not. But most authorities feel that estate planning is extremely important for anyone who has minor children; who has a family member who is exceptionally artistic or intellectually gifted; who has a retarded, emotionally disturbed, or physically handicapped child or other dependent; who has a spouse who cannot or does not want to handle money, securities, or your business. These are all what experts call "people-planning" indicators that some form of estate planning is needed.

Think about it: Is there someone in your family who needs, deserves, or would want special care?

"ASSET-PLANNING" INDICATORS

From an "asset-planning" point of view, estate planning is indicated if you are single, widowed, or divorced and have an estate of over $175,000 or if you are married and have assets exceeding $425,000. Even if people-planning is not important to you, if you own a business or own property in more than one state you should consider various forms of tax and administrative cost minimization devices.

Do one or more of these asset-planning indicators apply to you?

WHAT'S GOING TO STOP ME?

What stands between you and the security you'd like to provide for your family (or perhaps a friend or favorite charity)? There's a saying that an estate breaks up not because the estate owner has done anything wrong, but because he or she hasn't done anything—and that's wrong!

There are many causes of an estate break-up. Some of these problems are:

1. *Excessive transfer costs* (your taxes and estate administration expenses are higher than they need to be).

   There are some expenses, of course, that can't be avoided; these include last illness and funeral costs. Most of us will die with some current bills unpaid and long-term obligations such as mortgages, business loans, or installment contracts outstanding. And very few of us die without owing some income taxes as well as property taxes.

   But quite often attorney fees, appraisal fees, and accountant's fees and probate expenses—so-called "administrative" costs—could have been lowered substantially. In almost every unplanned estate, federal estate taxes and state death taxes are significantly higher than they need to be.

   What have you done to reduce these costs to the lowest possible amount?

2. *Lack of liquidity* (your executor doesn't have enough cash to pay death costs and other estate obligations as they come due).

When there are not enough assets that can be quickly and inexpensively converted into cash, the result is typically a forced (sacrifice) "cents-on-the-dollar" sale of your most valuable assets, the ones with substantial income-producing power. This results in a disproportionately large loss of financial security and family income. Worse yet, no one wants to buy the worst property you own. Usually it's the choicest parcel of land—or the business which has been in your family for three generations, or a precious family heirloom—that must be sold. Think of the psychological effect on your heirs if these assets are put on the auction block. The outcome is quite often a devastating emotional crush as well as financial shock.

Have your advisors computed a "hypothetical probate" to determine the potential cash needs your executor will have? Will there be enough ready cash to meet those needs?

3. *Improper disposition of assets* (would you put a high-powered sports car into the hands of a child?)

Many times beneficiaries are left either the wrong asset or the right asset in the wrong manner, or at the wrong time. Beneficiaries are often unable or unwilling to handle large sums of money. But quite often that's exactly what happens; substantial sums are left outright as life insurance proceeds, or through joint ownership or a savings account, or as a payment from an employee fringe benefit plan. Such beneficiaries often fall prey to well-intended (and sometimes not so well-intended) but misleading or misguided (and almost always harmful) advice.

Do you have particular assets, mementos, or other types of property that will need special management? Have you thought about whether your beneficiaries are both capable and willing to manage and invest the assets you will leave them?

4. *Inadequate income at retirement* (it's too late when the time comes to remedy the problem of insufficient capital or capital which is not producing enough income to satisfy the needs of your current living standard).

There's an old saying that the difference between an old man and an elderly person is money. Do you have a systematic program in which you are setting aside dollars for retirement?

5. *Inadequate income if disabled* (extremely high medical costs coupled with capital which is either insufficient or which is not readily convertible to income-producing status).

   Estate planning authorities often call inadequate income at disability "a living death." Problems associated with loss of income due to disability are often compounded by a massive financial drain caused by the illness itself. Further complications are triggered by inattention to the management of currently owned assets, which reduces the rate of growth of estate assets and diminishes the value of the estate with incredible rapidity.

   What have you done to provide yourself a steady stream of dollars if you become sick or have an accident? Have you considered the effect of prolonged disability on your business?

6. *Special problems* (if a member of your family has a serious illness or is physically or mentally disturbed or emotionally troubled, estate planning is more important than ever. Other special problems include provisions for children of a prior marriage, beneficiaries who have extraordinary financial needs, business problems, and unusual business or educational opportunities).

   Is there someone who will need special care when you are unable to provide it?

WHERE DO I START?

The many problems listed above have solutions. The answers are more easily secured by you the estate owner than they will be by you the disabled person, or by you the retiree, or by your survivors. Ignoring these problems or shifting them to others merely delays the decisions. Problems which can be handled relatively easily—if action is taken while you are alive and healthy—often seems insurmountable to those grief-stricken, leaderless individuals you may leave behind.

If not all your people- or asset-planning objectives are assured, you should be engaged in what is called "the estate-planning process." Essentially, this process has four steps:

Step 1: Gathering the Information

You, your attorney, your life insurance agent, your trust officer, and other financial advisors must gather comprehensive and accurate data on your family, your property, your business interests, benefits available to you as an employee, your family income and finances, your income and capital needs, your liabilities, various factors which affect the plan you have devised, and an in-depth knowledge of your people- and asset-planning wishes and desires.

Step 2: Analyzing Needs

The data gathered has to be arranged so that the problems that stand between you and your objectives are apparent. One very important part of this process is the estimation of what it will cost to transfer your assets to your intended beneficiaries. This is often called a "hypothetical probate" or "liquidity-needs" analysis.

Step 3: Formulating a Plan

Once this information is compiled, an estate plan must be formulated and preparations must be made to implement it. If your plan is arranged properly, you will have maximized the usefulness of the assets you already own. That means you can personally enjoy them during your lifetime and your family will obtain maximum utility from them after your death.

Step 4: Testing and Implementing the Plan

The final step in the estate-planning process is to test and implement the proposed plan.

It is very important to remember that estate planning is a continual process: once you have implemented a plan, it remains useful only so long as it fits your needs, your desires, and the circumstances of all the parties involved. As your needs and the needs of your family members change, the estate plan must also be modified.

Review of the Plan

Examples of events which trigger the need to reassemble the estate-planning team and recheck the plan are: (a) the birth of a child, (b) a change of residence to another state, (c) substantial changes in income, health, or living standards.

Even if none of these occur, you should review your life insurance needs at least once every two years and obtain a full audit of your estate plan at least every five to seven years.

WITHOUT A WILL, WHAT?

Who needs a will? What can a will give me that I can't get without one? Those are good questions and should have answers.

A will is the legal expression of what you want to happen to your property when you die. The easiest way to understand why it is so important is to find out what happens if you die without one.

The absence of a valid will is called "intestacy." In essence, everyone has a will; if *you* don't draw one, your *state* —through its intestacy laws—will "draw the will" you failed to make. In other words, the laws of the state in which you live will determine, automatically and regardless of what you really wanted, the disposition of your "probate" (that term is explained below) property.

Typically, intestacy laws spell out certain preferred classes of survivors. Usually, if you die survived by a spouse, that person will receive all or the bulk of your estate. Any children and other descendants you have will share what's left. They will divide your estate in the proportions and manner specified by your state's intestacy laws. Other relatives or organizations you care about may receive nothing.

Generally, if no spouse, children, or other descendants survive you, then your parents, brothers, and sisters will receive equal shares of your estate. (One quick and inexpensive way of finding out how your state's intestacy laws work is to visit your local bank's trust department. They generally have free brochures as well as a helpful staff that can explain, in general and understandable terms, the intestacy laws of your state.)

Without a will, you can't direct that any of your property go to a non-related individual or to a charity. You've lost control not only over who will receive your property at your death but also how or when they will receive it. You've also forfeited the privilege of naming a personal respresentative to guide the disposition of your estate and to make sure things go as you'd want them to. The person appointed by the court will have minimal flexibility in dealing with your assets or your loved ones.

Without a will you can't name guardians for minor or disabled children. If you let the state draw your will, you give up the opportunity to use certain deductions, exclusions, and various planning techniques to minimize administrative expenses and federal estate and state death tax shrinkage.

A valid will, regardless of how large or how small your estate, is the cornerstone of the estate planning process because it allows you, rather than the state, to control the disposition of your property.

WHAT DOES A WILL WILL?

A few paragraphs above, you noticed the term "probate" property. Your estate is your property. It is whatever you own at the time you die. Your "probate" estate is the real and personal property that you own in your own name that you personally have a right to transfer according to the terms of the will that you write and which takes effect at your death. Essentially, probate property consists of the assets you own solely in your own name—the assets disposed of by state intestacy laws if you don't draw a valid will.

There is a difference between your "probate" estate (that's a property law concept essentially encompassing assets which will either pass under your will or under your state's intestacy laws) and your "gross" estate (this is a term used for federal and state death tax purposes) which typically encompasses a much larger amount of property.

Your gross estate (a tax concept) includes all the property subject to federal estate tax at your death (both probate and nonprobate). For example, typically life insurance is not probate property because it passes by contract and not under your will. Regardless of what your will says, life insurance proceeds pass directly to the beneficiary you have named in your policy. (Unless you have named your estate as beneficiary, a designation that is rarely recommended by estate planners.) Likewise, jointly held property with rights of survivorship and property passing under certain employee benefit plans are nonprobate assets that are probably subject to federal and state estate taxes. But they will not be probate property because you can't dispose of those assets by will.

There may be some assets you have which are neither probate property nor part of your gross estate for federal estate-tax purposes. Yet they are important because they may form a significant part of your financial security program.

There are two types of such assets: one is death benefit that your family can receive from your pension, profit sharing, or HR-10 plan. If you are covered under an IRA (Individual Retirement Account), death benefits from this source might also escape both probate and the burden of federal taxation. Arranged properly, the death proceeds from all these plans will pass outside your probate estate because of their contractual nature. Likewise, they can be federal estate-tax free and in many states can also escape state death taxation.

The death benefit from a corporate pension or profit-sharing or HR-10 plan can be federal estate-tax free if you make it payable to anyone other than your executor—and if the recipient takes it over more than one tax year. Alternatively, it could be taken in a lump sum all in one tax year, and your beneficiary would still be entitled to receive it without causing any federal estate tax in your estate. But to obtain both the estate-tax exclusion and still receive the retirement plan distribution in a lump sum, your beneficiary must elect to forgo the favorable 10-year income averaging available only for lump sum distributions. It's an either/or choice. It can be federal estate-tax free in your estate, or the beneficiary can use special 10-year averaging—but it's not possible to have both.

An IRA (Individual Retirement Account) death benefit will be estate-tax free only if it is payable as an annuity (i.e., over more than 36 months in a series of substantially equal increments).

The second type of financial asset that is not probate property and will not typically be subject to death taxes is Social Security income. Payments made to your surviving spouse and minor children through the Social Security system will not be subject to probate nor will your executor have to pay federal estate (or state death) taxes. Because of this freedom from administrative costs and taxes, these two types of assets are unique and present significant estate planning opportunities.

I'D RATHER DO IT MYSELF

Who needs an attorney, why not draw my own will? There are so many reasons why homemade wills are good examples of the old adage, "He who has himself for attorney has a fool for client."

No matter how small your estate or how simple your desires, it's worth the expense to employ a qualified attorney. The complexity and interrelationships of tax, property, domestic relations, and other laws make a homemade will a frivolous, dangerous, and highly expensive way to cut corners. The ultimate cost of a homemade will will be at least the same—and is typically much greater—than one drawn by a qualified attorney. But it will be your heirs who pay the price.

What would it cost to have the will drawn by someone who knows how to do it? The answer is, that depends. The more assets, the more complex your dispositive desires, and the more factors that have to be considered, the more money you'll have to pay. Quite often a two- or three-page will may be adequate and you should be billed accordingly. In many other cases the will may be much longer or complex (and the bill higher) because of the time the attorney must spend in drafting it. Don't forget, your will must not only effectively accomplish the personal objectives you specified with respect to how your assets are to be distributed but must also take into consideration the federal and state income, estate, and gift-tax laws. Quite often, the person who drafts your will must also understand corporate, trust, real estate, and security laws.

No matter how few or how many pages, a properly prepared will must provide a plan for distributing your assets the way you want them distributed. But that will must also consider the needs of your beneficiaries as well as the federal and state laws which will affect your dispositive plans. Obviously, your will must be unambiguous and completely describe what you want accomplished. Furthermore, the will must be flexible enough to take into consideration any of the many changes in family circumstances which might occur after you sign your will.

Don't forget to ask the attorney's hourly charge before he or she begins to work—or agree in advance on a total fee. Just like any other contract for services to be performed, have the attorney put down the terms of the agreement in writing so there'll be no misunderstanding.

TURN AROUNDS

The one thing you can be sure of in life is change. Your feelings about your property and the people you want to receive your property will change. And so will those people—and their needs. Fortunately, a will is inoperative until you die and therefore you can change it any time until then.

There are many very good reasons why people change or revoke their wills. For example, modification should be considered if your health or your beneficiary's health or financial circumstances have changed. A birth, a death, a marriage, a divorce all change to some extent the circumstances that were operative at the time you signed your will. Furthermore, when the tax law changes in a significant manner, your will should, at the very least, be reexamined.

How can you change your will? Changing the will can be as simple as having the attorney draft a "codicil." A codicil is a legal means of modifying an existing will without rewriting the entire document. It is typically used when the will needs only minor modifications. A codicil is often a document of a page or two that reaffirms everything you've already stated in your will except the specific provisions which need to be changed. Just like your will, your codicil should be typed, signed, and properly witnessed according to the requirements of your own state's law.

If substantial changes are needed, you probably should have a new will. You may want to draw a new will in some cases even though you haven't made substantial changes. For example, if you decide not to leave property to someone who is named in your original will, to avoid offending the omitted beneficiary, you may want to destroy the old will after a new one is drawn and properly executed.

There are times, however, when you should not destroy a prior will even after a new one is made and signed. A good example is if you are older or in poor health and you feel someone may contest the will. If the new will for some reason fails, the prior will may qualify. Another reason for keeping old wills is that a prior will could help to prove "a continuity of testamentary purpose." In other words, your executor may have to prove that the last will you drew—which may have provided a large gift to a friend or favorite charity—was not a last-minute thought that was the result of an unduly influenced mind. If you had made a gift to the same friend or charity in an earlier will, the existence of that provision could help your executor avoid or defeat a contest of your latest will.

Your state has specific laws that provide how a will can be revoked. Actually, there are two ways common to most states: You can revoke your will by (1) making a later will which expressly revokes prior wills, or (2) making a codicil which specifically revokes any wills.

Your will can also be revoked by making a later will inconsistent with a former will or by physically mutilating, burning, or defacing your will with the intent of revoking it.

State law in many cases will *automatically* revoke or modify your will if certain events occur. The most common automatic will-revoking triggers are: (1) marriage, (2) divorce, (3) birth or adoption of a child, and (4) slaying. For instance, if you legally divorce your spouse, in many states all provisions in your will relating to your spouse become inoperative. Or if you are single when you make your will and then marry, automatically, and regardless of what you do or do not say, your spouse has a right to receive that portion of your estate that would have been received had you died without a valid will. Your spouse has a right to his (or her) "intestate" share—the share that he or she would have received had you died without a valid will. But if your will actually gives your spouse more than an intestate share, then the intestate-share provision would not apply.

What if you didn't provide for a child born or adopted after you wrote your will? In many states, the state "writes" that child into the will for you. Your state may provide that a child born or adopted after you wrote your will will receive that share of your estate not passing to your spouse that would have been given to the child if you didn't have a will (unless it appears in the will by specific direction that you intended that child should not benefit under your will).

Almost all states have "slayers statutes." These laws forbid anyone who participates in a willful and unlawful killing from acquiring property as a result.

There is one further way your will can be changed. You may not like it but many states give a surviving spouse what is known as a "right of election." In other words your surviving spouse might have a right to "take against your will"—to take a specified portion of your estate regardless of what you gave your spouse in your will. One state, for example, allows a surviving spouse to demand at least that share that would have been allowed had the decedent died without a valid will. If an individual leaves his entire estate to his son, absent a pre- or post-nuptial agreement to the contrary, his wife can take the same one-third share of his estate she would have received had her husband died intestate.

Some states even give these "rights of election" to children. There are ways to avoid these rights of election but they can't be accomplished by your executor. You must do the planning.

DOS AND DON'TS

Do remember that both you and your spouse should have wills. Those wills should be coordinated. Insist that your attorney examine documents relating to all your assets including your life insurance policies, the deeds to jointly held property such as your home and bank accounts, and your certificates for company-sponsored pension and group insurance benefits before your will is drafted. A will should not be drawn in a vacuum. It must consider and be tied to the values and ownership arrangement of your assets, your overall employee benefit program, and your personal financial plans.

Do keep your will where it can be found quickly. The person you have named as executor should know where it can be found (your safe deposit box is a good place). Make sure your attorney or perhaps some other advisor has a copy.

Don't name anyone as guardian or executor without conferring with them first. Both jobs involve awesome responsibilities, are highly time-consuming, can be extremely complicated, and, if handled improperly, can be personally costly to your executor.

Name a backup executor, guardian, and trustee such as a bank or trust company in case the person you have named for some reason will not or cannot serve or, once having agreed to serve, is unable to continue serving.

Most importantly, don't make changes in your will—even minor changes—without consulting your attorney.

PROBATE: WHAT'S TO AVOID?

When you die, like most people, you probably will own property and owe debts. You may have claims against other persons, such as accounts receivable or law suits in progress. Your executor has the duty of collecting money that is owed to you.

He or she then must satisfy any debts to your creditors (including the federal and state government to whom you or your estate owe income, gift, or death taxes).

The third major duty of an executor is to distribute what is left to the appropriate individuals or organizations. This three part process is called "probate" and is generally supervised by a local court known as the Probate Court, the Surrogate's Court, or Orphan's Court.

You may have designated a person in your will to take charge of this process. That person is called an "executor." If you die intestate, that is, without a valid will, the court will appoint someone to do the executor's job. That person will be called an "administrator" and has essentially the same duties and legal privileges as an executor.

Your executor or administrator (quite often also referred to as a decedent's "personal representative") must perform a number of extremely important and often highly complex tasks (see Fig. 8.1). For example, your executor may have to bring suit on your estate's behalf or release some party from liability. Without the probate process, there would be no one legally entitled to do these things. Titles to real estate could not be made marketable because no one would be legally empowered to act on behalf of your estate.

Probate is therefore a very important process in which your executor carries out his or her tasks under court supervision and scrutiny. In fact your personal representative will not be discharged from his or her duties by the court until an extensive accounting of all assets, liabilities, income, and dispositions has been made.

Why, then, do you hear so much talk about avoiding probate? Frankly, because at one time, courts charged high probate fees and lawyers based their fee on the size of your probate estate. In most states probate is now a relatively inexpensive process (call your local probate court for a list of the charges). Attorneys are more commonly billing clients by the hours they actually spend rather than for a percentage of the probate estate.

There are still good reasons, however, for avoiding probate with respect to certain assets. For example, if you own property in more than one state, multiple probates (these are called "ancillary administrations") will be required. Property will have to be probated in each state where property is owned. This could be both aggravating and expensive.

Another reason for avoiding probate with respect to assets such as the family home or checking accounts is that the probate procedure can be time-consuming. Typically, the entire procedure takes from a minimum of nine months to as long as two or three years in some cases. Your attorney will point out those assets which should be held in a manner that will not pass through probate.

If privacy is important (once the will is probated, it becomes a public document) then avoiding probate is essential.

CHECKLIST OF EXECUTOR'S PRIMARY DUTIES

1. Probate of will.
2. Advertise Grant of Letters.
3. Inventory of safe deposit box.
4. Claim for life insurance benefits—obtain Form 712.
   a. Consider mode of payment.
5. Claim for pension and profit-sharing benefits.
   a. Consider mode of payment.
   b. Obtain copies of plan, IRS approval and beneficiary designation.
6. Apply for lump sum Social Security benefits and V.A. benefits.
7. File Form 56—Notice of Fiduciary Relationship.
8. Open estate checking and savings accounts.
9. Write to banks for date of death value.
10. Value securities.
11. Appraisal of real property and personal property.
12. Obtain 3 years of U.S. Individual income tax returns and 3 years of cancelled checks.
13. Obtain 5 years financials on business interest plus all relevant agreements.
14. Obtain copies of all U.S. gift tax returns filed by decedent.
15. Obtain evidence of all debts of decedent and costs of administering estate.
16. Were any of decedent's medical expenses unpaid at death?
17. Has the estate received after death income taxable under Section 691 of the IRC?
18. Prepayment of inheritance tax—check local state law to determine if permissible and if so, the applicable deadlines.
19. Consider requesting prompt assessment of decedent's U.S. income taxes.
20. File personal property tax returns—due February 15 of each year estate in administration.
21. File final U.S. and state individual income tax return (IRS Form 1040)—due April 15 of the year after the year in which death occurs.
22. Is the estate subject to ancillary administration?
23. Are administration expenses and losses to be claimed as an income or estate tax deduction?
24. Obtain alternate valuation date values for U.S. estate tax.
25. Payment of U.S. estate tax with flower bonds—must be tendered to Federal Reserve with Form within 9 months of death.
26. Consider election of extension of time to pay U.S. estate tax (Sections 6161, 6166, or 6166A)—must be filed on or before due date of U.S. estate tax return.
27. Consider election to defer payment of inheritance tax on remainder interests—where permitted, determine deadline for election.
28. Consider election for special valuation of farm or business real estate under IRC Section 2032A—must be made with timely filed U.S. estate tax return.
29. File form notice to IRS required by Section 6039A of IRC—due with final U.S. individual income tax return or U.S. estate tax return.
30. File inheritance and federal estate tax return—federal due within 9 months of death—extensions may be requested—check local state law for due date and possible extensions.
31. File inventory—check local state law for requirements and due date.
32. Consider requesting prompt assessment of U.S. estate tax return.
33. Apply for U.S. I.D. number if estate will file U.S. income tax returns.
34. File U.S. Fiduciary Income Tax Return (Form 1041)—choice of fiscal year.
35. Consider redemption under IRC Section 303.
36. Apply for tax waivers
37. File account or prepare informal family agreement.
38. Prepare audit notices and statement of proposed distribution.
39. File schedule of distribution if applicable.

SOURCE: Tools and Techniques of Estate Planning, *3d edition, The National Underwriter Co.,* Cincinnati, Ohio

FIGURE 8.1

Two last comments about probate: First, the fees your estate will pay the estate's attorney can (and should) be negotiated by your executor *before* hiring the attorney. (This is one good reason that an attorney should seldom be named as executor. The avoidance of conflicts of interest is another. In most states the executor you've nominated can use any attorney he or she would like to use and is not bound to use the attorney who drew your will—regardless of what the attorney wrote into the will.)

Second, although there are many advantages to passing property outside of probate (for example, property passing through a life insurance contract is less likely to become subject to contest than the provisions of a will), probate equates to court supervision. That means a disinterested party will be safeguarding the interests of your beneficiaries. This "watchful" control over the executor often outweighs the relatively minor costs involved in probate.

TWISTED JOINTS

Bob and Jean, when they purchased their new home, took title as "tenants by the entireties." Many people take title to real property (and in some states personal property) jointly either through "a joint tenancy" or tenancy by the entirety." There are both advantages and disadvantages to these ownership forms. A joint tenancy and a tenancy by the entirety have these characteristics:

First, in both cases, at the death of one of the joint tenants, the interest of the decedent passes directly to the surviving joint tenant by operation of law and in either case is free from the claims of the decedent's creditors, heirs, or personal representatives.

Second, a joint tenancy with right of survivorship may consist of any number of persons, whether or not they are related by blood or marriage. The tenancy by the entirety, on the other hand, exists only between husband and wife.

Third, in the case of a joint tenancy, each joint tenant can, unilaterally, partition (sever) the tenancy and sell or give away his or her share. However, in the case of a tenancy by the entirety, severance can only occur by mutual agreement, termination by divorce, or conveyance by both spouses to a third party. For example, Bob could not sell his "share" of the house unless Jean agreed in writing to the conveyance.

What are the advantages of joint tenancy? Typically, joint tenancy gives the psychological sense of family unity and security. At one joint owner's death, the property is quickly, easily, and (in most states) automatically transferred to the coowner.

In many states, certain jointly owned property is not subject to claims asserted by creditors of a deceased coowner. For this reason many homes are titled jointly with right of survivorship. Separately owned property is normally subject to such claims.

Furthermore, some states exempt jointly owned property from state death taxes. This is a considerable advantage, especially if there is no state limit to the amount of jointly held property that is exempt.

Since jointly owned property with right of survivorship does not pass through probate, there is no delay in estate administration, and such property avoids the publicity that arises from the probate of a will.

But there are disadvantages you should consider. Once the property is titled jointly, you have lost control as to the property's use and management. That control is split between you and the other joint owner(s).

For instance, neither Bob or Jean would be able to unilaterally rent their home or give it away. (This "disadvantage" has the obvious advantage of protecting the interest of the other joint owner.)

Second, property held in joint ownership *cannot* be disposed of by your will. In other words, if you were a joint tenant with right of survivorship and you die first, *regardless* of what your will says, the property will pass directly to your cotenant.

Third, since title to the property does pass immediately and automatically to the surviving cotenant, you cannot provide for any management of the property (such as trust management) or specify any limitations or restrictions on the survivor. The new owner may then have an asset he or she is incapable of wisely investing or handling.

There may also be hidden potential gift tax costs at both the creation and severance of a joint tenancy or a tenancy by the entirety. For instance, suppose Bob calls his stockbroker and has him purchase 1000 shares of Texas Oil and Gas "in my name and my wife Jean's name as joint tenants with the right of survivorship." Since Jean is receiving a property interest she did not previously have, Bob is making a gift to her.

Furthermore, where property is held jointly between husband and wife, if the surviving spouse receives all or a substantial portion of your estate through jointly held property, you may have needlessly subjected too much property to taxation at your surviving spouse's death. Estate planners refer to this as "overqualification of the marital deduction." It means more property than necessary to maximize the use of the so called "marital deduction" (explained below) went to the surviving spouse. The result of over-qualifying the marital deduction is that additional property could be taxed again when the surviving spouse dies. It may have been possible to avoid such needless taxation at the surviving spouse's later death if the property was owned in your name alone and the appropriate will and trust provisions were used. Through the so-called marital deduction clause, property in excess of the maximum marital deduction could be held in a special trust for children in a way that will avoid a second tax at the surviving spouse's death.

For example, assume Bob's entire estate was worth $1,000,000 (after debts and expenses). If the entire estate were jointly held with Jean, at Bob's death Jean would receive all of it. The federal estate tax law, as explained below, allows Bob to pass half of that "adjusted" gross estate (the gross estate less certain debts and expenses) free of federal estate tax. In other words half—and only half in this example—would be deductible. The other $500,000 is subject to tax when Bob dies. Then, when Jean dies, the entire $1,000,000 (to the extent not consumed or given away) could be subject to tax again. Alternatively, Bob could have given Jean only the deductible $500,000 and left the other $500,000 to a trust that would provide security for Jean during her lifetime but at her death would go to their children—without being taxed in Jean's estate.

TRUST ME

What is a trust and how does it work? Stated simply, a trust is the relation-ship which occurs when one party (often called a "grantor, settlor," or "creator") transfers property to a second party (the "trustee") who must use those assets solely for the benefit of a third party (the "beneficiary"). The third party beneficiary(ies) may or may not include the grantor himself. The property placed in the trust is called "trust principal," *"corpus,"* or *"res."*

The whole idea is that the trustee holds legal title to the property in the trust but can only use the property and the income produced by it for the benefit of trust beneficiaries.

Generally, the trust is created by a written document called a "trust agreement." The grantor spells out the substantive provisions, such as who is to receive most assets, how the property in the trust is to be allocated, how income is to be distributed, as well as certain administrative provisions.

A trust can be "testamentary" (created in a will and taking effect at death) or "*inter vivos*" (this is a trust you create while you are alive and is often referred to as a "living" trust). A trust can be "revocable" (you can change the terms or get back the property) or "irrevocable" (you can't change the terms or get the property back once it is set up).

These terms will be discussed in more detail below.

What's in It for me?

Why set up a trust? The answer is that you may want to establish a trust for any one or more of a number of reasons. Most people create trusts to obtain significant income and estate tax savings and/or to provide management and conservation services for their property. Although trusts are not for everyone (and in fact are typically for those with substantial assets), even people with moderate or modest means should sometimes consider the use of a trust.

In an irrevocable trust you can actually shift the burden of income taxes from you—at *your* income tax rates—to the trust itself and/or to its beneficiary, both of whom are typically in lower income tax brackets than you are. The difference in tax rates could amount to a substantial annual savings. Coupled with the personal income tax exemption allowed to each beneficiary, those savings can be significant.

Even better, dramatic federal and often state estate tax savings are available because once you place property into an irrevocable trust it's no longer in your estate (assuming the trust is drafted properly and you live for more than three years after the transfer).

Any appreciation from the date of the gift grows in the hands of your beneficiaries and will not be taxed in your estate. (There may, however, be gift tax implications when you place property into the trust.) That's because when you put property into an irrevocable trust you are really making an absolute gift to the trust's beneficiaries. If the gift is large enough, you'll have to pay gift taxes.

Regardless of the size of your estate, you may have family members who *can't* handle money (or who don't *want* to handle particular types of assets) on their own. Good examples of such beneficiaries are minors, spendthrifts, and mental or emotional incompetents. These people need asset management for obvious reasons.

Trusts are often set up by people perfectly capable of handling assets but who can't—or don't want to—take the time to do so. They want to relieve themselves of these burdens and do so by using trusts. The trustee assumes the responsibility for investing, managing, and conserving the property on behalf of the beneficiaries (including you, if that's what you want).

A trust may be a great way for helping a vigorous person to protect himself or herself in the event of unexpected incapacitation and inability or unwillingness to manage his or her assets.

Who Should Watch the Store?

Who should you pick as your trustee? First of all, you can pick more than one trustee. In that case, each party would be considered a "cotrustee" and they would make decisions jointly.

What do you look for in selecting a trustee? First, a trustee should have sound knowledge of investment principles and asset management, good financial judgment, and an intimate knowledge of the needs of each beneficiary. Further, the trustee should be available to the beneficiaries, which means that he or she should be young enough to survive through the term of the trust.)

Often a corporate trustee, such as a trust company or a bank authorized to perform trust duties, may be the best choice to meet these requirements. A bank probably has investment experience and will not be incapacitated by death, disability, or absence. Unlike a family member, a corporate trustee can obey the directions of the trust instrument impartially and objectively. This objectivity can be particularly important in avoiding the conflicts of interest that may occur where a number of beneficiaries are members of the same family.

But on the other hand a corporate trustee may be overly conservative in making investments, impersonal, and lacking in a familiarity and understanding of family problems and needs that someone in your family might have. You may gain the advantages of both a personal trustee and a corporate trustee by appointing one (or more) individual(s) and a corporate trustee as cotrustees.

ARMS IN THE ARSENAL

What types of trusts are available for me to meet my objectives?

There are a number of types of trusts and the terms of those trusts can be as wide and varied as the imagination of your attorney and the needs and desires of the parties involved.

The most common types of trust are the "living" trusts, "testamentary" trusts, and the life insurance trust/pour-over will combination.

A living (*inter vivos*) trust is one created during your lifetime. It can either be "revocable" or "irrevocable." You can set it up to last for a specified period or it can go on long after your death and even your spouse's death and children's death.

Revocable Living Trust

If you make the trust revocable, you can change your mind and regain the trust property (or income) at any time or change the terms of the trust as often as you'd like. You could also direct who is to receive either income or principal. For federal income and estate tax purposes, you are treated just as if you never gave up the property you've placed in the trust. Therefore, if property in the trust earns income, you'll be taxed on it. If someone else receives it, you'll still be subject to income tax on it—and you may also be liable for gift taxes (just as if you received the income and then gave it away).

Why then set up a revocable living trust? Basically, a living trust makes it possible to provide management continuity and income flow even after you die. No probate is necessary since the trust continues to operate after you die in the same way it did while you are alive.

The second advantage of a living trust is that the burdens of investment decisions and management responsibility may be taken from your shoulders and assumed by your trustee. You may want to control investment decisions and management policy as long as you are alive and healthy, but you may want to set up a trust to provide backup help in case you become unable or unwilling to manage your own assets. This type of revocable living trust is called a "stepup" trust because the trustee "steps up" to take your place in decision-making and in day-to-day management if you want relief from the burden of managing the trust or if you become incapable of acting on your own behalf.

A further advantage of the revocable living trust is that the terms of the trust and the amount of assets placed into it will never become known to the public. Unlike the terms of your will, the public has no right to know the terms or conditions of a revocable living trust.

But there are disadvantages. The trustee will charge fees to manage property placed into the trust and attorneys will, of course, charge legal fees for drafting such instruments.

Irrevocable Living Trust

You may want to consider establishing an irrevocable living trust. The advantage of such a trust is that you can substantially reduce income taxes and possibly save estate taxes. Keep in mind, however, that once you put property into an irrevocable trust, you relinquish the right to receive the property back, terminate the trust, or change its terms. Another drawback is that you may be making taxable gifts. Each time you put property into the trust you are really making a gift to each of the trust's beneficiaries.

Additional disadvantages include fees charged by trustees for asset management, the loss of your use of trust property and any income it may produce, and the forfeiture of your right to change the terms of the trust even if circumstances (yours *or* your beneficiary's) change.

Testamentary Trust

Another type of trust is one created by and in your will; it is called a testamentary trust. This type of trust comes into existence only after your will is probated. There are no income or estate tax savings because you don't give up property until you die.

The testamentary trust does have the advantage of shifting the burdens of asset management and investment decision-making from your beneficiaries to the trustee. It also can be used to delay or control who receives what and when and how money or other assets will be paid out.

Life Insurance Trust with Pour-Over Will

One of the most common types of trust is the type coupled with the provisions of your will. This is called a life insurance trust and pour-over will combination. Your will can be written so that it "pours over" (think of a funnel) certain assets into a previously established (living) life insurance trust. You can make this type of trust revocable or irrevocable. It is called a life insurance trust because while you are alive you name the trust as beneficiary of specified life insurance policies and perhaps employee benefits. In many states you don't have to fund a life insurance trust with any other assets. Then you state in your will that probate assets—after payment of debts, expenses, taxes, and specific bequests—are to go (pour over) into the life insurance trust.

The trust contains provisions as to how all the assets will be administered and distributed. The big advantage of the life insurance trust—pourover will combination is that all your assets are easily coordinated and administered in a unified manner according to your wishes.

IS IT BETTER TO GIVE?

Lifetime gifts may be one of the very best ways of beating federal death taxes. Through what is known as the "gift-tax exclusion," a person can give any number of donees as much as $3000 each and every year and not pay one dime in gift tax. Neither you nor the person receiving your gift (called the "donee") pays any income or gift tax.

If you are married and your spouse consents, you may increase the gift tax-free limit to as much as $6000 a year even if the entire gift was made from your personal assets. This is called "gift splitting," since your spouse is treated as if he or she had made half the gift regardless of the actual contribution. So if you are married and have four children, you could give them as much as $24,000 each and every year without paying one dime in gift tax. At the end of just 20 years, you will have given away almost half a million dollars (plus the income that money or other asset produced).

If you assume that your beneficiaries have invested that money (or if you've made gifts of stock in your closely held corporation or rapidly appreciating land), the total value of the estate you have shifted from your high bracket to the beneficiaries' lower brackets could well have doubled.

A recent addition to the provisions of the tax law makes it possible to give gifts within three years of your death and—regardless of your motive—the gift will not be treated as part of your estate. In other words, certain gifts can be excluded from your estate even if you have made them within three years of your death and regardless of your intentions.

This exclusion from the federal estate tax applies, however, only to gifts you personally make that are worth $3000 or less and only if the recipient can immediately use, possess, or enjoy the gift. (This special estate tax exclusion will be lost if you are required to file a gift tax return for *any* reason.) For instance, assume you "split" gifts with your spouse to increase the annual exclusion from $3000 to $6000. You must file a gift tax return even though there may be no tax to pay. For gift tax purposes, the additional amounts (up to $3000) you give would be gift tax free but for estate tax purposes all your gifts (the $3000 your spouse is deemed to have made plus the $3000 you are treated as having made) are includable in your estate if you die within three years of your gift. If you make a gift of a "future interest" in property, i.e., a gift where your beneficiary's use, possession, or enjoyment is delayed or subject to certain conditions, regardless of the amount of that gift, you must file a gift tax return. That will cause the property to be includable in your estate if you die within three years of the transfer.

Another provision in the tax law allows you to take a credit against any gift or estate tax otherwise payable. That credit (the so-called "unified credit") equates to $175,625.00. In other words, each taxpayer on a "one-shot" basis can make gifts during lifetime or transfers at death totaling $175,625 without paying any taxes—and this amount is over and above the $3000 annual exclusion. However, to the extent this offset is used during lifetime, it does not regenerate. That means it is no longer available to offset future lifetime or "deathtime" gifts.

Herb Cheesman, a widower who has never made any prior gifts, gives his son, Mark, property worth $103,000. He applies his $3000 annual exclusion and reduces the gift to $100,000. He may then take a credit which reduces to zero the gift tax that would otherwise be payable. But the use of this "unified credit" means that he can give only another $75,625 (over and above any allowable $3000 annual exclusion) without paying gift tax. At his death, if he has made no further lifetime gifts, he may leave up to $75,625 estate tax free. The value of any other assets would be taxable in his estate.

A further provision in the tax law, called a "marital" deduction, makes it possible for you to give $100,000 to a spouse (in excess of the $3000 annual exclusion and the unified credit) entirely gift tax free. This marital deduction is allowable only for gifts made to a spouse.

It is possible, therefore, to combine the annual exclusion ($3000) with the gift tax marital deduction ($100,000), and the one-time credit (equivalent to $175,625) to give to a spouse up to $278,625 during your lifetime without paying one cent in federal gift taxes.

What's the Cost?

There is, of course, no free lunch in the tax law. Gifts in excess of the annual exclusion, marital deduction, and unified credit mentioned above will be taxable. The gift tax rates are progressive and start at a rate of 18% (but only on the taxable portion of the gift—that portion over and above the allowable exclusion, deduction, and unified credit). Table 8.1 gives a breakdown of gift tax rates.

What to Give

The best types of property to give away depends on the circumstances and objectives of the parties. Usually high income-producing property is good property for you to give away if you are in a high income bracket and your recipients are in relatively lower brackets.

Property which is likely to grow substantially in value is also excellent property for giving, since future appreciation can be removed from your estate and the gift can be made when the gift tax values (and therefore gift tax transfer costs) are lowest.

Property which has already appreciated should be given away if you contemplate that it will be sold in the near future and your recipient is in a lower income tax bracket than you are. That's because he or she will net more after-tax income than the donor would have received. Property with relatively low gift tax value and high estate tax value (such as life insurance) is also an excellent gift. And that's because you get a lot out of your estate at minimal cost.

Typically, it is not a good idea to give away "loss property." Loss property is an asset, which, if sold, would result in a loss. The reason this type of property is typically not a good asset for giving is that no one but you can use your loss for tax purposes. You should sell that property yourself, take the loss deduction on your own return, and then give away the cash proceeds. Let's say, for example, that you bought land for $10,000. Due to a change in nearby zoning, your property drops in value to $7000. It

TABLE 8.1 UNIFIED RATE SCHEDULE FOR ESTATE AND GIFT TAXES (IRC Sec. 2001(c))

IF THE AMOUNT WITH RESPECT TO WHICH THE TENTATIVE TAX TO BE COMPUTED IS:	THE TENTATIVE TAX IS:
Not over $10,000	18% of such amount.
Over $10,000 but not over $20,000	$1,800 plus 20% of the excess of such amount over $10,000.
Over $20,000 but not over $40,000	$3,800 plus 22% of the excess of such amount over $20,000.
Over $40,000 but not over $60,000	$8,200 plus 24% of the excess of such amount over $40,000.
Over $60,000 but not over $80,000	$13,000 plus 26% of the excess of such amount over $60,000.
Over $80,000 but not over $100,000	$18,200 plus 28% of the excess of such amount over $80,000.
Over $100,000 but not over $150,000	$23,800 plus 30% of the excess of such amount over $100,000.
Over $150,000 but not over $250,000	$38,800 plus 32% of the excess of such amount over $150,000.
Over $250,000 but not over $500,000	$70,800 plus 34% of the excess of such amount over $250,000.
Over $500,000 but not over $750,000	$155,800 plus 37% of the excess of such amount over $500,000.
Over $750,000 but not over $1,000,000	$248,300 plus 39% of the excess of such amount over $750,000.
Over $1,000,000 but not over $1,250,000	$345,800 plus 41% of the excess of such amount over $1,000,000.
Over $1,250,000 but not over $1,500,000	$448,300 plus 43% of the excess of such amount over $1,250,000.
Over $1,500,000 but not over $2,000,000	$555,800 plus 45% of the excess of such amount over $1,500,000.
Over $2,000,000 but not over $2,500,000	$780,800 plus 49% of the excess of such amount over $2,000,000.
Over $2,500,000 but not over $3,000,000	$1,025,800 plus 53% of the excess of such amount over $2,500,000.
Over $3,000,000 but not over $3,500,000	$1,290,800 plus 57% of the excess of such amount over $3,000,000.
Over $3,500,000 but not over $4,000,000	$1,575,800 plus 61% of the excess of such amount over $3,500,000.
Over $4,000,000 but not over $4,500,000	$1,880,800 plus 65% of the excess of such amount over $4,000,000.
Over $4,500,000 but not over $5,000,000	$2,205,800 plus 69% of the excess of such amount over $4,500,000.
Over $5,000,000	$2,550,800 plus 70% of the excess over $5,000,000.

SOURCE: *National Underwriter Co.,* The Tools and Techniques of Estate Planning, *3rd edition, 1980.*

would be better to sell it for $7000, report a $3000 tax loss, and give the net proceeds to your donee.

Another type of property which might be considered as a gift is property you own in a state other than that of your residence. This would help avoid the costly process known as "ancillary administration," that is, probate in both the state of your residence and the state where the property is situated at the time of your death. It would also reduce the administrative problems of your personal representative.

WILL I DIE FOR ALL I'M WORTH?

Right behind death in seriousness is the threat of death taxes. There are both federal and state taxes to consider. Death is inevitable but you don't (if you plan properly) have to pay (much in) death taxes.

The federal estate tax is a tax levied on the privilege of transferring property at death. Taxes are measured by the value of the property which you transfer—or are deemed to transfer—to others. The phrase "deemed to transfer" is highlighted because the federal estate tax (and the death tax law of many states) reaches not only transfers that a decedent *actually* makes at death, but also certain transfers made during lifetime. In other words, to thwart estate tax avoidance schemes, the federal estate (death) tax is imposed as well on certain lifetime gifts made "to beat the estate tax" or transfers which are essentially the same as dispositions of property made at death. To take an extreme example, assume Bob gives his daughter, Laura, stock worth $100,000 the day before his death. The tax law treats the gift as though it were actually made at Bob's death even though Laura had become the lawful owner of the stock by that date. The $100,000 would therefore become subject to the federal estate tax.

There are many ways of minimizing or even avoiding both federal and state death taxes but they require careful planning *now*, while you are alive and while you have time to make well-considered decisions.

What the Feds Get

It's important to know how the federal estate tax is computed so that you can take full advantage of the various tax minimization tools and techniques available.

In a nutshell, the federal estate tax is computed in five stages. The first stage involves determining the "gross estate," the total of all the property which you own at the date of your death or property which you are deemed to own for the reasons discussed above. If you will examine Fig. 8.2 you will see that "gross estate" is given as item 1, and for our example we are assuming that the amount is $440,000.

The second state is called the "adjusted gross estate" (item 5). This is found by subtracting from your gross estate any allowable funeral and administration expenses (item 2), debts and certain taxes (such as income or property taxes) (item 3), and losses (item 4) incurred during the administration of your estate. Assume these costs aggregate $40,000 ($25,000 of funeral and administrative costs and $15,000 of debts).

The third stage is called the "taxable estate" (item 9). This is computed by subtracting from your adjusted gross estate (item 5) deductions for property you leave to your surviving spouse (the "marital" deduction: item 6) and deductions for property you leave to certain charities (the "charitable" deduction: item 8). In some cases—where a person dies with no surviving spouse and leaves minor children—a deduction is allowed for property left to his or her children (the "orphans'" deduction: item 7).

The orphans' deduction is allowable only if immediately after your death your children have no surviving parent, you leave no surviving spouse, and the property which you leave to each child is includable in your estate. The amount of the deduction is the lower of (a) the net value of the property the child receives or (b) $5000 multiplied by the difference between 21 and the age of your child (or children) at the time of your death. So the deduction for property passing to a two-year-old child, for example, could be as much as $95,000 ($5000 × 19).

Assume for the purposes of our example that you are single, childless, and make no charitable contributions. Therefore, you'd have no marital deduction, charitable deduction, or orphans' deduction.

The fourth stage is the computation of the "estate tax payable before credits" (item 14). It is important to note that certain taxable lifetime gifts (co-called "adjusted taxable gifts": item 10) you made will affect the tax payable at your death. Therefore, you must consider the effect of these lifetime gifts on your executor's need for cash to pay taxes at your death.

Assume all your lifetime gifts were $3000 or less and therefore not subject to tax.

	(1)	Gross Estate			$440,000
	(2)	Funeral and administration expenses			25,000
	(3)	Debts and taxes			15,000
	(4)	Losses			0
		Total Deductions			40,000
Equals	(5)	Adjusted Gross Estate			$400,000
Minus	(6)	Marital deduction (max.-greater of ½ of A.G.E. or $250,000)			0
	(7)	Orphans' deduction			0
	(8)	Charitable deduction			0
		Total Deductions			0
Equals	(9)	Taxable Estate			$400,000
Plus	(10)	Adjusted taxable gifts (post '76 lifetime taxable transfers not included in Gross Estate)			0
Equals	(11)	Tentative tax base (total of taxable estate and adjusted taxable gifts)			$400,000
Compute	(12)	Tentative tax			121,800
Minus	(13)	Gift taxes payable on post '76 gifts			0
Equals	(14)	Tax payable before credits			$121,800
Minus	(15)	Tax credits			
		(a) Unified credit		47,000	
		(b) State death tax credit	State Death Tax Payable 6,800	6,800	
		(c) Credit for tax on prior transfers		0	
		(d) Credit for foreign death taxes		0	
		Total reduction		53,800	
Equals	(16)	Net Federal Estate Tax Payable			$ 68,000
Plus	(17)	Total cash bequests			0
Equals	(18)	Total cash requirements (sum of: 2, 3, state death tax payable, 16, 17)			$114,800

SOURCE: The Tools and Techniques of Estate Planning, 3rd edition, The National Underwriter Company, Cincinnati, Ohio

FIG. 8.2 DETERMINING ESTATE LIQUIDITY NEEDS

The fifth and final stage involves the determination of "net" federal estate tax (item 16). Certain credits are allowed against the federal estate tax otherwise payable. These credits result in a dollar-for-dollar reduction of the estate tax. For example, a credit is allowed (up to certain limits) against the federal estate tax for state inheritance or other death taxes (item 15b) actually paid. Assume your executor must pay $6800 in death taxes to your state government. This is within the estate death tax credit limit. Therefore, a reduction of $6800 will be allowed.

An extremely important credit that will be available to almost every individual's estate is the "unified credit" (item 15a)—the credit described above that is allowed for both "lifetime and deathtime" gifts. To the extent the credit is not used up during your lifetime, it will be available to offset taxes when you die. The credit is $47,000. That is equivalent to allowing you to own and transfer up to $175,625 worth of otherwise taxable property at your death and have no federal estate tax liability.

After reducing the estate tax payable for any of the allowable credits, the net federal estate tax (item 16) is payable by your executor in cash, generally within nine months of your death. The net federal estate tax payable in the example is $6800. But note that total cash requirements (item 18) would be $114,800. That's because your executor will have to pay off debts and other estate settlement costs.

The State of State Death Taxes

Almost every estate will have to pay state death taxes regardless of the size of the estate. Certain deductions allowed under federal estate tax law (such as the marital deduction) are not available under many state death tax laws. So many estates that will pay little or no federal estate taxes will have sizable state death tax costs.

Furthermore, federal law exempts certain transfers that are not protected under many state laws. For example, under federal law, employer-generated death benefits under a pension plan may be totally excludable from estate taxation. These same benefits may be totally subject to tax for state death tax purposes.

Also, the amount of property exempted from tax under federal law is larger than that exempted by the laws of most states.

The rates at which transfers or receipts of property are taxed vary widely from state to state. Some states have graduated rates similar to the federal tax law while others, such as Pennsylvania, have flat rates (e.g., 6% for transfers to children and spouses and 15% to siblings and friends) that do not grow progressively as the size of your estate increases. Some states have sizable deductions or exemptions not allowed by other states.

Because the impact of state death taxes can be so significant, many individuals go "domicile shopping" at retirement. In other words they look for a state with favorable rates, exemptions, and deductions. If your estate is large enough, it may pay to do some looking around before you settle down.

THE ALPHABET SYSTEM OF ESTATE PLANNING

The federal and state tax laws described above can be a disaster to someone who has not planned. But looking at the problem positively, the tax laws provide an opportunity for great savings if you invest the time to take advantage of them. You can maximize the financial security of your family by judicially using a system of tax-oriented arrangements and maneuvers.

These tools and techniques of estate planning can be categorized into what one estate planner calls the "alphabet" system. It is comprised of a *C*—creation of tax exempt wealth; four *D*s—*d*ivide, *d*educt, *d*efer, and *d*iscount; an *E*—*e*limination or reduction of tax on existing wealth; and an *F*—*f*reezing techniques. Let's look at these one at a time.

C—Creation of Tax-Exempt Wealth

Here are some tools that can provide security for your family—at no death tax cost:

1. Life insurance can be arranged so that it is federal estate tax free, exempt from state death taxes, and is not subject to either income or gift taxes. This is accomplished with the advice and guidance of your insurance agent and your counsel—through third party ownership. Your spouse, child, or irrevocable trust on their behalf owns and is the beneficiary of the insurance.

2. Qualified retirement plans such as pension- and profit-sharing plans can provide estate tax free death benefits—not only at your death but also, if arranged properly, at your spouse's death. Name the trustee of a "family" (nonmarital) trust as beneficiary. This could pro-

vide income to the surviving spouse for his or her lifetime. If pension proceeds are received over more than one tax year, they will be excludable in your estate. Although the trust provides substantial economic security for your spouse, it is limited so that, at the death of the spouse none of the assets will be in that person's estate.

3. There are certain plans available to corporate employees known as "Death Benefit Only (DBO) plans." These arrangements allow substantial amounts of income to be paid from a corporation to the surviving spouse of an employee but do not generate any federal estate tax (and in some states may be exempt from state death tax as well). For example, your employer might call you in and say, "In return for your valuable and continued services—and in addition to your other salary and your corporate pension, our firm will make the following promise. If you die between now and age 65 while working for us, we will pay your surviving spouse $20,000 a year for 10 years." Although the income she receives would be taxable as salary to her, the entire $200,000 could be federal estate tax free.

D—Dividing the Estate

Each time a new taxpaying entity can be created, income taxes are saved and estate accumulation is stimulated.

Some of the more popular "dividing" techniques are as follows:

1. Income-producing property may be given to minor children either outright or in a trust. The difference between your tax bracket and the children's tax bracket represents income tax savings. Furthermore, since each child has his or her own $1000 personal exemption, by increasing the amount of income that can be received within your family without paying tax, you have conquered by dividing. Income paid to each of four minor children, for example, creates four new tax exempt "wallets." In total, four children can receive up to $4000 of income each year—every year—without paying tax.

2. Short-term trusts (also called "reversionary" or "Clifford" trusts) are trusts which last for the lifetime of the beneficiary or for at least 10 years and one day more. At the end of the specified period of time, all the property you have placed into the trust comes back to you.

But during the term of the trust the income earned by trust property is taxed to the trust or its low bracket beneficiary(ies) rather than to you at your higher bracket. The income tax savings can be used to provide income and financial security for your beneficiaries. For example, Steve and Rosetta, who have never made any gifts in prior years, could place $150,000 worth of high grade bonds in trust for their two-year-old son. The trust would last 15 years. Then trust assets would return to Steve and Rosetta. During the 15 years all the income would be taxed—not to Steve and Rosetta but to their son, who is in a much lower bracket.

3. Establishing a corporation is like creating a "tax wallet" because it permits individuals who are in high personal income tax brackets to split income between themselves and their corporation. This technique projects the progressive nature of our income tax structure against itself by dividing income into two (lower) tax brackets and also takes advantage of the lower corporate rates. For instance, $100,000 of taxable income would subject a single taxpayer to about $50,000 in tax. If that same person split income evenly between himself or herself and the corporation he or she established ($50,000 each), the tax would drop to personal tax (about $18,000) and corporate tax (about $9000)—a total of approximately $27,000 for a saving of around $23,000 ($50,000 minus $27,000) a year.

4. The estate tax marital deduction for certain property your spouse receives at your death allows you to pass—estate tax free—up to $250,000 or one-half of your adjusted gross estate, whichever is larger and helps you take full advantage of your surviving spouse's unified credit.

D—Deduct

Deductible dollars you set aside to provide for your own retirement are more valuable than nondeductible (expensive) dollars. Here are just some of the ways of using deductions in estate planning:

1. Qualified corporate pension and profit-sharing plans allow a tax deduction for money put aside for your own retirement. These are among the most important of all estate planning tools.

2. HR-10 (Keogh) plans are excellent means of providing tax deductible retirement security for a sole proprietor or partner. These plans can also provide substantial federal estate tax-free death benefits.

3. IRAs (Individual Retirement Accounts) can be established for those who are not covered by a qualified retirement plan such as those mentioned above. This is yet another way to take a tax deduction for money you set aside for your own retirement and is an important estate planning device.

4. Latest in the estate planner's arsenal is the simplified employee pension plan. These can be "super IRAs" since the maximum $7500 deductible limit is considerably higher than the $1500 deduction limitation in an IRA.

D—Defer

The progressive tax rates (rates that increase as the income or size of the estate increases) penalize taxpayers whose minimum earnings—or estates—are high. Of course this makes it difficult to attain and retain financial wealth. But there are tools and techniques that help minimize the total tax burden by spreading income over more than one tax year or defer the tax to a later period so that the taxpayer can invest money otherwise payable in taxes for a longer period of time. Some of these deferral devices include the following:

1. Private annuities are arrangements under which one person transfers property to another (usually younger) family member. In return, the recipient promises to pay an income to the original owner for as long as he or she lives. The income tax attributable to the gain realized on the "sale" is spread over a number of years (the lifetime of the person transferring the property) and therefore reduced.

    For example, a 65-year-old farmer owns farmland worth $100,000. He paid only $10,000 for it many years ago. He'd like to sell it to his son but doesn't want to pay tax on his $90,000 gain this year. He's planning on retiring sometime in the next five years and he'd like to pay the tax over as many years as possible. His son could promise to pay him $12,445 a year for the rest of the father's life. Of each payment the farmer receives, part is a tax-free recovery of his $10,000 investment, part is reportable as a portion of his $90,000 capital gains, and the balance would be ordinary income.

The total tax payable would be thousands of dollars less than if the farmer took a lump sum payment in a year when he had substantial income from other sources.

2. An installment sale, like a private annuity, is an alternative to a lump sale. It enables the taxable gain to be spread over a number of years. That may drop it into lower tax brackets because the recipient has less taxable income (such as at retirement) or greater deductions.

3. Certain selective deferred compensation plans are available to corporate employees to help defer income from high tax-bracket years (such as working years) to lower bracket years (such as retirement years) so that you can net more after taxes. For instance, instead of taking $100,000 salary of today, a 60-year-old married taxpayer employee defers receipt of a portion of it for five years and then takes the deferred money over a number of years, when his or her "outside" income is lower.

4. Qualified pension and profit-sharing plans are also useful in deferring taxes since typically you pay no tax on income received or capital gains earned on your behalf within the retirement plan's trust until you receive payments from the trust.

5. Depreciable real estate—real estate that yields high write-offs in years when you are earning large amounts of taxable income—enables you to defer the tax burden until a date when you are either in a lower tax bracket or have additional deductions available.

D—Discount

After you have done all you can to build your estate to its maximum and reduce the income and estate tax burdens on it, you may still have an estate tax payable. There are two ways to—in effect—pay your federal estate taxes at a discount:

1. Government bonds (no longer issued by the federal government but still available through trust or bond departments or banks and stock brokers) called "flower bonds" are sold at less than par value but are redeemed by the government at par (plus accrued interest) in payment of the federal estate tax. Unfortunately, the "discount" is re-

duced because the bond must be included in your gross estate at its par value and may be used to pay only the federal estate tax—not any of the other death costs.

2. Life insurance can be purchased on your life by a family member or by a trust for an annual premium that is between three and six percent of the face (death) value of the policy. Proceeds of such insurance should pass to your beneficiaries free of income tax, estate tax, inheritance tax, and probate costs. They can be used to pay death taxes, debts, and other probate costs and administrative expenses.

E—Elimination or Reduction of Tax on Existing Wealth

Taxes can be eliminated or reduced—even on assets you already own—by either of these methods:

1. Although taxable gifts you make during lifetime may affect the rate at which your estate will be taxed at your death, substantial amounts of gifts—and all the appreciation from the time of each gift on—can and should be removed from your estate by lifetime gifts, thus eliminating the estate tax. Through careful planning, substantial amounts of gifts can be made free of gift tax.

2. Charitable deduction techniques allow unlimited gifts to charity at no gift or estate tax cost. A number of creative techniques enable these charitable gifts to be used to increase the income and capital of your family.

F—Freezing Techniques

How can we stop the growth in your estate and shift growth to a new generation? Estate planners call these "freezing" techniques because they freeze the growth in your estate and help you shift growth to a new generation. Here are four popular freezing techniques:

1. Preferred stock recapitalizations: If you are presently in business in a corporate form you may want to consider changing the nature of your stock so that you own nonappreciating preferred stock. Then you could give away (or sell) to your children or other relatives

common stock which represents the future growth in your business. There are unlimited variations of this concept.

2. Installment sale—private annuity: These two techniques are means of exchanging property for cash that will be paid to you over an extended period of time. For instance, if you were 65 years old, you could transfer farmland worth $100,000 to your son in return for his promise to pay you an income of $12,445 a year for the rest of your life—no matter how long you live. Since you can no longer own the property itself (that is growing in your children's hands), at your death the asset will not be includable in your estate. Much of the cash you receive through the installment sale or private annuity can be given away or used for current living expenses.

3. Family partnership: This is a device similar to the preferred stock recapitalization in the sense that it allows you to spread not only income but also capital and have that capital grow in the hands of your children or other relatives. You give interests in your proprietorship or existing partnership to your children. They own the interest (and they, rather than you, will be taxable on the income it produces) but you continue to run the business. In this manner the family partnership avoids many of the problems of joint ownerships with children.

4. Diversions of services, capital, and business opportunities are the fourth type of freezing technique. These are known to estate planners as "self-help" planning techniques. By devoting your time, money, and business opportunities to enrich your children rather than yourself, you are building their security and at the same time reducing or eliminating the growth in your own estate at no tax cost. For instance, a father could consult for or even work in his son's business. By charging no fee or salary, he could enrich his son at no gift, income, or estate tax cost.

WRAPPING IT UP

We have seen that the estate planning process is a continual exercise in the accumulation, conservation, and distribution of your estate in the manner that most effectively achieves your own goals. But there are forces that stand between you and the accomplishment of financial security for yourself and your family. These include death-related costs, improper asset management, insufficient cash to pay debts and expenses, improper or insufficient use of the vehicles of asset transfer, and the costs that will be incurred if you become disabled.

The estate planning process itself consists of gathering data, identifying the potential problems, formulating a plan, delegating the responsibilities for executing that arrangement, testing the plan, implementing it, and periodic and regularly scheduled reviews.

One of the key tools of estate planning is a properly arranged will. Important privileges are forfeited if you should die without one. These include the right to decide who will receive your property, how that property will be transferred at your death, and who will administer your estate. Without a will you also forfeit the right to nominate a guardian and decide who will bear the burden of taxes and administrative expenses.

Your will should be clear and unambiguous. It should be flexible enough to encompass the changes in tax laws as well as in your family's circumstances which may occur after it is drawn. Your will should as effectively as possible minimize or eliminate federal and state death taxes. Fortunately, because change occurs so rapidly, your will itself can be modified by a codicil or revoked by a later will.

At death, the process known as estate administration or "probate" occurs. This is essentially a three-part process in which the executor you have selected (or the administrator you neglected to select and which the court has selected for you) (1) collects your assets, (2) pays your debts and taxes, and (3) distributes what is left to the appropriate beneficiaries.

Another major tool for estate owners of moderate and large estates is the trust. A trust relationship arises when one party, the grantor, transfers property to a second party, the trustee, for the benefit of third parties, the beneficiaries. A trust may be testamentary or *inter vivos* and revocable or irrevocable. The tax consequences of placing property in trust depend on which of these types of trusts are used. The primary purposes of trusts are to save income and estate taxes, provide asset management, and conserve the property you place in the trust.

It is often better to give than to receive—especially if you're trying to reduce the estate tax burden your executor will face. The gift tax law imposes a graduated tax on the right to transfer property during your lifetime. The estate tax is essentially a levy on the privilege of making gifts at death. It is unified (coordinated) with the gift tax so that the rates and credits are the same for both. Taxable gifts you make during your lifetime may affect rates at which your remaining estate will be taxed. After the estate tax has been computed, certain credits will be allowed. The net tax payable is the result. This amount is usually payable within nine months of the day you die. Your executor must also have cash to pay state death taxes.

There are many tools and techniques available to help you accumulate, conserve, and distribute your estate. The most essential of these tools can be classified into the following categories:

1. Creation of tax-exempt wealth.

2. Dividing wealth among family members.

3. Deducting money you set aside for your own retirement and family security.

4. Deferring the payment of taxes whenever possible to shift the impact of taxes to years when you'll be in a lower bracket.

5. Discounting—to pay estate taxes through either flower bonds or life insurance at a "discount."

6. Elimination or reduction of tax on existing wealth.

7. Freezing techniques—stopping the growth in your estate and shifting it to your children and other beneficiaries.

The tools and techniques—and the experts who can make them work for you —are available, but you must make the first step. You must call together the estate planning team: your attorney, accountant, trust officer, and life insurance agent. After all, it's your estate!

9
TIMETABLE FOR RETIREMENT PLANNING

IN YOUR 40s

1. Periodically send a "statement of earnings" postcard to Social Security requesting your wage records to assure that they are being properly credited to your account and correct address. Social Security record errors become difficult to have changed further back than three years. A request postcard may be obtained at your local Social Security office. (Keep several on hand.)

2. If you have a pension, understand the details of the plan and what it promises.

3. Inventory your assets and project an estimated retirement income. Financial planning is something you don't want to postpone until you're 60 or 65. Since it takes time to acquire assets, start early—not later than in your forties. Develop a plan that will supplement com-

pany income and Social Security, if necessary, by considering the following options:

a)   Start a long-term savings program with automatic payroll deductions, certificates of deposit, or various savings plans. A good plan would be one that pays from day of deposit to day of withdrawal and compounds "continuously."

b)   If you have an employee contribution plan, increase the annuity that you will receive upon retirement by increasing your personal contribution now.

c)   If you are eligible to contribute to a tax-deferred annuity account, investigate the advantages. (Employees of hospitals, foundations, nonprofit organizations, and public schools usually qualify.)

d)   If you are self-employed or without a company pension program, consider opening a Keogh or IRA account. The money can go into various investment vehicles and accumulates tax-deferred interest. Inquire at your bank, savings and loan association, insurance agency, or brokerage firm.

e)   If you earn above the FICA earnings base and your company participates in the bond-a-matic plan administered under Social Security, you may elect to continue the regular deductions until the end of the year; the additional money is then placed in Government Series EE Bonds in your account.

f)   Consider a savings plan which would shelter your interest income during your high earnings/high tax years until you are presumably in a lower tax bracket. Some considerations include: Government Series EE Bonds, Freedom Shares, Deferred Annuities, Municipal Bond Mutual Funds. See your banker, insurance agent, or broker.

4. If you have not already done so, make out a will! If you have a will, review it regularly every three years *or* if you move to another state *or* if your family circumstances change.)

5. The best way to be young for your years at 60 and 70 is to begin to take better care of yourself at 40 and 50.

IN YOUR 50s

1. Continue to keep in touch with Social Security as to the accuracy of your withholdings.

2. Update your financial plan, keeping in mind increasing inflation. If you're living a very comfortable lifestyle today, you won't be able to continue that lifestyle in retirement unless you do some realistic planning.

3. To determine whether or not you are fully vested in your company's pension plan—that is, whether you have worked long enough to qualify for pension benefits at retirement age—consult the personnel director of your company.

4. If you have accumulated a large amount of assets, in order to save on taxes you might need an elaborate estate plan which includes a type of trust fund. Check with an estate planner or bank official. Whether or not you end up employing their services, their suggestions are worth considering.

5. Check to make sure the beneficiary designation on your life insurance policy is up-to-date. Have you provided for alternate or contingent beneficiaries? Remember that life insurance and company retirement plan death benefits do not pass to your heirs under your will; they go instead to the designated beneficiary.

6. Take advantage of a preretirement seminar which may be scheduled through your company or available in your local community. The purpose of these seminars is to provide you with practical information on a variety of retirement matters such as: housing, community resources, Social Security, Medicare, financial planning, leisure opportunities, legal affairs, and health maintenance; and they help you develop realistic expectations of retirement.

IN YOUR EARLY 60s

1. This is an ideal opportunity to determine whether early retirement (between 62 and 65) would be to your financial (and emotional?) advantage. Check with both your personnel officer and the Social

Security Administration. For Social Security benefits, it generally takes you 12 years to make up the financial reduction of early retirement at age 62.

2. Begin to put in order the documents necessary to process Social Security benefits:

   a)   Husband's Social Security card

   b)   Wife's Social Security card

   c)   Proof of husband's age

   d)   Proof of wife's age

   e)   Your marriage certificate

   f)   Copy of your latest income tax "withholding statement" (Form W–2). If you are self-employed, a copy of your latest income-tax return.

3. If you decide upon early retirement, determine whether your company medical insurance will carry over prior to age 65 and Medicare (and after).

4. If you are thinking of selling your home, you may want to wait until you are 65 to take advantage of the special tax breaks. By all means see a tax expert before you sell.

5. Don't put your will away and forget it as years go by. Wills should be reviewed and revised periodically. Through a properly prepared will, your property will pass on to your heirs exactly as you wish.

6. Determine what ongoing financial obligations you have for how long; for example, mortgage, or education payments.

7. If you have been part of a payroll savings plan, you may wish to transfer Series EE to Series HH bonds, arranging bond maturities to fall at staggered intervals. While you hold onto the principal, having the interest become available semiannually may answer your need for supplemental income.

8. Practice living on your anticipated retirement income for a month or so.

BEFORE RETIREMENT

1. Know your retirement income. Estimate your cost of living: rent, food, insurance, health care, transportation, clothing, recreation, etc. In order to get a complete financial picture, you'll need to know what you'll have, as well as what you'll need to spend.

2. Have the personnel officer of your company determine the following:

   a) Exactly how much your pension will be

   b) What company or bank will send your pension and when your first check will arrive

   c) What you can do about accrued vacation time

   d) Whether there are any special annuitant benefits

   e) Whether you qualify for supplemental medical or hospital insurance

3. Register with your Social Security office at least three months prior to retirement (processing records takes time). Take with you the necessary documents to apply. Generally you can avoid the crowds and a waiting line at the Social Security office if you plan to apply late in the afternoon and/or late in the week.

4. If you anticipate a second career, get a copy of the pamphlet *You Can Work and Still Get Social Security* from your local Social Security office.

5. If you have changed jobs several times, you could be entitled to partial pensions based on a company's contributions to its pension plan while you worked there. Vesting qualifications vary greatly. Check.

6. Certain retirement benefits are available to veterans. To see if you qualify, check with the Veterans Administration or any of the local service clubs.

7. If you have little or no cash income or assets, you may be eligible to receive Supplementary Security Income (SSI) and food stamps. Check with the Social Security office or your county welfare office.

8. Begin "setting your house in order." Compile your important papers, something your family can rely on should something happen to you. File the following in a safe deposit box or disaster-proof container at home:

a) Birth certificates, adoption papers, marriage certificate, divorce record, and death certificates

b) Military service records

c) Pension papers

d) The wills of you and your spouse

e) Mortgages, security agreements, installment contracts, and other evidences of your debt

f) Copies of all contracts you hold, abstracts of titles and deeds

g) Lists of debts owed to you

h) All stocks, bonds, and other certificates of investment plus notations of all savings accounts

9. If your car is more than four years old, you should think about dropping the collision insurance you have; it might not be worth its cost to you. If you're thinking about buying a new car, it's a good idea to check with your insurance agent on which models are less expensive to insure.

10. If you receive a lump-sum distribution from a qualified pension or profit-sharing plan, you can avoid any current income tax on those funds by transferring them to an Individual Retirement Account within 60 days.

11. Don't procrastinate in making realistic plans for your day-to-day living.

AFTER RETIREMENT

1. If you become 65 but continue to work, you are still eligible for Medicare benefits. Initiate procedures on your own. You'll need your birth certificate and Social Security card.

2. On the average, Medicare pays 72% of hospital costs and 54% of doctor bills. You may wish to consider buying private insurance to dovetail Medicare coverage. What you will need will be supplemental insurance, not major medical. Questions on Medicare Supplemental insurance may be directed to:

> Health Insurance Institute
> 1850 K Street, N.W.
> Washington, D.C. 20006

3. One tax advantage occurs once you reach the age of 65. You are now entitled to collect double exemptions.

4. Although Social Security benefits are tax-free, part or all of your pension will be subject to income tax. If you are required to estimate your taxes quarterly, check out the procedures and appropriate forms with your tax accountant or the IRS. Become a knowledgeable "tax" expert yourself.

5. If you sell your home after 55, part or all of the profit will be tax free. A guide to tax information for retirees, entitled *Tax Facts* is available through the American Association of Retired Persons. Consult your local chapter or write to:

> Tax Facts
> c/o NRTA-AARP
> 1909 K Street, N.W.
> Washington, D.C. 20049

6. All states have special departments that can provide you with specific information about agencies and organizations operating within your local area for retirees. To receive a directory of the state agencies, write to:

> U.S. Department of Health and Human Services
> Office of Human Development
> Administration on Aging
> Washington, D.C. 20201

7. Some auto insurance companies offer premium reductions to drivers of retirement age. Be sure to ask your agent.

8. Home repairs cost more from year to year. Ask for a property insurance assessment every year to be certain your property is adequately covered from fire and other hazards. Avoid suffering a loss you can't afford to replace.

9. If your car is more than four years old, you should think about dropping the collision insurance you have; it might not be worth its cost to you. If you're thinking about buying a new car, it's a good idea to check with your insurance agent on which models are less expensive to insure.

10

IMPORTANT QUESTIONS AND ANSWERS—About Social Security, IRAs, and Keogh Plans

SOCIAL SECURITY

What benefits are provided under the Old-Age, Survivors, and Disability Program (OASDI)?

- Monthly benefits for workers who are retired, or partially retired, and at least 62 years old, and monthly benefits for their spouses and dependents.
- Monthly benefits for disabled workers and their dependents.
- Monthly benefits for the survivors of deceased workers.
- A lump-sum death benefit payment for each worker.

How can I check on my Social Security earnings record?

By filling out form OAR-7004 (Request for Statement of Earnings). The form (see Fig. 10.1) can be picked up at any district office and must be mailed to the Social Security Administration, P.O. Box 57,

REQUEST FOR STATEMENT OF EARNINGS

SOCIAL SECURITY → NUMBER

DATE OF BIRTH →

MONTH	DAY	YEAR

Please send a statement of my social security earnings to:

NAME _____

STREET & NUMBER _____

CITY & STATE _____ ZIP CODE _____

} Print Name and Address In Ink Or Use Type-writer

SIGN YOUR NAME HERE
(DO NOT PRINT) _____

Sign your own name only. Under the law, information in your social security record is confidential and anyone who signs another person's name can be prosecuted.
If you have changed your name from that shown on your social security card, please copy your name below exactly as it appears on your card.

☆ U.S. Government Printing Office: 1978—270-383

YOUR SOCIAL SECURITY EARNINGS RECORD

For a *free* statement of earnings credited to your social security record, complete other side of this card. Use card for only *one* person.

All covered wages and self-employment income are reported under your *name* and social security *number.* So show your name and number *exactly* as on your card. If you ever used another name or number, show this too.

Be sure to put a stamp on this card or it won't be delivered. You can mail the card in a stamped envelope if you wish.

If you have a separate question about social security, or want to discuss your statement when you get it, the people at any social security office will be glad to help you.

Form SSA-7004 PC (1-79)
(Prior Editions May Be Used Until Supply Is Exhausted)

POSTAGE REQUIRED

SOCIAL SECURITY ADMINISTRATION
P. O. BOX 57
BALTIMORE, MARYLAND 21203

FIGURE 10.1

Baltimore, Maryland, 21203. The form must include your name, address, Social Security number, and the date of birth. The Social Security Administration will mail you a statement of total wages and self-employment income credited to your account, together with an estimate of benefits based on your earnings up to the date the estimate is requested. If a portion of your earnings is not credited, you can ask the district office how to go about correcting the records.

Are Social Security benefits subject to federal taxes?

No. All benefits, whether payable to retired or disabled workers, dependents or survivors, are exempt from federal income tax. (Rev. Rul. 70-217, 1970-1 C.B. 12.) Neither the value of survivor's benefits nor the lump-sum death benefit is includable in the worker's gross estate for federal estate tax purposes. (Rev. Rul. 67-277, 1967-2 C.B. 323; Rev. Rul. 55-87, 1955-1 C.B. 112.)

How are quarters of coverage determined for an employee?

1. For years prior to 1978, an employee in covered employment receives one quarter of coverage for each quarter in which earnings were $50 or more.

2. For years prior to 1978, each quarter of the year is counted as a quarter of coverage if the employee's total wages (or wages and self-employment income) for any calendar year exceed the maximum Social Security earnings base for that year. This is true even if the employee receives no wages in some of the quarters.

   Example: Mr. Smith was unemployed from January 1, 1977, to April 1, 1977. During the last nine months of the year he worked in covered employment and earned over $16,500 (the maximum Social Security earnings base for 1977). He is credited with four quarters of coverage for 1977 even though he received no wages in the first quarter.

3. For 1978, an employee received one quarter of coverage for each $250 of earnings, up to a maximum of four. For 1979, one quarter of coverage is received for each $260 of earnings up to a maximum of four.

Example: Mrs. Hall worked for two months in 1979 and earned $700. She was credited with two quarters of coverage for the year because she received one quarter of coverage for each $260 of earnings, up to a maximum of four. In order to receive four quarters of coverage in 1979, Mrs. Hall would have needed earnings totaling $1,040 ($260 × 4 = $1,040). This method of determining quarters of coverage will be used for years after 1979 also, but the measure of earnings ($260 in 1979) will automatically increase each year to take account of increases in average wages.

Are quarters of coverage used in determining the size of my Social Security benefits?

No, quarters of coverage are used only to determine your insured status. The law provides an exact method for computing benefits based on your average monthly earnings. Calendar years are used in making the computation.

How do I become fully insured?

By acquiring a sufficient number of quarters of coverage to meet *either* of the following two tests:

1. You are fully insured if you have 40 quarters of coverage (a total of 10 years in covered work). Once you have acquired 40 quarters of coverage you are fully insured for life, even if you spend no further time in covered employment or covered self-employment.

2. You are fully insured if: (a) you have at least six quarters of coverage, and (b) you have acquired at least as many quarters of coverage as there are years elapsing after 1950 (or, if later, after the year in which you become disabled, reach or will reach age 62, or die, whichever occurs first.)

Tests serve only to determine the number of quarters of coverage you need to be fully insured. It doesn't matter when these quarters of coverage were acquired so long as it was after 1936. Also, in applying test No. 2, it is not necessary to count the quarters of coverage, whether within or without the elapsed period, to determine whether you have the required number.

How do I determine the number of quarters of coverage needed to be fully insured for old-age benefits?

Count the number of years after 1950 (or, if later, after the year in which you attained age 21), and before the year of your 62nd birthday. (But do not count a year of which any part was in an established period of disability.) Generally, this is the minimum number of quarters of coverage you will need to be fully insured. However, you must have at least six quarters of coverage to be fully insured; and you are fully insured in any event if you have 40 or more quarters of coverage.

Example 1. Mr. Brown applied for old-age benefits in 1980; he attained age 62 in 1978. He needed 27 quarters of coverage to be fully insured (there are 27 years between 1950 and 1978, the year of his 62nd birthday).

Example 2. Mr. Jones applied for old-age benefits in 1980, the year he reached age 65. He needed at least 27 quarters of coverage to be fully insured (there are 27 years between 1950 and 1978, the year of his 63rd birthday).

Example 3. Miss Smith applied for old-age benefits in 1980, the year she attained age 65. She needed 25 quarters for coverage to be fully insured (there are 25 years between 1950 and 1976, the year of her 62nd birthday).

Do I need to file an application for old-age benefits?

Yes. You can file application within three months before the first month in which you are entitled to benefits. The earliest date for filing would be three months before the month of your 62nd birthday.

As evidence of age, you must ordinarily submit one or more of the following: birth certificate; church record of birth or baptism; Census Bureau notification of registration of birth; hospital birth record; physician's birth record; family Bible; naturalization record; immigration record; military record; passport; school record; vaccination record; insurance policy; labor union or fraternal record; marriage record; other evidence of probate value.

Can I receive old-age benefits regardless of the amount of my wealth or the amount of my retirement income?

Yes. You are entitled to old-age benefits regardless of how wealthy you are. Also, the amount of retirement income you receive (e.g. dividends, interest, rents, etc.) is immaterial. You are subject to loss of benefits only because of excess earnings arising from your personal services.

Can a husband and wife both receive old-age benefits?

Yes. If each is entitled to receive benefits based on their own earnings record, each can receive old-age benefits independently of the other's benefits. However, a woman who is entitled to both an old-age benefit and a wife's benefit cannot receive both in full.

Is the wife of a retired or disabled worker entitled to benefits?

Yes, the wife of a man who is receiving old-age or disability benefits is entitled to a wife's benefit if: (1) she is at least 62 years old, or she is caring for at least one child, under age 18 or disabled, who is entitled to a child's benefit based on the retired or disabled worker's Social Security account; and (2) she is not entitled to an old-age or disability benefit that is larger than one-half her husband's benefit; and (3) she has filed application for benefits.

Is the divorced *wife of a retired or disabled worker entitled to a wife's benefit?*

She is entitled to a divorced wife's benefit if: (1) she is at least 62 years old; (2) she was married to the worker for *10 years or longer* before the date of divorce; (3) she has not remarried, or her subsequent marriage has ended in death or divorce; (4) she is not entitled to an old-age benefit or disability benefit that is larger than one-half her divorced husband's benefit; and (5) she has filed application for benefits.

Under what circumstances is the widow of an insured worker entitled to benefits if she has no child in her care?

She is entitled to a widow's benefit if: (1) she is at least 60 years old; (2) her husband was fully insured at death; (3) she is not entitled to an old-age or disability benefit that is equal to or larger than her widow's benefit; (4) she has filed application for a widow's benefit or was receiving a wife's benefit when her husband died.

Can the divorced wife of a deceased man qualify for a widow's benefit?

Yes, if she was married to him for *at least 10 years* before the divorce. In addition, she must be at least 60 years old and must meet the other requirements for entitlement to a widow's benefit. The benefit she receives is called a "surviving divorced wife's benefit." If a woman was entitled to a "divorced wife's benefit" before her former husband's death, she will be entitled to a "surviving divorced wife's benefit."

What is the earliest age at which a woman can receive a widow's benefit?

She can elect to start receiving a reduced widow's benefit at age 60, but a disabled widow can start receiving benefits at age 50.

Can a widow lose her benefits by working?

Yes. Although benefits are payable regardless of how wealthy a widow is, she will lose some or all of her benefits if she is under age 72 but over age 64 and earnings exceed $4500 in 1979; or if she is under age 65 for all of 1979 and earnings exceed $3480.

What is the amount of the Social Security lump sum death payment?

A lump sum death benefit of $255 is paid when an insured worker dies. The lump sum is payable in addition to any monthly survivor benefits that are due. The death benefit is payable for every insured worker.

What earnings are used in computing a person's Average Indexed Monthly Earnings (AIME)?

Generally, the AIME is based on Social Security earnings for years after 1950. This includes wages earned as an employee and/or self-employment income.

Only earnings credited to the person's Social Security account can be used and maximum earnings creditable for specific years are as follows:

$29,700 for 1981
$25,900 for 1980
$22,900 for 1979
$17,700 for 1978
$16,500 for 1977
$15,300 for 1976
$14,100 for 1975
$13,200 for 1974
$10,800 for 1973
$ 9,000 for 1972
$ 7,800 for years 1968–1971
$ 6,600 for years 1966–1967
$ 4,800 for years 1959–1965
$ 4,200 for years 1955–1958
$ 3,600 for years 1951–1954
$ 3,000 for years 1940–1950
$ 3,000 for each employee for years 1937–1939

Do benefits increase when the cost-of-living increases?

The Social Security Act provides for automatic increases in benefits and in the maximum earnings base (earnings subject to Social Security taxes) due to changing economic conditions.

The automatic increases are determined by increases in the Consumer Price Index (CPI) prepared by the Department of Labor. Each year the Secretary of Health and Human Services (i.e., the Social Security Administration) determines whether the "base quarter" in the calendar year is a "cost-of-living computation quarter."

Whenever the Secretary determines that the base quarter in a calendar year is a cost-of-living computation quarter, benefits will be increased, starting with June of that year. Automatic cost-of-living benefit increases are based on the rise in the Consumer Price Index from the first quarter of one year to the first quarter of the following year.

Benefits are automatically increased by the same percentage (rounded to the nearest $\frac{1}{10}$ of 1%) as the percentage by which the Consumer Price Index for the cost-of-living computation quarter exceeds the Consumer Price Index for the later of: (1) the most recent cost-of-living computation quarter or; (2) the most recent calendar quarter in which a general benefit increase became effective.

The maximum earnings base will be automatically adjusted each January after 1982 if average taxable wages have increased sufficiently. Most benefits may be increased, including the special benefits payable to persons age 72 or over who are not fully insured. Also, the amount of excess earnings that results in loss of benefits may be increased whenever there is an automatic cost-of-living benefit increase.

Can I obtain higher old-age benefits by working past retirement age?

Yes, in two ways. First, if you continue working you will receive an increase in old-age benefits equal to 1% for each year ($\frac{1}{12}$ of 1% for each month) you work between ages 65 and 72. Note that this is not an increase in your PIA. Other benefits based on your PIA, such as those payable to your wife, are not affected.

For workers reaching age 62 after 1978, the delayed retirement credit is 3% per year (¼ of 1% per month). However, since workers reaching age 62 in 1980 will not reach age 65 until 1983, this provision will have relatively little effect before 1984. The delayed retirement credit is also payable to a worker's surviving spouse receiving a widow's or widower's benefit, beginning in June 1978.

Second, work past retirement age frequently results in a higher AIME. In determining the number of years to be used in the computation, the year in which you reach retirement age, and succeeding years, are not counted. But those years can be selected as years of highest earnings.

Can I lose some or all of my Social Security benefits by working?

Yes, if you are under age 72 but over age 64 and earn over $5500 in 1981. A person who is age 72 or older will not lose benefits by working no matter how much he or she earns. Beginning in 1982, the age at which the retirement test no longer applies will be lowered from 72 to 70, and for beneficiaries age 65 and over the annual exempt amount will be increased to $6000. After 1982, the $6000 level will be increased automatically as wage levels rise. The annual exempt amounts for beneficiaries under age 65 will also be increased each year as age levels rise.

What are the general rules for loss of benefits because of excess earnings?

If you are age 72 or older, no benefits will be lost because of your earnings. If you are under age 72, the following rules apply:

- If not more than $5500 is earned in 1981 by a beneficiary over age 64, no benefits will be lost for that year.
- If more than $5500 is earned in 1981 by a beneficiary over age 64, $1 of benefits will ordinarily be lost for each $2 of earnings over $5000.
- If not more than $4080 is earned in 1981 by a beneficiary under age 65 for the entire year, no benefits will be lost for that year.
- If more than $4080 is earned in 1981 by a beneficiary under age 65 for the entire year, $1 of benefits will ordinarily be lost for each $2 of earnings over $3720.

What is the rate of Social Security tax for a self-employed person?

The tax on self-employed persons is imposed under the Self-Employment Contributions Act. The maximum earning base (the maximum amount of net earnings subject to tax) is $29,700 in 1981, subject to increases in future years. Net earnings in excess of this amount are not taxable.

The self-employment tax consists of two taxes: the OASDI tax (the tax for old-age, survivors, and disability insurance) and the Hospital Insurance Tax (for the hospital insurance part of Medicare). For 1981, the rate of the OASDI tax is 8.00%, and the rate of the HI tax is 1.30%, resulting in a combined rate of 9.30%. Thus, the maximum tax in 1981 (for a self-employed person earning at least $29,700) is $2,762.10.

Must a Social Security beneficiary who works pay Social Security taxes?

Yes, even though you are receiving Social Security benefits, you must pay taxes at the same rate as other individuals.

Example: In 1981, Mr. Anderson, age 73, receives $183.50 a month on old-age benefits; he also works as an employee and earns $6000 for the year. Mr. Anderson must pay $399.00 in Social Security taxes for 1981.

When should a person file for retirement benefits?

A person should contact the nearest Social Security district office within three months of retirement age (age 62 or later). The district office will provide the information needed to decide whether or not to file an application for retirement benefits at that time.

INDIVIDUAL RETIREMENT ACCOUNTS (IRAs)

Who is eligible to set up a Regular IRA?

Usually, any working individual under age 70½ who is *not* an active participant at *any time* during the year in a retirement plan sponsored by an employer. These include pension plans, profit-sharing plans, thrift and savings plans, Keogh plans, or any deferred compensation plans sponsored by the United States or a state government.

Do married couples with two incomes contribute to one or two Regular IRAs?

Two. Each may establish a separate IRA account if eligible. Contributions and eligibility are based on each separate income and each contribution is a separate tax deduction. This is true even though a couple may live in a community property state.

What happens if I establish an IRA and then become covered by a retirement plan where I work?

You won't be able to make any more tax deductible contributions to your IRA and your account will be frozen. The earnings will continue to accumulate tax free until they are distributed to you.

Can the assets of a Regular IRA be rolled over to an employer-sponsored retirement program?

No, the assets in a Regular IRA cannot be rolled over into any employer-sponsored retirement program. If you become an active participant in an employer's plan, your Regular IRA will be "frozen" until distributions are to begin, or until you are again eligible to make contributions.

What do I do if I receive company stock or other property as part of a lump-sum distribution?

In most cases, it is probably easiest to sell the property and rollover all or part of the proceeds.

If only part of the distribution is placed in a Special IRA, how is the remainder taxed?

Any amount attributable to employer contributions or investment earnings is taxed as ordinary income. Any portion representing employee contributions is not taxed.

How are benefits paid?

Benefits must be paid in one of two ways: (a) a single lump-sum payment, or (b) in substantially equal installments over a period which is not longer than a period equal to the life expectancy of the contributor or the joint life expectancies of the contributor and his or her spouse.

What happens if I contribute too much to an IRA account in any one year?

If more than the maximum allowable in any year is contributed, a 6% excise tax will be imposed on the excess contribution. However, the 6% tax can be avoided by withdrawing the excess contribution and earnings prior to the filing date for your Federal income tax return (normally April 15). If the excess contribution plus earnings is not withdrawn by the tax return filing date, the 6% excise tax will be imposed in each succeeding year until the excess is eliminated.

Are my IRA contributions locked into any one particular investment?

No. First you may select more than one organization which sponsors IRA programs as long as the total of all deductible investments made each year is within your personal contribution limit. For example, you could place part of your contribution in a savings account and the remainder in a mutual fund plan. Second, you may transfer IRA assets from one sponsoring organization to another. However, the reinvestment must take place within 60 days and you are allowed to make such rollovers only once every 12 months.

If I become disabled, can I make an early withdrawal from my IRA account?

Yes. In order to avoid the 10% IRS Premature Distribution Tax, a person under age 59½ must have a total and permanent physical or mental disability which prevents gainful employment and which is determined by a physician to be terminal or expected to continue for at least one year.

If I die, will my IRA account be included in my taxable estate?

Not if certain conditions are met. In order to be excluded, the death benefit must be paid to a beneficiary in a series of substantially equal payments for a period of 36 months or longer. Any death benefit paid over less than 36 months, or any death benefit not paid in substantially equal installments, will be included in your taxable estate.

When do you pay taxes on IRA plans?

If you take out your IRA funds in a lump sum, the entire account, including principal and earnings is ordinary income in the year of receipt. But, you may be able to use the five-year income averaging available to all taxpayers. If money is withdrawn periodically in installments or an annuity, you pay taxes only on what you receive each year.

What is an IRA "rollover"?

The IRA rollover is a special kind of IRA that can be used for many purposes. It is especially useful for avoiding an immediate tax on a lump-sum distribution from a company plan (which is terminated, or if an employee leaves the job, or if he or she retires or dies). If an IRA rollover account is set up within 60 days from the distribution, an immediate tax is avoided, and the funds in the account may continue compounding on a tax-deferred basis until withdrawn at a later time.

KEOGH PLANS

Who can establish a Keogh retirement plan?

Any sole proprietor or partnership, whether or not the business has employees; for example: doctors, lawyers, accountants, writers, etc. Any employees of the business *must* be included as participants in the plan on the same general basis as owner-employees.

How much can I contribute to a Keogh plan?

Employers may contribute 15% of *earned* income—or $7500, whichever is less—in each taxable year. If the participant's adjusted gross income is less than $15,000, the allowable minimum contribution is $750 or 100% of earned income, whichever is less.

When can Keogh plan benefits be paid?

Distributions to *owner-employees* can begin upon termination of employment, but not earlier than age 59½ nor later than age 70½. Benefits can be paid to *other employees* upon termination of employment without regard to age.

Can I collect benefits if I become disabled?

In the event that any participant in the plan becomes so disabled as to render him or her unable to engage in any substantial gainful activity, all contributed amounts plus interest may be paid immediately.

What happens to my plan if I die?

In the event that any participant dies, all contributed amounts plus interest may be immediately paid to the participant's designated beneficiary or estate. The portion of these contributed amounts which represents contributions made to the plan on a tax-deductible basis, plus the earnings on those contributions, may pass to the participant's designated beneficiary free of federal estate tax if the beneficiary receives the distribution in installments.

What happens if I make withdrawals before age 59½?

All contributed amounts plus interest must be declared as income in the year withdrawn, and a 10% penalty tax must be paid to the Federal Government.

APPENDIX

TABLE A.1 Present Value of $1 Received Annually at the End of Each Period for N Periods

Years (N)	1%	2%	4%	6%	8%	10%	12%	14%	15%	16%	18%	20%	22%	24%	25%	26%	28%	30%	35%	40%	45%	50%
1	0.990	0.980	0.962	0.943	0.926	0.909	0.893	0.877	0.870	0.862	0.847	0.833	0.820	0.806	0.800	0.794	0.781	0.769	0.741	0.714	0.690	0.667
2	1.970	1.942	1.886	1.833	1.783	1.736	1.690	1.647	1.626	1.605	1.566	1.528	1.492	1.457	1.440	1.424	1.392	1.361	1.289	1.224	1.165	1.111
3	2.941	2.884	2.775	2.673	2.577	2.487	2.402	2.322	2.283	2.246	2.174	2.106	2.042	1.981	1.952	1.923	1.868	1.816	1.696	1.589	1.493	1.407
4	3.902	3.808	3.630	3.465	3.312	3.170	3.037	2.914	2.855	2.798	2.690	2.589	2.494	2.404	2.362	2.320	2.241	2.166	1.997	1.849	1.720	1.605
5	4.853	4.713	4.452	4.212	3.993	3.791	3.605	3.433	3.352	3.274	3.127	2.991	2.864	2.745	2.689	2.635	2.532	2.436	2.220	2.035	1.876	1.737
6	5.795	5.601	5.242	4.917	4.623	4.355	4.111	3.889	3.784	3.685	3.498	3.326	3.167	3.020	2.951	2.885	2.759	2.643	2.385	2.168	1.983	1.824
7	6.728	6.472	6.002	5.582	5.206	4.868	4.564	4.288	4.160	4.039	3.812	3.605	3.416	3.242	3.161	3.083	2.937	2.802	2.508	2.263	2.057	1.883
8	7.652	7.325	6.733	6.210	5.747	5.335	4.968	4.639	4.487	4.344	4.078	3.837	3.619	3.421	3.329	3.241	3.076	2.925	2.598	2.331	2.108	1.922
9	8.566	8.162	7.435	6.802	6.247	5.759	5.328	4.946	4.772	4.607	4.303	4.031	3.786	3.566	3.463	3.366	3.184	3.019	2.665	2.379	2.144	1.948
10	9.471	8.983	8.111	7.360	6.710	6.145	5.650	5.216	5.019	4.833	4.494	4.192	3.923	3.682	3.571	3.465	3.269	3.092	2.715	2.414	2.168	1.965
11	10.368	9.787	8.760	7.887	7.139	6.495	5.988	5.453	5.234	5.029	4.656	4.327	4.035	3.776	3.656	3.544	3.335	3.147	2.752	2.438	2.185	1.977
12	11.255	10.575	9.385	8.384	7.536	6.814	6.194	5.660	5.421	5.197	4.793	4.439	4.127	3.851	3.725	3.606	3.387	3.190	2.779	2.456	2.196	1.985
13	12.134	11.343	9.986	8.853	7.904	7.103	6.424	5.842	5.583	5.342	4.910	4.533	4.203	3.912	3.780	3.656	3.427	3.223	2.799	2.468	2.204	1.990
14	13.004	12.106	10.563	9.295	8.244	7.367	6.628	6.002	5.724	5.468	5.008	4.611	4.265	3.962	3.824	3.695	3.459	3.249	2.814	2.477	2.210	1.993
15	13.865	12.849	11.118	9.712	8.559	7.606	6.811	6.142	5.847	5.575	5.092	4.675	4.315	4.001	3.859	3.726	3.483	3.268	2.825	2.484	2.214	1.995
16	14.718	13.578	11.652	10.106	8.851	7.824	6.974	6.265	5.954	5.669	5.162	4.730	4.357	4.033	3.887	3.751	3.503	3.283	2.834	2.489	2.216	1.997
17	15.562	14.292	12.166	10.477	9.122	8.022	7.120	6.373	6.047	5.749	5.222	4.775	4.391	4.059	3.910	3.771	3.518	3.295	2.840	2.492	2.218	1.998
18	16.398	14.992	12.659	10.828	9.372	8.201	7.250	6.467	6.128	5.818	5.273	4.812	4.419	4.080	3.928	3.786	3.529	3.304	2.844	2.494	2.219	1.999
19	17.226	15.678	13.134	11.158	9.604	8.365	7.366	6.550	6.198	5.877	5.316	4.844	4.442	4.097	3.942	3.799	3.539	3.311	2.848	2.496	2.220	1.999
20	18.046	16.351	13.590	11.470	9.818	8.514	7.469	6.623	6.259	5.929	5.353	4.870	4.460	4.110	3.954	3.808	3.546	3.316	2.850	2.497	2.221	1.999
21	18.857	17.011	14.029	11.764	10.017	8.649	7.562	6.687	6.312	5.973	5.384	4.891	4.476	4.121	3.963	3.816	3.551	3.320	2.852	2.498	2.221	2.000
22	19.660	17.658	14.451	12.042	10.201	8.772	7.645	6.743	6.359	6.011	5.410	4.909	4.488	4.130	3.970	3.822	3.556	3.323	2.853	2.498	2.222	2.000
23	20.456	18.292	14.857	12.303	10.371	8.883	7.718	6.792	6.399	6.044	5.432	4.925	4.499	4.137	3.976	3.827	3.559	3.325	2.854	2.499	2.222	2.000
24	21.243	18.914	15.247	12.550	10.529	8.985	7.784	6.835	6.434	6.073	5.451	4.937	4.507	4.143	3.981	3.831	3.562	3.327	2.855	2.499	2.222	2.000
25	22.023	19.523	15.622	12.783	10.675	9.077	7.843	6.873	6.464	6.097	5.467	4.948	4.514	4.147	3.985	3.834	3.564	3.329	2.856	2.499	2.222	2.000
26	22.795	20.121	15.983	13.003	10.810	9.161	7.896	6.906	6.491	6.118	5.480	4.956	4.520	4.151	3.988	3.837	3.566	3.330	2.856	2.500	2.222	2.000
27	23.560	20.707	16.330	13.211	10.935	9.237	7.943	6.935	6.514	6.136	5.492	4.964	4.524	4.154	3.990	3.839	3.567	3.331	2.856	2.500	2.222	2.000
28	24.316	21.281	16.663	13.406	11.051	9.307	7.984	6.961	6.534	6.152	5.502	4.970	4.528	4.157	3.992	3.840	3.568	3.331	2.857	2.500	2.222	2.000
29	25.066	21.844	16.984	13.591	11.158	9.370	8.022	6.983	6.551	6.166	5.510	4.975	4.531	4.159	3.994	3.841	3.569	3.332	2.857	2.500	2.222	2.000
30	25.808	22.396	17.292	13.765	11.258	9.427	8.055	7.003	6.566	6.177	5.517	4.979	4.534	4.160	3.995	3.842	3.569	3.332	2.857	2.500	2.222	2.000
40	32.835	27.355	19.793	15.046	11.925	9.779	8.244	7.105	6.642	6.234	5.548	4.997	4.544	4.166	3.999	3.846	3.571	3.333	2.857	2.500	2.222	2.000
50	39.196	31.424	21.482	15.762	12.234	9.915	8.304	7.133	6.661	6.246	5.554	4.999	4.545	4.167	4.000	3.846	3.571	3.333	2.857	2.500	2.222	2.000

TABLE A.2   Present Value of $1 Received at the End of Period

Years Hence	1%	2%	4%	6%	8%	10%	12%	14%	15%	16%	18%	20%	22%	24%	25%	26%	28%	30%	35%	40%	45%	50%
1	0.990	0.980	0.962	0.943	0.926	0.909	0.893	0.877	0.870	0.862	0.847	0.833	0.820	0.806	0.800	0.794	0.781	0.769	0.741	0.714	0.690	0.667
2	0.980	0.961	0.925	0.890	0.857	0.826	0.797	0.769	0.756	0.743	0.718	0.694	0.672	0.650	0.640	0.630	0.610	0.592	0.549	0.510	0.476	0.444
3	0.971	0.942	0.889	0.840	0.794	0.751	0.712	0.675	0.658	0.641	0.609	0.579	0.551	0.524	0.512	0.500	0.477	0.455	0.406	0.364	0.328	0.296
4	0.961	0.924	0.855	0.792	0.735	0.683	0.636	0.592	0.572	0.552	0.516	0.482	0.451	0.423	0.410	0.397	0.373	0.350	0.301	0.260	0.226	0.198
5	0.951	0.906	0.822	0.747	0.681	0.621	0.567	0.519	0.497	0.476	0.437	0.402	0.370	0.341	0.328	0.315	0.291	0.269	0.223	0.186	0.156	0.132
6	0.942	0.888	0.790	0.705	0.630	0.564	0.507	0.456	0.432	0.410	0.370	0.335	0.303	0.275	0.262	0.250	0.227	0.207	0.165	0.133	0.108	0.088
7	0.933	0.871	0.760	0.665	0.583	0.513	0.452	0.400	0.376	0.354	0.314	0.279	0.249	0.222	0.210	0.198	0.178	0.159	0.122	0.095	0.074	0.059
8	0.923	0.853	0.731	0.627	0.540	0.467	0.404	0.351	0.327	0.305	0.266	0.233	0.204	0.179	0.168	0.157	0.139	0.123	0.091	0.068	0.051	0.039
9	0.914	0.837	0.703	0.592	0.500	0.424	0.361	0.308	0.284	0.263	0.225	0.194	0.167	0.144	0.134	0.125	0.108	0.094	0.067	0.048	0.035	0.026
10	0.905	0.820	0.676	0.558	0.463	0.386	0.322	0.270	0.247	0.227	0.191	0.162	0.137	0.116	0.107	0.099	0.085	0.073	0.050	0.035	0.024	0.017
11	0.896	0.804	0.650	0.527	0.429	0.350	0.287	0.237	0.215	0.195	0.162	0.135	0.112	0.094	0.086	0.079	0.066	0.056	0.037	0.025	0.017	0.012
12	0.887	0.788	0.625	0.497	0.397	0.319	0.257	0.208	0.187	0.168	0.137	0.112	0.092	0.076	0.069	0.062	0.052	0.043	0.027	0.018	0.012	0.008
13	0.879	0.773	0.601	0.469	0.368	0.290	0.229	0.182	0.163	0.145	0.116	0.093	0.075	0.061	0.055	0.050	0.040	0.033	0.020	0.013	0.008	0.005
14	0.870	0.758	0.577	0.442	0.340	0.263	0.205	0.160	0.141	0.125	0.099	0.078	0.062	0.049	0.044	0.039	0.032	0.025	0.015	0.009	0.006	0.003
15	0.861	0.743	0.555	0.417	0.315	0.239	0.183	0.140	0.123	0.108	0.084	0.065	0.051	0.040	0.035	0.031	0.025	0.020	0.011	0.006	0.004	0.002
16	0.853	0.728	0.534	0.394	0.292	0.218	0.163	0.123	0.107	0.093	0.071	0.054	0.042	0.032	0.028	0.025	0.019	0.015	0.008	0.005	0.003	0.002
17	0.844	0.714	0.513	0.371	0.270	0.198	0.146	0.108	0.093	0.080	0.060	0.045	0.034	0.026	0.023	0.020	0.015	0.012	0.006	0.003	0.002	0.001
18	0.836	0.700	0.494	0.350	0.250	0.180	0.130	0.095	0.081	0.069	0.051	0.038	0.028	0.021	0.018	0.016	0.012	0.009	0.005	0.002	0.001	0.001
19	0.828	0.686	0.475	0.331	0.232	0.164	0.116	0.083	0.070	0.060	0.043	0.031	0.023	0.017	0.014	0.012	0.009	0.007	0.003	0.002	0.001	
20	0.820	0.673	0.456	0.312	0.215	0.149	0.104	0.073	0.061	0.051	0.037	0.026	0.019	0.014	0.012	0.010	0.007	0.005	0.002	0.001	0.001	
21	0.811	0.660	0.439	0.294	0.199	0.135	0.093	0.064	0.053	0.044	0.031	0.022	0.015	0.011	0.009	0.008	0.006	0.004	0.002	0.001		
22	0.803	0.647	0.422	0.278	0.184	0.123	0.083	0.056	0.046	0.038	0.026	0.018	0.013	0.009	0.007	0.006	0.004	0.003	0.001	0.001		
23	0.795	0.634	0.406	0.262	0.170	0.112	0.074	0.049	0.040	0.033	0.022	0.015	0.010	0.007	0.006	0.005	0.003	0.002	0.001			
24	0.788	0.622	0.390	0.247	0.158	0.102	0.066	0.043	0.035	0.028	0.019	0.013	0.008	0.006	0.005	0.004	0.003	0.002	0.001			
25	0.780	0.610	0.375	0.233	0.146	0.092	0.059	0.038	0.030	0.024	0.016	0.010	0.007	0.005	0.004	0.003	0.002	0.001	0.001			
26	0.772	0.598	0.361	0.220	0.135	0.084	0.053	0.033	0.026	0.021	0.014	0.009	0.006	0.004	0.003	0.002	0.002	0.001				
27	0.764	0.586	0.347	0.207	0.125	0.076	0.047	0.029	0.023	0.018	0.011	0.007	0.005	0.003	0.002	0.002	0.001	0.001				
28	0.757	0.574	0.333	0.196	0.116	0.069	0.042	0.026	0.020	0.016	0.010	0.006	0.004	0.002	0.002	0.002	0.001	0.001				
29	0.749	0.563	0.321	0.185	0.107	0.063	0.037	0.022	0.017	0.014	0.008	0.005	0.003	0.002	0.002	0.001	0.001	0.001				
30	0.742	0.552	0.308	0.174	0.099	0.057	0.033	0.020	0.015	0.012	0.007	0.004	0.003	0.002	0.001	0.001	0.001	0.001				
40	0.672	0.453	0.208	0.097	0.046	0.022	0.011	0.005	0.004	0.003	0.001	0.001										
50	0.608	0.372	0.141	0.054	0.021	0.009	0.003	0.001	0.001	0.001												

TABLE A.3 Compound Interest Table

THE AMOUNT TO WHICH ONE DOLLAR WILL ACCUMULATE AT COMPOUND INTEREST

ONE DOLLAR PER ANNUM IN ADVANCE DEPOSITED AT THE BEGINNING OF EACH YEAR

Years	3%	3½%	4%	4½%	5%	5½%	6%	5¾%	6½%	7%	7½%	8%	8½%	9%	9½%	10%
1	1.030	1.035	1.040	1.045	1.050	1.055	1.060	1.058	1.065	1.070	1.075	1.080	1.085	1.090	1.095	1.100
2	2.091	2.106	2.122	2.137	2.153	2.168	2.184	2.176	2.199	2.215	2.231	2.246	2.262	2.278	2.294	2.310
3	3.184	3.215	3.246	3.278	3.310	3.342	3.375	3.358	3.407	3.440	3.473	3.506	3.540	3.573	3.607	3.641
4	4.309	4.362	4.416	4.471	4.526	4.581	4.637	4.609	4.694	4.751	4.808	4.867	4.925	4.985	5.045	5.105
5	5.468	5.550	5.633	5.717	5.802	5.888	5.975	5.932	6.064	6.153	6.244	6.336	6.429	6.523	6.619	6.716
6	6.662	6.779	6.898	7.019	7.142	7.267	7.394	7.330	7.523	7.654	7.787	7.923	8.061	8.200	8.343	8.487
7	7.892	8.052	8.214	8.380	8.549	8.722	8.897	8.809	9.077	9.260	9.446	9.637	9.831	10.029	10.230	10.436
8	9.159	9.368	9.583	9.802	10.027	10.256	10.491	10.373	10.732	10.978	11.230	11.488	11.751	12.021	12.297	12.580
9	10.464	10.731	11.006	11.288	11.578	11.875	12.181	12.027	12.494	12.816	13.147	13.487	13.835	14.193	14.560	14.937
10	11.808	12.142	12.486	12.841	13.207	13.583	13.972	13.776	14.372	14.784	15.208	15.645	16.096	16.560	17.039	17.531
11	13.192	13.602	14.026	14.464	14.917	15.386	15.870	15.626	16.371	16.888	17.424	17.977	18.549	19.141	19.752	20.384
12	14.618	15.113	15.627	16.160	16.713	17.287	17.882	17.582	18.500	19.141	19.806	20.495	21.211	21.953	22.724	23.523
13	16.086	16.677	17.292	17.932	18.599	19.293	20.015	19.650	20.767	21.550	22.366	23.215	24.099	25.019	25.977	26.975
14	17.599	18.296	19.024	19.784	20.579	21.409	22.276	21.841	23.182	24.129	25.118	26.152	27.232	28.361	29.540	30.773
15	19.157	19.971	20.825	21.719	22.657	23.641	24.673	24.151	25.754	26.888	28.077	29.324	30.632	32.003	33.442	34.950
16	20.762	21.705	22.698	23.742	24.840	25.996	27.213	26.597	28.493	29.840	31.258	32.750	34.321	35.974	37.714	39.545
17	22.414	23.500	24.645	25.855	27.132	28.481	29.906	29.184	31.410	32.999	34.647	36.450	38.323	40.301	42.391	44.599
18	24.117	25.357	26.671	28.064	29.539	31.103	32.760	31.919	34.517	36.379	38.353	40.446	42.665	45.018	47.514	50.159
19	25.870	27.280	28.778	30.371	32.066	33.868	35.786	34.812	37.825	39.995	42.305	44.762	47.377	50.160	53.122	56.275
20	27.676	29.269	30.969	32.783	34.719	36.786	38.993	37.871	41.349	43.865	46.553	49.423	52.489	55.765	59.264	63.002
21	29.537	31.329	33.248	35.303	37.505	39.864	42.392	41.106	45.102	48.006	51.119	54.457	58.036	61.873	65.989	70.403
22	31.453	33.460	35.618	37.937	40.430	43.112	45.996	44.528	49.098	52.436	56.028	59.893	64.054	68.532	73.353	78.543
23	33.426	35.667	38.083	40.689	43.502	46.538	49.816	48.145	53.355	57.177	61.305	65.765	70.583	75.790	81.416	87.347
24	35.459	37.950	40.646	43.565	46.727	50.153	53.864	51.971	57.883	62.249	66.978	72.106	77.668	83.701	90.246	97.347
25	37.553	40.313	43.312	46.571	50.113	53.966	58.156	56.017	62.715	67.676	73.076	78.954	85.355	92.324	99.914	108.182
26	39.710	42.759	46.084	49.711	53.669	57.989	62.706	60.296	67.857	73.484	79.632	86.351	93.695	101.723	110.501	120.100
27	41.931	45.291	48.968	52.993	57.403	62.233	67.528	64.820	73.333	79.698	86.679	94.339	102.744	111.968	122.094	133.210
28	44.219	47.911	51.966	56.423	61.323	66.711	72.640	69.605	79.164	86.347	94.255	102.966	112.562	123.135	134.788	147.631
29	46.575	50.623	55.085	60.007	65.439	71.435	78.058	74.665	85.375	93.461	102.399	112.283	123.215	135.308	148.688	163.494
30	49.003	53.429	58.328	63.752	69.761	76.419	83.802	80.015	91.989	101.073	111.154	122.346	134.773	148.575	163.908	180.943
31	51.503	56.334	61.701	67.666	74.299	81.677	89.890	85.674	99.033	109.218	120.566	133.213	147.314	163.037	180.574	200.138
32	54.078	59.341	65.209	71.756	79.064	87.225	96.343	91.657	106.536	117.933	130.683	144.951	160.920	178.800	198.824	221.252
33	56.730	62.453	68.858	76.030	84.067	93.077	103.184	97.985	114.525	127.259	141.560	157.627	175.684	195.982	218.807	244.477
34	59.462	65.674	72.652	80.497	89.320	99.251	110.435	104.677	123.035	137.237	153.252	171.317	191.702	214.711	240.689	270.024
35	62.276	69.008	76.598	85.164	94.836	105.765	118.121	111.753	132.097	147.913	165.820	186.102	209.081	235.125	264.649	298.127
36	65.174	72.458	80.702	90.041	100.628	112.637	126.268	119.236	141.748	159.337	179.332	202.070	227.938	257.376	290.886	329.039
37	68.159	76.029	84.970	95.138	106.709	119.887	134.904	127.150	152.027	171.561	193.857	219.316	248.398	281.630	319.615	363.043
38	71.234	79.725	89.409	100.464	113.095	127.536	144.058	135.519	162.974	184.640	209.471	237.941	270.597	308.066	351.073	400.448
39	74.401	83.550	94.025	106.030	119.800	135.605	153.762	144.368	174.632	198.635	226.256	258.056	294.683	336.882	385.520	441.593
40	77.663	87.510	98.826	111.847	126.840	144.119	164.048	153.727	187.048	213.610	244.301	279.781	320.816	368.292	423.239	486.852

Example: $500.00 deposited at the beginning of each year for 10 years at 4% interest will amount to 500 × 12.486 or $6,243.00.

TABLE A.4 Compound Discount Table

THE PRESENT VALUE OF ONE DOLLAR DUE AT THE END OF A GIVEN NUMBER OF YEARS AT COMPOUND INTEREST

Years	3%	3½%	4%	4½%	5%	5½%	5¾%	6%	6½%	7%	7½%	8%	8½%	9%	9½%	10%
1	.9709	.9662	.9615	.9569	.9524	.9479	.9456	.9434	.9390	.9346	.9302	.9259	.9217	.9174	.9132	.9091
2	.9426	.9335	.9246	.9157	.9070	.8985	.8942	.8900	.8817	.8734	.8653	.8573	.8495	.8417	.8340	.8264
3	.9151	.9019	.8890	.8763	.8638	.8516	.8456	.8396	.8278	.8163	.8050	.7938	.7829	.7722	.7617	.7513
4	.8885	.8714	.8548	.8386	.8227	.8072	.7996	.7921	.7773	.7629	.7488	.7350	.7216	.7084	.6956	.6830
5	.8626	.8420	.8219	.8025	.7835	.7651	.7561	.7473	.7299	.7130	.6965	.6806	.6651	.6499	.6352	.6209
6	.8375	.8135	.7903	.7679	.7462	.7253	.7150	.7050	.6853	.6663	.6480	.6302	.6130	.5963	.5801	.5645
7	.8131	.7860	.7599	.7348	.7107	.6874	.6761	.6651	.6435	.6227	.6028	.5835	.5649	.5470	.5298	.5132
8	.7894	.7594	.7307	.7032	.6768	.6516	.6394	.6274	.6042	.5820	.5607	.5403	.5207	.5019	.4838	.4665
9	.7664	.7337	.7026	.6729	.6446	.6176	.6046	.5919	.5673	.5439	.5216	.5002	.4799	.4604	.4418	.4241
10	.7441	.7089	.6756	.6439	.6139	.5854	.5717	.5584	.5327	.5083	.4852	.4632	.4423	.4224	.4035	.3855
11	.7224	.6849	.6496	.6162	.5847	.5549	.5406	.5268	.5002	.4751	.4513	.4289	.4076	.3875	.3685	.3505
12	.7014	.6618	.6246	.5897	.5568	.5260	.5113	.4970	.4697	.4440	.4198	.3971	.3757	.3555	.3365	.3186
13	.6810	.6394	.6006	.5643	.5303	.4996	.4835	.4688	.4410	.4150	.3906	.3677	.3463	.3262	.3073	.2897
14	.6611	.6178	.5775	.5400	.5051	.4726	.4572	.4423	.4141	.3878	.3633	.3405	.3191	.2992	.2807	.2633
15	.6419	.5969	.5553	.5167	.4810	.4479	.4323	.4173	.3888	.3624	.3380	.3152	.2941	.2745	.2563	.2394
16	.6232	.5767	.5339	.4945	.4581	.4246	.4088	.3936	.3651	.3387	.3144	.2919	.2711	.2519	.2341	.2176
17	.6050	.5572	.5134	.4732	.4363	.4025	.3866	.3714	.3428	.3166	.2925	.2703	.2499	.2311	.2138	.1978
18	.5874	.5384	.4936	.4528	.4155	.3815	.3656	.3503	.3219	.2959	.2721	.2502	.2303	.2120	.1952	.1799
19	.5703	.5202	.4746	.4333	.3957	.3616	.3457	.3305	.3022	.2765	.2531	.2317	.2122	.1945	.1783	.1635
20	.5537	.5026	.4564	.4146	.3769	.3427	.3269	.3118	.2838	.2584	.2354	.2145	.1956	.1784	.1628	.1486
21	.5375	.4856	.4388	.3968	.3589	.3249	.3091	.2942	.2665	.2415	.2190	.1987	.1803	.1637	.1487	.1351
22	.5219	.4692	.4220	.3797	.3418	.3079	.2923	.2775	.2502	.2257	.2037	.1839	.1662	.1502	.1358	.1228
23	.5067	.4533	.4057	.3634	.3256	.2919	.2764	.2618	.2349	.2109	.1895	.1703	.1532	.1378	.1240	.1117
24	.4919	.4380	.3901	.3477	.3101	.2767	.2614	.2470	.2206	.1971	.1763	.1577	.1412	.1264	.1133	.1015
25	.4776	.4231	.3751	.3327	.2953	.2622	.2472	.2330	.2071	.1842	.1640	.1460	.1301	.1160	.1034	.0923
26	.4637	.4088	.3607	.3184	.2812	.2486	.2337	.2198	.1945	.1722	.1525	.1352	.1199	.1064	.0945	.0839
27	.4502	.3950	.3468	.3047	.2678	.2355	.2210	.2074	.1825	.1609	.1419	.1252	.1105	.0976	.0863	.0763
28	.4371	.3817	.3335	.2916	.2551	.2233	.2090	.1956	.1715	.1504	.1320	.1159	.1019	.0895	.0788	.0693
29	.4243	.3687	.3207	.2790	.2429	.2117	.1976	.1846	.1610	.1406	.1228	.1073	.0939	.0822	.0719	.0630
30	.4120	.3563	.3083	.2670	.2314	.2006	.1869	.1741	.1512	.1314	.1142	.0994	.0865	.0754	.0657	.0573
31	.4000	.3442	.2965	.2555	.2204	.1902	.1767	.1643	.1420	.1228	.1063	.0920	.0797	.0691	.0600	.0521
32	.3883	.3326	.2851	.2445	.2099	.1803	.1671	.1550	.1333	.1147	.0988	.0852	.0735	.0634	.0548	.0474
33	.3770	.3213	.2741	.2340	.1999	.1709	.1580	.1462	.1252	.1072	.0919	.0789	.0677	.0582	.0500	.0431
34	.3660	.3105	.2636	.2239	.1904	.1620	.1494	.1379	.1175	.1002	.0855	.0730	.0624	.0534	.0457	.0391
35	.3554	.3000	.2534	.2143	.1813	.1535	.1413	.1301	.1103	.0937	.0796	.0676	.0575	.0490	.0417	.0356
36	.3450	.2898	.2437	.2050	.1727	.1455	.1336	.1227	.1036	.0875	.0740	.0626	.0530	.0449	.0381	.0323
37	.3350	.2800	.2343	.1962	.1644	.1379	.1264	.1158	.0973	.0818	.0689	.0580	.0489	.0412	.0348	.0294
38	.3252	.2706	.2253	.1878	.1566	.1307	.1195	.1092	.0913	.0765	.0640	.0537	.0451	.0378	.0318	.0267
39	.3158	.2614	.2166	.1797	.1492	.1239	.1130	.1031	.0858	.0715	.0596	.0497	.0415	.0347	.0290	.0243
40	.3066	.2526	.2083	.1719	.1420	.1175	.1069	.0972	.0805	.0668	.0554	.0460	.0383	.0318	.0265	.0221

Example: To find the value now (present value) of $500 to be paid 15 years from now at 3% interest, multiply 500 by .6419. Answer $320.95.

To find the amount necessary now to pay a premium of $75.00 due 5 years from now, 3½% interest, multiply 75 by .8420. Answer $63.15.

TABLE A.5 Compound Discount Table

THE PRESENT VALUE OF ONE DOLLAR DUE AT THE END OF EACH YEAR
FOR A GIVEN NUMBER OF YEARS AT COMPOUND INTEREST

Years	3%	3½%	4%	4½%	5%	5½%	5¾%	6%	6½%	7%	7½%	8%	8½%	9%	9½%	10%
1	.971	.966	.962	.957	.952	.948	.946	.943	.939	.935	.930	.926	.922	.917	.913	.909
2	1.913	1.900	1.886	1.873	1.859	1.846	1.840	1.833	1.821	1.808	1.796	1.783	1.771	1.759	1.747	1.735
3	2.829	2.802	2.775	2.749	2.723	2.698	2.685	2.673	2.648	2.624	2.601	2.577	2.554	2.531	2.509	2.487
4	3.717	3.673	3.630	3.588	3.546	3.505	3.485	3.465	3.426	3.387	3.349	3.312	3.276	3.240	3.204	3.170
5	4.580	4.515	4.452	4.390	4.329	4.270	4.241	4.212	4.156	4.100	4.046	3.993	3.941	3.890	3.840	3.791
6	5.417	5.329	5.242	5.158	5.076	4.996	4.956	4.917	4.841	4.767	4.694	4.623	4.554	4.486	4.420	4.355
7	6.230	6.115	6.002	5.893	5.786	5.683	5.632	5.582	5.485	5.389	5.297	5.206	5.119	5.033	4.950	4.868
8	7.020	6.874	6.733	6.596	6.463	6.335	6.272	6.210	6.089	5.971	5.857	5.747	5.639	5.535	5.433	5.335
9	7.786	7.608	7.435	7.269	7.108	6.952	6.876	6.802	6.656	6.515	6.379	6.247	6.119	5.995	5.875	5.759
10	8.530	8.317	8.111	7.913	7.722	7.538	7.448	7.360	7.189	7.024	6.864	6.710	6.561	6.418	6.279	6.144
11	9.253	9.002	8.760	8.529	8.306	8.093	7.989	7.887	7.689	7.499	7.315	7.139	6.969	6.805	6.647	6.495
12	9.954	9.663	9.385	9.119	8.863	8.619	8.500	8.384	8.159	7.943	7.735	7.536	7.345	7.161	6.984	6.814
13	10.635	10.303	9.986	9.683	9.394	9.117	8.983	8.853	8.600	8.358	8.126	7.904	7.691	7.487	7.291	7.103
14	11.296	10.921	10.563	10.223	9.899	9.590	9.441	9.295	9.014	8.745	8.489	8.244	8.010	7.786	7.572	7.367
15	11.938	11.517	11.118	10.740	10.380	10.038	9.873	9.712	9.403	9.108	8.827	8.559	8.304	8.061	7.828	7.606
16	12.561	12.094	11.652	11.234	10.838	10.462	10.282	10.106	9.768	9.447	9.142	8.851	8.575	8.313	8.062	7.824
17	13.166	12.651	12.166	11.707	11.274	10.865	10.668	10.477	10.111	9.763	9.434	9.122	8.825	8.544	8.276	8.021
18	13.754	13.190	12.659	12.160	11.690	11.246	11.034	10.828	10.432	10.059	9.706	9.372	9.055	8.756	8.471	8.201
19	14.324	13.710	13.134	12.593	12.085	11.608	11.380	11.158	10.735	10.336	9.959	9.604	9.268	8.950	8.649	8.365
20	14.877	14.212	13.590	13.008	12.462	11.950	11.706	11.470	11.019	10.594	10.194	9.818	9.463	9.129	8.812	8.513
21	15.415	14.698	14.029	13.405	12.821	12.275	12.016	11.764	11.285	10.836	10.413	10.017	9.644	9.292	8.961	8.649
22	15.937	15.167	14.451	13.784	13.163	12.583	12.308	12.042	11.535	11.061	10.617	10.201	9.810	9.442	9.097	8.771
23	16.444	15.620	14.857	14.148	13.489	12.875	12.584	12.303	11.770	11.272	10.807	10.371	9.963	9.580	9.221	8.883
24	16.936	16.058	15.247	14.496	13.799	13.152	12.846	12.550	11.991	11.469	10.983	10.529	10.104	9.707	9.334	8.985
25	17.413	16.482	15.622	14.828	14.094	13.414	13.093	12.783	12.198	11.654	11.147	10.675	10.234	9.823	9.437	9.077
26	17.877	16.890	15.983	15.147	14.375	13.662	13.327	13.003	12.392	11.826	11.299	10.810	10.354	9.929	9.532	9.161
27	18.327	17.285	16.330	15.451	14.643	13.898	13.548	13.211	12.575	11.987	11.441	10.935	10.465	10.027	9.618	9.237
28	18.764	17.667	16.663	15.743	14.898	14.121	13.757	13.406	12.746	12.137	11.573	11.051	10.566	10.116	9.697	9.306
29	19.188	18.036	16.984	16.022	15.141	14.333	13.954	13.591	12.907	12.278	11.696	11.158	10.660	10.198	9.769	9.370
30	19.600	18.392	17.292	16.289	15.372	14.534	14.141	13.765	13.059	12.409	11.810	11.258	10.747	10.274	9.835	9.427
31	20.000	18.736	17.588	16.544	15.593	14.724	14.318	13.929	13.201	12.532	11.917	11.350	10.827	10.343	9.895	9.479
32	20.389	19.069	17.874	16.789	15.803	14.904	14.485	14.084	13.334	12.647	12.015	11.435	10.900	10.406	9.949	9.526
33	20.766	19.390	18.148	17.023	16.003	15.075	14.643	14.230	13.459	12.754	12.107	11.514	10.968	10.464	9.999	9.569
34	21.132	19.701	18.411	17.247	16.193	15.237	14.792	14.368	13.577	12.854	12.193	11.587	11.030	10.518	10.045	9.608
35	21.487	20.001	18.665	17.461	16.374	15.391	14.934	14.498	13.687	12.948	12.273	11.655	11.088	10.567	10.087	9.644
36	21.832	20.290	18.908	17.666	16.547	15.536	15.067	14.621	13.791	13.035	12.347	11.717	11.141	10.612	10.125	9.676
37	22.167	20.571	19.143	17.862	16.711	15.674	15.194	14.737	13.888	13.117	12.415	11.775	11.190	10.653	10.160	9.706
38	22.492	20.841	19.368	18.050	16.868	15.805	15.313	14.846	13.979	13.193	12.479	11.829	11.235	10.691	10.192	9.733
39	22.808	21.103	19.584	18.230	17.017	15.929	15.426	14.949	14.065	13.265	12.539	11.879	11.276	10.726	10.221	9.757
40	23.115	21.355	19.793	18.402	17.159	16.046	15.533	15.046	14.146	13.332	12.594	11.925	11.315	10.757	10.247	9.779

Example: The present value of $50 due at the end of each year for the next 10 years at 3½% interest is $415.85 (50 multiplied by 8.317).

TABLE A.6　Annual Investment to Accumulate $1,000

AMOUNT OF MONEY THAT MUST BE INVESTED ANNUALLY IN ADVANCE, AT COMPOUND INTEREST, TO AMOUNT TO $1,000 IN A GIVEN NUMBER OF YEARS.

Years	3%	3½%	4%	4½%	4¾%	5%	5¼%	5½%	5¾%	6%	7%	8%
1	970.87	966.18	961.54	956.94	954.65	952.38	950.12	947.87	945.63	943.40	934.58	925.93
2	478.26	474.78	471.34	467.94	466.25	464.58	462.91	461.25	459.60	457.96	451.49	445.16
3	314.11	311.05	308.03	305.05	303.57	302.10	300.65	299.20	297.76	296.33	290.70	285.22
4	232.07	229.23	226.43	223.68	222.32	220.96	219.62	218.29	216.97	215.65	210.49	205.48
5	182.87	180.18	177.53	174.92	173.63	172.36	171.09	169.84	168.59	167.36	162.51	157.83
6	150.09	147.51	144.96	142.47	141.24	140.02	138.81	137.61	136.42	135.25	130.65	126.22
7	126.71	124.20	121.74	119.33	118.15	116.97	115.81	114.66	113.52	112.39	107.99	103.77
8	109.18	106.74	104.35	102.02	100.87	99.74	98.61	97.50	96.40	95.32	91.09	87.05
9	95.57	93.18	90.86	88.59	87.47	86.37	85.28	84.21	83.15	82.10	78.02	74.15
10	84.69	82.36	80.09	77.87	76.79	75.72	74.66	73.62	72.59	71.57	67.64	63.92
11	75.80	73.52	71.30	69.14	68.08	67.04	66.01	65.00	64.00	63.01	59.21	55.63
12	68.41	66.17	63.99	61.88	60.85	59.83	58.83	57.85	56.88	55.92	52.24	48.79
13	62.16	59.96	57.83	55.77	54.76	53.77	52.79	51.83	50.89	49.96	46.40	43.08
14	56.82	54.66	52.57	50.55	49.56	48.59	47.64	46.71	45.79	44.89	41.44	38.24
15	52.20	50.07	48.02	46.04	45.08	44.14	43.21	42.30	41.41	40.53	37.19	34.10
16	48.17	46.07	44.06	42.12	41.18	40.26	39.35	38.47	37.60	36.75	33.51	30.53
17	44.61	42.55	40.58	38.68	37.76	36.86	35.97	35.11	34.27	33.44	30.30	27.43
18	41.46	39.44	37.49	35.63	34.73	33.85	32.99	32.15	31.33	30.53	27.49	24.72
19	38.65	36.66	34.75	32.93	32.05	31.19	30.35	29.53	28.73	27.94	25.00	22.34
20	36.13	34.17	32.29	30.50	29.64	28.80	27.98	27.18	26.41	25.65	22.80	20.23
21	33.86	31.92	30.08	28.33	27.48	26.66	25.86	25.09	24.33	23.59	20.83	18.36
22	31.79	29.89	28.08	26.36	25.54	24.73	23.95	23.20	22.46	21.74	19.07	16.70
23	29.92	28.04	26.26	24.58	23.77	22.99	22.23	21.49	20.77	20.07	17.49	15.21
24	28.20	26.35	24.60	22.95	22.17	21.40	20.66	19.94	19.24	18.57	16.06	13.87
25	26.63	24.81	23.09	21.47	20.70	19.95	19.23	18.53	17.85	17.20	14.78	12.67
26	25.18	23.39	21.70	20.12	19.36	18.63	17.93	17.24	16.58	15.95	13.61	11.58
27	23.85	22.08	20.42	18.87	18.13	17.42	16.73	16.07	15.43	14.81	12.55	10.60
28	22.61	20.87	19.24	17.72	17.00	16.31	15.64	14.99	14.37	13.77	11.58	9.71
29	21.47	19.75	18.15	16.66	15.96	15.28	14.63	14.00	13.39	12.81	10.70	8.91
30	20.41	18.72	17.14	15.69	15.00	14.33	13.70	13.09	12.50	11.93	9.89	8.17
31	19.42	17.75	16.21	14.78	14.11	13.46	12.84	12.24	11.67	11.12	9.16	7.51
32	18.49	16.85	15.34	13.94	13.28	12.65	12.04	11.46	10.91	10.38	8.48	6.90
33	17.63	16.01	14.52	13.15	12.51	11.90	11.31	10.74	10.21	9.69	7.86	6.34
34	16.82	15.23	13.76	12.42	11.80	11.20	10.62	10.08	9.55	9.06	7.29	5.84
35	16.06	14.49	13.06	11.74	11.13	10.54	9.99	9.45	8.95	8.47	6.76	5.37
36	15.34	13.80	12.39	11.11	10.51	9.94	9.39	8.88	8.39	7.92	6.28	4.95
37	14.67	13.15	11.77	10.51	9.93	9.37	8.84	8.34	7.86	7.41	5.83	4.56
38	14.04	12.54	11.18	9.95	9.38	8.84	8.33	7.84	7.38	6.94	5.42	4.20
39	13.44	11.97	10.64	9.43	8.87	8.35	7.85	7.37	6.93	6.50	5.03	3.88
40	12.88	11.43	10.12	8.94	8.40	7.88	7.40	6.94	6.51	6.10	4.68	3.57
45	10.47	9.13	7.94	6.89	6.41	5.96	5.54	5.15	4.78	4.43	3.27	2.40
50	8.61	7.38	6.30	5.36	4.94	4.55	4.19	3.85	3.54	3.25	2.30	1.61

TABLE A.7 Compound Interest Table

ONE DOLLAR PRINCIPAL
Showing the Accumulations of One Dollar Principal
Sum at Various Interest Rates

10%	9½%	9%	8½%	8%	7½%	7%	6½%	Years	6%	5¾%	5½%	5%	4½%	4%	3½%	3%
1.100	1.095	1.090	1.085	1.080	1.075	1.070	1.065	1	1.060	1.058	1.055	1.050	1.045	1.040	1.035	1.030
1.210	1.199	1.188	1.177	1.166	1.156	1.145	1.134	2	1.124	1.118	1.113	1.103	1.092	1.082	1.071	1.061
1.331	1.313	1.295	1.277	1.260	1.242	1.225	1.208	3	1.191	1.183	1.174	1.158	1.141	1.125	1.109	1.093
1.464	1.438	1.412	1.386	1.360	1.335	1.311	1.286	4	1.262	1.251	1.239	1.216	1.193	1.170	1.148	1.126
1.610	1.574	1.539	1.504	1.469	1.436	1.403	1.370	5	1.338	1.323	1.307	1.276	1.246	1.217	1.188	1.159
1.771	1.724	1.677	1.631	1.587	1.543	1.501	1.459	6	1.419	1.399	1.379	1.340	1.302	1.265	1.229	1.194
1.949	1.887	1.828	1.770	1.714	1.659	1.606	1.554	7	1.504	1.479	1.455	1.407	1.361	1.316	1.272	1.230
2.143	2.067	1.993	1.921	1.851	1.783	1.718	1.655	8	1.594	1.564	1.535	1.477	1.422	1.369	1.317	1.267
2.358	2.263	2.172	2.084	1.999	1.917	1.838	1.763	9	1.689	1.654	1.619	1.551	1.486	1.423	1.363	1.305
2.594	2.478	2.367	2.261	2.159	2.061	1.967	1.877	10	1.791	1.749	1.708	1.629	1.553	1.480	1.411	1.344
2.853	2.714	2.580	2.453	2.332	2.216	2.105	1.999	11	1.898	1.850	1.802	1.710	1.623	1.539	1.460	1.384
3.138	2.971	2.813	2.662	2.518	2.382	2.252	2.129	12	2.012	1.956	1.901	1.796	1.696	1.601	1.511	1.426
3.452	3.254	3.066	2.888	2.720	2.560	2.410	2.267	13	2.133	2.068	2.006	1.886	1.772	1.665	1.564	1.469
3.797	3.563	3.342	3.133	2.937	2.752	2.579	2.415	14	2.261	2.187	2.116	1.980	1.852	1.732	1.619	1.513
4.177	3.901	3.642	3.400	3.172	2.959	2.759	2.572	15	2.397	2.313	2.232	2.079	1.935	1.801	1.675	1.558
4.595	4.272	3.970	3.689	3.426	3.181	2.952	2.739	16	2.540	2.446	2.355	2.183	2.022	1.873	1.734	1.605
5.054	4.678	4.328	4.002	3.700	3.419	3.159	2.917	17	2.693	2.587	2.485	2.292	2.113	1.948	1.795	1.653
5.560	5.122	4.717	4.342	3.996	3.676	3.380	3.107	18	2.854	2.736	2.621	2.407	2.208	2.026	1.857	1.702
6.116	5.609	5.142	4.712	4.316	3.951	3.617	3.309	19	3.026	2.893	2.766	2.527	2.308	2.107	1.923	1.754
6.727	6.142	5.604	5.112	4.661	4.248	3.870	3.524	20	3.207	3.059	2.918	2.653	2.412	2.191	1.990	1.806
7.400	6.725	6.109	5.547	5.034	4.556	4.141	3.753	21	3.400	3.235	3.078	2.786	2.520	2.279	2.059	1.860
8.140	7.364	6.659	6.018	5.437	4.909	4.430	3.997	22	3.604	3.421	3.248	2.925	2.634	2.370	2.132	1.916
8.954	8.063	7.258	6.530	5.871	5.277	4.741	4.256	23	3.820	3.618	3.426	3.072	2.752	2.465	2.206	1.974
9.850	8.829	7.911	7.085	6.341	5.673	5.072	4.533	24	4.049	3.826	3.615	3.225	2.876	2.563	2.283	2.033
10.835	9.668	8.623	7.687	6.848	6.098	5.427	4.828	25	4.292	4.046	3.813	3.386	3.005	2.666	2.363	2.094
11.918	10.587	9.399	8.340	7.396	6.566	5.807	5.141	26	4.549	4.279	4.023	3.556	3.141	2.772	2.446	2.157
13.110	11.593	10.245	9.049	7.988	7.047	6.214	5.476	27	4.822	4.525	4.244	3.733	3.282	2.883	2.532	2.221
14.421	12.694	11.167	9.818	8.627	7.576	6.649	5.832	28	5.112	4.785	4.478	3.920	3.430	2.999	2.620	2.288
15.863	13.900	12.172	10.653	9.317	8.144	7.114	6.211	29	5.418	5.060	4.724	4.116	3.584	3.119	2.712	2.357
17.449	15.220	13.268	11.588	10.063	8.755	7.612	6.614	30	5.743	5.351	4.984	4.322	3.745	3.243	2.807	2.427
19.194	16.666	14.462	12.541	10.868	9.412	8.145	7.044	31	6.088	5.658	5.258	4.538	3.914	3.373	2.905	2.500
21.114	18.249	15.763	13.607	11.737	10.117	8.715	7.502	32	6.453	5.984	5.547	4.765	4.090	3.508	3.007	2.575
23.225	19.983	17.182	14.763	12.676	10.876	9.325	7.990	33	6.841	6.328	5.852	5.003	4.274	3.648	3.112	2.652
25.548	21.882	18.728	16.018	13.690	11.692	9.978	8.509	34	7.251	6.692	6.174	5.253	4.466	3.794	3.221	2.732
28.102	23.960	20.414	17.380	14.785	12.569	10.677	9.062	35	7.686	7.076	6.514	5.516	4.667	3.946	3.334	2.814
30.913	26.237	22.251	18.857	15.968	13.512	11.424	9.651	36	8.147	7.483	6.872	5.792	4.877	4.104	3.450	2.898
34.004	28.729	24.254	20.460	17.246	14.525	12.224	10.279	37	8.636	7.914	7.250	6.081	5.097	4.268	3.571	2.985
37.404	31.458	26.437	22.199	18.625	15.614	13.079	10.947	38	9.154	8.369	7.649	6.385	5.326	4.439	3.696	3.075
41.145	34.447	28.816	24.086	20.115	16.785	13.995	11.658	39	9.704	8.850	8.069	6.705	5.566	4.616	3.825	3.167
45.259	37.719	31.409	26.133	21.725	18.044	14.974	12.416	40	10.286	9.359	8.513	7.040	5.816	4.801	3.959	3.262

Example: To find how much $5,000 principal sum will amount to in 15 years if all interest at 5% is allowed to accumulate, multiply $5,000 by 2.079. Answer $10,395.00.

ACCUMULATION FOR SPECIFIC OBJECTIVE(S)

Specific Objective: _____

Target Date for Accumulation (p. 5) ....   _____

Years from Present to Target Date (p. 5) ....   _____ years

Amount of Capital Desired (p. 5).. $ _____

Capital Currently Available
 for this Purpose.. $ _____

Amount Present Capital Will Grow to
 During Accumulation Period at _____% Interest $ _____

Estimated Balance to be Provided... $ _____

To Provide for Deficit (if any):

 Amount of Annual Invested Capital @ _____%
 to Achieve Objective .... $ _____

Details of Plans:

Type(s) of Investments and Expected Return(s): _____

_____

_____

_____

_____

_____

Funding Vehicles, Trusts, Etc.: _____

_____

_____

_____

_____

_____

Special Considerations: _____

_____

_____

_____

_____

_____

_____

_____

FIGURE A.1

FINANCIAL INDEPENDENCE (RETIREMENT)

Estimated Required Monthly Income at Age _____ $_____

Source	Estimated Amount Monthly	Benefits Begin at Age:
Amount of Income Available:		
Social Security		
Other Government Pension		
Self-Employed Retirement Plan (Keogh)		
Individual Retirement Account (IRA)		
Pension Plan		
Profit-Sharing Plan		
Tax-Deferred Annuity		
Non-Qualified Deferred Compensation		
Non-Qualified Annuity		
Life Insurance Cash Values		
Unearned Income		
Liquidation of Assets		
Other (Specify)		
TOTAL		
Estimated Balance to Be Provided	$_____	

To provide for deficit,

Capital Required @ _____% is $_____

FIGURE A.2

INCOME/EXPENDITURE—CURRENT/PROJECTED

ANNUAL INCOME	CURRENT	PROJECTED ONE YEAR	ACTUAL ONE YEAR	PROJECTED THREE YEARS	ACTUAL THREE YEARS
Salary, Bonus, etc.					
Self-Employment (Business)					
Real Estate (net after taxes, etc.)					
Dividends—(a) Close Corporation Stock					
(b) Investments					
Interest—(a) Bonds					
(b) Savings Accounts					
Trust Income					
Life Insurance Settlement Options					
Other Sources					
TOTAL ANNUAL INCOME					

ANNUAL EXPENDITURES

FIXED:

Housing (Mortgage/Rent)					
Utilities and Telephone					
Food, Groceries, etc.					
Clothing and Cleaning					
Income Taxes, Social Security, etc.					
Property Taxes					
Transportation (Auto, Commuting)					
Medical/Dental/Drugs (include insurance)					
Debt Repayment					
Housing Supplies/Repairs/Maintenance					
Life Insurance					
Property and Liability Insurance					
Current School Expenses					
TOTAL FIXED EXPENSES					

DISCRETIONARY:

Vacations, Travel, Camps, etc.					
Recreation/Entertainment/Club Dues					
Contributions/Gifts					
Household Furnishings					
Fund for Education					
Savings					
Investments					
Other					
TOTAL DISCRETIONARY EXPENSES					
TOTAL ANNUAL EXPENDITURES					
NEW BORROWING OR ASSET LIQUIDATION (total expenditures minus total income)					

FIGURE A.3

FINANCIAL POSITION—CURRENT/PROJECTED

ASSETS LIQUID ASSETS	CURRENT	PROJECTED ONE YEAR	ACTUAL ONE YEAR	PROJECTED THREE YEARS	ACTUAL THREE YEARS
Cash					
Savings Accounts					
Savings Certificates, etc.					
Cash Value of Life Insurance					
Life Insurance Dividend Accumulations					
Other					
TOTAL LIQUID ASSETS					
OTHER FINANCIAL ASSETS					
Corporate Bonds (market value)					
Municipal Bonds (market value)					
U.S. Government Bonds					
Listed Common Stock					
Listed Preferred Stock					
Mutual Funds					
Annuities					
Nonmarketable Stocks and Bonds					
Equity in Business					
Real Estate Investment (market value)					
Vested Value of Pension/Retirement Funds					
Accounts Receivable					
Other					
TOTAL OTHER FINANCIAL ASSETS					
PERSONAL ASSETS					
Residence (market value)					
Seasonal Residence (market value)					
Automobiles (current value)					
Household					
Jewelry — Furs					
Collections					
Other					
TOTAL PERSONAL ASSETS					
TOTAL ASSETS					
LIABILITIES					
Charge Accounts/Credit Cards, etc.					
Installment Debts					
Notes Payable					
Mortgages					
Other Debts					
TOTAL LIABILITIES					
NET WORTH (Assets Minus Liabilities)					

FIGURE A.4

GLOSSARY

ACCELERATION The legal clause in a note, bond, or mortgage giving the creditor (mortgagee) the right to demand, upon default of the debtor (mortgagor), the immediate payment of the unpaid balance of the loan or mortgage.

ACCRUED INTEREST Interest accrued on a bond since the last interest payment was made. The buyer of the bond pays the market price plus accrued interest. Exceptions include bonds that are in default and income bonds.

ADJUSTED GROSS ESTATE An amount calculated for the purpose of determining the maximum allowable marital deduction and arrived at by reducing the gross estate allowable debts, funeral and medical costs, and administrative expenses.

ADJUSTED TAXABLE ESTATE This phrase is now substituted for "taxable estate." It means the taxable estate reduced by $60,000.

ADMINISTRATION The management of a decedent's estate, including the marshaling of assets; the payment of expenses, debts, and charges; the payment or delivery of legacies; and the rendition of an account.

ADMINISTRATOR–EXECUTOR An administrator is a man appointed by the court to settle an estate. An executor is a man named by the estate owner in the will as the one to settle that estate. The administrator is always named by the court, the executor by the deceased in the will.

ADMINISTRATRIX–EXECUTRIX A woman appointed by the court (administratrix) or named in the will (executrix) to settle the estate.

AFTER-BORN CHILD A child born after the execution of a parent's will.

ANNUAL EXCLUSION An exclusion of $3000 allowed the donor each year for each donee, provided the gift is one of present interest (donee must be given an immediate right to possession or enjoyment of the property interest).

ANNUAL REPORT The formal financial statement issued yearly by a corporation.

ASSESSED VALUE Value assigned to property by a public body for tax purposes.

ASSIGNMENT The act of transferring any interest in property to another party. The one who transfers the right is the *assignor*; the receiver of the right is *assignee*.

BALANCE SHEET A condensed financial statement showing the nature and amount of a company's assets, liabilities, and capital on a given date.

BALLOON PAYMENT The balance due on a debt instrument at maturity that is in excess of a regular principal payment.

BEAR Someone who believes the market will decline. *See* Bull.

BEAR MARKET A declining market. *See* Bull Market.

BEARER BOND A bond which does not have the owner's name registered on the books of the issuing company and which is payable to the holder. *See* Coupon Bond, Registered Bond.

BENEFICIARY (a) One who inherits a share or part of a decedent's estate or (b) one who takes the beneficial interest under a trust.

BID AND ASKED Often referred to as a quotation or quote. The bid is the highest price anyone has declared that he or she wants to pay for a security at a given time; the asked is the lowest price anyone will take at the same time.

BIG BOARD A popular term for the New York Stock Exchange.

BOND Basically an IOU or promissory note of a corporation, usually issued in multiples of $1000 or $5000, although $100 and $500 denominations are not unknown. A bond is evidence of a debt on which the issuing company usually promises to pay the bondholders a specified amount of interest for a specified length of time, and to repay the loan on the expiration date.

BROKER An agent who handles the public's orders to buy and sell securities, commodities, or other property. For this service a commission is charged.

BULL One who believes the market will rise. *See* Bear.

BULL MARKET An advancing market. *See* Bear Market.

CAPITALIZATION Determining value by evaluating Net Income as a percentage that represents a reasonable return on the total investment.

CAPITAL GAIN OR CAPITAL LOSS Profit or loss from the sale of a capital asset. A capital gain, under current federal income tax laws, may be either short-term (6 months or less) or long-term (more than 6 months). A short-term capital gain is taxed at the reporting individual's full income tax rate. A long-term capital gain is subject to a lower tax.

CAPITAL STOCK All shares representing ownership of a business, including preferred and common. *See* Common Stock, Preferred Stock.

CASH FLOW The amount of cash generated over time from an investment, usually after any tax effects.

CERTIFICATE The actual piece of paper which is evidence of ownership of stock in a corporation.

CHARITABLE DEDUCTION A deduction allowed against a reportable gift to a charitable organization (equal to the value of the gift).

CLOSING The conclusion or consummation of the real estate transaction where all documents are signed and deed or land contract, etc., is transferred.

CODICIL A supplement or addition to an existing will, to effect some revision, change, or modification of that will. A codicil must meet the same requirements regarding execution and validity as a will.

COMMITMENT An agreement, usually in writing, to undertake or agree to do something; usually a promise by a lender to loan money on a project.

COMMITMENT FEE   Fee paid for a binding agreement to lend monies at a future date. May be refunded upon completion of the commitment or retained for damages in the event of noncompliance.

COMMON STOCK   Securities which represent an ownership interest in a corporation.

COMMUNITY PROPERTY   Property acquired during marriage in which both husband and wife have an undivided one-half interest. Not more than half can be disposed of by will. In some community property states the husband can control and dispose of community property during marriage. There are presently eight community property states: Arizona, California, Idaho, Louisiana, New Mexico, Nevada, Texas, and Washington.

CONGLOMERATE   A corporation that has diversified its operations usually by acquiring enterprises in widely varied industries.

CONVERTIBLE   A bond, debenture, or preferred share which may be exchanged by the owner for common stock or another security, usually of the same company, in accordance with the terms of the issue.

CORPUS   A term used to describe the principal or trust estate as distinguished from the income. Also the property transferred to the trust.

COUPON BOND   Bond with interest coupons attached. The coupons are clipped as they come due and are presented by the holder for payment of interest. *See* Bearer Bond, Registered Bond.

CUMULATIVE PREFERRED   A stock having a provision that if one or more dividends are omitted, the omitted dividends must be paid before dividends may be paid on the company's common stock.

DEBENTURE   A promissory note backed by the general credit of a company and usually not secured by a mortgage or lien on any specific property. *See* Bond.

DEBT SERVICE   The amount of cash needed to cover periodic mortgage payments, including interest and principal.

DEVISE   A gift of real estate under a will, as distinguished from a gift of personal property.

DISCOUNT   The amount by which a preferred stock or bond may sell below its par value. Also used as a verb to mean "takes into account," as "the price of the stock has discounted the expected dividend cut." *See* Premium.

DIVIDEND A payment made from earnings to the stockholders of a corporation. It is authorized by the board of directors and paid on a pro rata basis among the shares outstanding.

DOLLAR COST AVERAGING A system of buying securities at regular intervals with a fixed dollar amount.

DOMICILE An individual's permanent home, the place to which he or she has the intention of returning.

DONEE The recipient of a gift. The term also is used to refer to the recipient of a power of appointment.

DONOR The person who makes a gift. The term also refers to the person who grants a power of appointment to another.

DOWER The provision that the law makes for a widow out of the real estate owned by her husband. At common law the widow was entitled to receive a one-third life interest in all the lands that her husband owned during their marriage. The amount to which the widow is entitled has been changed by statute in many states, and the term "dower" has been replaced by "statutory interest" in some jurisdictions.

ESTATE An interest in real property.

ESTATE TAX A tax imposed upon the right of a person to transfer property at death. This type of tax is imposed not only by the federal government but also by a number of states.

EXECUTOR–EXECUTRIX See Administrator and Administratrix.

EXTRA The short form of "extra dividend." A dividend in the form of stock or cash in addition to the regular or usual dividend the company has been paying.

FAIR MARKET VALUE The value at which estate property is included in the gross estate for federal estate tax purposes. The price at which property would change hands between a willing buyer and a willing seller, neither being under a compulsion to buy or sell and both having knowledge of the relevant facts.

FEDERAL ESTATE TAX An excise tax levied on the right to transfer property at death, imposed upon and measured by the value of the estate left by the deceased.

FEE SIMPLE   An estate in which the owner is entitled to the entire property, with unconditional power to dispose of it during lifetime and the power to bequeath it to anyone at death.

FIDUCIARY   One occupying a position of trust, e.g., executor, administrator, trustee.

FUTURE INTEREST   The postponed right of use or enjoyment of the property.

GIFT   (for gift tax purposes) Property or property rights or interest gratuitously passed on or transferred for less than an adequate and full consideration in money or money's worth (except for bona fide sales) to another, whether the transfer is in trust or otherwise, direct or indirect.

GIFT SPLITTING   A provision allowing a married couple to treat a gift made by one of them to a third party as having been made one-half by each, provided it is consented to by the other.

GIFT TAX   A tax imposed on transfers of property by gift during the donor's lifetime.

GOVERNMENT BONDS   Obligations of the U.S. Government, regarded as the highest grade issues in existence.

GRANTOR   A person who creates a trust; also called *settlor, creator, donor, trustor.*

GROSS ESTATE   An amount determined by totaling the value of all property in which decedent had an interest and which is required to be included in the estate by the Internal Revenue Code.

GROWTH STOCK   Stock of a company with a record of growth in earnings at a relatively rapid rate.

GUARDIAN   A person designated to represent the interests of minor children, whether named in a will or appointed by a court.

HEIR   Technically, a person designated by law to succeed to the estate of an intestate (also called *next of kin*).

HOLOGRAPHIC WILL   One entirely in the handwriting of the testator. In many states, such a will is not recognized unless it is published, declared, and witnessed as required by statute for other written wills.

INDENTURE A written agreement under which bonds and debentures are issued, setting forth maturity date, interest rate, and other terms.

INHERITANCE TAX A tax levied on the right of the heirs to receive property from a deceased person, measured by the share passing to each beneficiary, sometimes called a *succession tax.*

INSURANCE TRUST A trust composed partly or wholly of life insurance policy contracts.

INTANGIBLE PROPERTY Property that does not have physical substance. Examples: a certificate of stock or bond. The thing itself is only the evidence of value. Also, goodwill or an oral contract.

INTER VIVOS TRUST A trust created during the settlor's lifetime. It becomes operative during lifetime as opposed to a trust under will, which does not become operative until the settlor dies.

INTEREST Payments a borrower pays a lender for the use of money. A corporation pays interest on its bonds to its bondholders. *See* Bond, Dividend.

INTESTACY LAWS Individual state laws providing for distribution of property of a person who has died without leaving a valid will.

INTESTATE Without a will. A person who dies without a will dies intestate.

INVESTMENT COMPANY A company or trust that uses its capital to invest in other companies. There are two principal types: The closed-end and the open-end, or mutual fund. Shares in closed-end investment companies, some of which are listed on the New York Stock Exchange, are readily transferable in the open market and are bought and sold like other shares. Capitalization of these companies remains the same unless action is taken to change, which is seldom. Open-end funds sell their own new shares to investors, stand ready to buy back their old shares, and are not listed. Open-funds are so called because their capitalization is not fixed; they issue more shares as people want them.

IRREVOCABLE TRUST A trust that can be revoked or terminated by the grantor only with the consent of someone who has an adverse interest in the trust. The grantor cannot reclaim the trust property. To qualify as irrevocable for federal tax laws, the grantor cannot retain any right to alter, amend, revoke, or terminate.

JOINT TENANCY The holding of property by two or more persons in such a manner that, upon the death of one, the survivor or survivors take the entire property.

JOINT WILL   The same instrument is made the will of two or more persons and is jointly signed by them. When it is joint and mutual it contains reciprocal provisions.

LAND CONTRACT   A legal instrument that gives control but not title to land and enables the buyer to use the land while buying it on an installment basis.

LEASEHOLD (estate)   A contractual right to the use of real estate for a stated period of time upon payment of a stipulated consideration.

LEGACY   A gift of personal property by will.

LAGATEE   The person to whom a legacy is given.

LESSEE   The party to whom a lease is granted.

LESSOR   The party who grants a lease.

LEVERAGE   The act of borrowing funds at a fixed rate in an attempt to reinvest them at a higher rate. Borrowing against the established equity.

LIQUID ASSETS   Cash or assets that can be readily converted into cash without any serious loss. Examples: bonds, life insurance paid in lump sum.

LOAD   The portion of the offering price of shares of open-end investment companies which covers sales commissions and all other costs of distribution. The load is usually incurred only on purchase and not when shares are sold (redeemed).

LUMP-SUM DISTRIBUTION   Distribution or payment within one taxable year of the recipient of the balance to the credit of an employee, which becomes payable to the recipient on account of death or separation from the service *or* after age 59½.

MARITAL DEDUCTION   The portion of a decedent spouse's estate that may be passed to the surviving spouse without its becoming subject to the federal estate tax levied against the decedent spouse's estate, limited to the greater of (a) $250,000 or (b) 50 percent of the adjusted gross estate (but in no event more than the net value of the property passing to the surviving spouse in a qualifying manner).

MARKET PRICE   In the case of a security, market price is usually considered the last reported price at which the stock or bond sold.

MATURITY   The date on which a loan or a bond or debenture comes due and is to be paid off.

MORTGAGEE One who lends funds on the security of real estate (mortgage).

MORTGAGOR The borrower who gives as collateral real property.

MUNICIPAL BOND A bond issued by a state or a political subdivision, such as county, city, town, or village. The term also designates bonds issued by state agencies and authorities. In general, interest paid on municipal bonds is exempt from federal income taxes and state and local income taxes with the state of issue.

MUTUAL FUND *See* Investment Company.

MUTUAL WILLS The separate wills of two or more persons, with reciprocal provisions in favor of the other person contained in each will.

ODD LOT An amount of stock less than the established 100-share unit or 10-share unit of trading: from 1 to 99 shares for the great majority of issues, 1 to 9 for so-called inactive stocks. *See* Round Lot.

POWER OF APPOINTMENT A property right created (or reserved by a person having property subject to his or her disposition) enabling the donee of the power to designate, within such limits as the donor has prescribed, the transferees of the property or the shares in which it shall be received. A right given to a person to dispose of property that he or she does not fully own.

PREFERRED STOCK A class of stock with a claim on the company's earnings before payment may be made on the common stock and usually entitled to priority over common stock if company liquidates.

PREMIUM The amount by which a preferred stock or bond may sell above its par value.

PRICE-EARNINGS RATIO The price of a share of stock divided by earnings per share for a 12-month period. For example, a stock selling for $50 a share and earning $5 a share is said to be selling at a price-earnings ratio of 10 to 1.

PRINCIPAL The property comprising the estate or fund that has been set aside in trust, or from which income is expected to accrue (corpus). Trust principal is also known as the trust res.

PROBATE PROPERTY Property that can be passed under the terms of a will; if no will, it passes under the intestacy laws. Examples: individually held property, one-half of community property.

REGISTERED BOND A bond which is registered on the books of the issuing company in the name of the owner. It can be transferred only when endorsed by the registered owner. *See* Bearer Bond, Coupon Bond.

REVOCABLE TRUST A trust that can be changed or terminated during the grantor's lifetime and the property recovered by him or her.

ROUND LOT A unit of trading or a multiple thereof. On the NYSE the unit of trading is generally 100 shares in stocks and $1000 par value in the case of bonds. In some inactive stocks, the unit of trading is 10 shares.

SERIAL BOND An issue which matures in relatively small amounts at periodic stated intervals.

SHORT-TERM TRUST (also known as a CLIFFORD TRUST) An irrevocable trust running for a period of at least 10 years or the life of the beneficiary, whichever is shorter, in which the income is payable to a person other than the grantor, and established under the provisions of the Internal Revenue Code. The income is taxable to the income beneficiary and not to the grantor.

SOLE OWNERSHIP The holding of property by one person in such a manner that upon death it passes either by the terms of the will or if no will according to the intestacy laws.

SPRINKLING OR SPRAY TRUST A trust under which the trustee is given discretionary power to distribute any part of all of the income among beneficiaries in equal or unequal shares, and the direction to accumulate any income not distributed.

STOCK DIVIDEND A dividend paid in securities rather than cash.

TAXABLE ESTATE An amount determined by subtracting the allowable deductions from the gross estate.

TENANCY BY THE ENTIRETY The holding of property by a husband and a wife in such a manner that, except with the consent of each, neither husband nor wife has a disposable interest in the property during the lifetime of the other. Upon the death of either, the property goes to the survivor.

TENANCY IN COMMON The holding of property by two or more persons in such a manner that each has an undivided interest which, upon the death of one, is passed by probate. (It does not pass automatically to the surviving tenants in common.)

TESTAMENTARY The disposition of property by will. A testamentary document is an instrument disposing of property at death, either a will in fact or in the nature of a will.

TESTAMENTARY TRUST A trust of certain property passing under a will and created by the terms of the will.

TESTATE A term used when a person dies having left a will.

TESTATOR A person who leaves a will or testament in force at death.

TRUST A fiduciary arrangement whereby the legal title of property is held and the property managed by someone for the benefit of another.

WARRANTY DEED Conveys and guarantees the title in real property; safest form of deed.

YIELD Also known as return. The dividends or interest paid by a company expressed as a percentage of the current price. A stock with a current market value of $40 a share paying dividends at the rate of $2.00 is said to return 5% ($2.00 ÷ $40.00). The current return on a bond is figured the same way. A 3% $1000 bond selling at $600 offers a current yield return of 5% ($30 ÷ $600). *See* Dividend, Interest.

INDEX

Accidental death benefits, 124
Accumulation
  planning, 2, 60-61, 71
  worksheet, 62, 226

Bonds
  convertible, 95
  corporate, 92
  discount, 93
  municipal, 89
  savings, U.S., 86
Budgets, 53-54.

Certificates of deposit, 76
Charitable contributions, 16
Codicil, 163
Common stock, 96
Consumer Price Index, 27, 50

Convertible bonds, 95
Convertible term insurance, 111
Cost of living, 25-27
  regional, 26

Declining value of a $, 51
Defined-benefit plans, 150
Deposit term insurance, 113

Estate planning, 153
  executor's duties, 167
  joint tenancy, 168
  liquidity, 156
  probate, 165
  transfer costs, 155
  trusts, 170
  wills, 159
Estate tax schedule, 178

Executor (Executrix), 166
  duties, 167

Federal estate tax, 179–180
Financial position
  worksheet, 229
Financial tables, 219–225
Fixed expenses, 16

Gift tax schedule, 178
Gift taxes, 175–176
Gifts, 175
Glossary, 231
Government securities, 85
Guaranteed insurability, 126

Income
  disposable, 17
  projections, 18, 228
  required growth, 52–53
  retirement, 10, 55
  sources, 10–12, 55
  taxes, 13
  worksheet, 228
Individual Retirement Accounts (IRA)
  contributions, 141
  death benefits, 161, 186
  eligibility, 141
  questions and answers, 211
  rollovers, 144
  withdrawals, 143
Inflation
  effects, 49
  personal factor, 57
Insurance
  adjustable, 128
  dividends, 122
  participating, 121
  permanent, 115
  policy loans, 118
  premiums, 127

term, 109
  universal, 134
  waiver of premium, 125
Interest expense, 16
Intestacy laws, 159
Investment, 67
  life cycle, 83–84
  tax-sheltered, 100

Joint tenancy, 168

Keogh plans, 144, 214
  calculator, 146
  contributions, 147
  death benefits, 161, 186
  defined benefit plans, 150
  eligibility, 147
  questions and answers, 214
  withdrawals, 148

Life expectancy, 8–9
Life insurance
  adjustable, 128
  dividends, 122
  permanent, 115
  premiums, 127
  term, 109
  universal, 134
Living costs, 25–27

Medicaid, 30
Medical expenses, 16
Medicare, 30, 43, 45, 47
Money-market mutual funds, 78
Municipal bonds, 89
Mutual funds, 81

OASDI, 15; *see also* Social Security
Objectives, 68